SERVICE DESIGN

BCS, THE CHARTERED INSTITUTE FOR IT

BCS, The Chartered Institute for IT, is committed to making IT good for society. We use the power of our network to bring about positive, tangible change. We champion the global IT profession and the interests of individuals, engaged in that profession, for the benefit of all.

Exchanging IT expertise and knowledge
The Institute fosters links between experts from industry, academia and business to promote new thinking, education and knowledge sharing.

Supporting practitioners
Through continuing professional development and a series of respected IT qualifications, the Institute seeks to promote professional practice tuned to the demands of business. It provides practical support and information services to its members and volunteer communities around the world.

Setting standards and frameworks
The Institute collaborates with government, industry and relevant bodies to establish good working practices, codes of conduct, skills frameworks and common standards. It also offers a range of consultancy services to employers to help them adopt best practice.

Become a member
Over 70,000 people including students, teachers, professionals and practitioners enjoy the benefits of BCS membership. These include access to an international community, invitations to a roster of local and national events, career development tools and a quarterly thought-leadership magazine. Visit bcs.org to find out more.

Further information
BCS, The Chartered Institute for IT,
3 Newbridge Square,
Swindon, SN1 1BY, United Kingdom.
T +44 (0) 1793 417 417
(Monday to Friday, 09:00 to 17:00 UK time)
bcs.org/contact

shop.bcs.org/
publishing@bcs.uk

bcs.org/qualifications-and-certifications/certifications-for-professionals/

This book is both an excellent introduction to service design and a practical guide to its application. Clear, actionable, and rich with real-world examples, it is essential reading for anyone engaged in shaping services.

Pip Hall, *Service Design Manager, Founding Member, Service Design Forum*

A practical, clearly structured guide that brings service design to life through actionable frameworks and insights. Essential for teams seeking to embed consistent, customer centric thinking across their services.

Michael Greenhalgh, *Head of Business Architecture, Places for People*

The service sector requires new skills and scientific rigor in practice, including knowledge of business, information technology and human factors; this book offers a practical roadmap for effective service design.

Yin Leng Tan, *Associate Professor of Digital Futures and Programme Area Director of Digital Business Masters Programmes, Henley Business School, University of Reading*

Service Design is a wonderfully accessible compendium of essential techniques and frameworks for the service design and broader change communities. The book is packed full of clearly laid out approaches set within relatable, real world context and is abundant with detailed templates to provide structure. This is a must-have resource for anyone working in the service design space, you will find yourself pulling it off the shelf time and again for guidance and inspiration.

Colleen Henderson, *Co-Founder, Service Design Forum*

True to its name, *Service Design* is a masterpiece of a resource! It brilliantly pulls together invaluable tools, like Nielsen's usability components, to bridge design theory with real-world execution. The ultimate friendly guide for building a truly customer-centric business and support a service designers toolkit!

Paula Harrington, *Principal Service Designer, Acacium Group, Healthcare and Services*

A comprehensive, go-to guide that brings service design to life by combining methodology, practice and real examples, while showing how it integrates across disciplines to deliver meaningful, end-to-end customer experience improvements.

Anne-Louise Arkle, *Head of Service Design and Digital Adoption, Member of Service Design Forum*

A definitive and exceptionally practical guide that connects service design with the author's previous book, *Business Architecture*, bringing together mindset, methods and delivery into a clear, cohesive framework. Strongly recommended and particularly timely in an age of increasing organisational and technological complexity.

Chloe Gray, *Director of Enterprise and Business Architecture at The University of Manchester*

Some authors preach and others teach. This book does the latter, bringing together diverse disciplines, practical tools and complementary frameworks to demonstrate that effective service design is about informed choice rather than rigid methodology, empowering practitioners to select the right approach for the context and deliver meaningful outcomes.

Sara Mubasshir, *Head of Data, Digital and AI at Royal Mencap Society*

If you've ever been asked 'so what is service design, exactly?', I'd recommend this book. It's a practical, no nonsense guide that cuts through the noise, showing what service design really is and how to do it well. Packed with useful tools and techniques, including a few that were new to me, I can't wait to put them into practice on my next project.

Emma Whitelam, *Lead Designer*

Among the many books available on service design, this latest from BCS stands out for its highly practical application of a wide range of models and techniques. Any practising enterprise or business architect, service designer, CX specialist or business analyst will benefit from the breadth of resources and models provided. All are well explained in an easy-to-navigate structure, and particularly useful is the clear guidance given on how they can be used to contribute to delivering valuable business or customer outcomes. Highly recommended!

Joanna Goodrick, *Deputy Director and Head of Business Architecture, Cambridge University Press and Assessment*

At last! The essential and comprehensive guide to service design that everyone needs! Debra and Jonathan have brought to life the mindset and techniques that everyone aspiring to create better services will rely on again and again. This book isn't just for designers, it's for business leaders, public sector leaders and entrepreneurs whose aim is to create great services - offering better value to their customers, users and stakeholders.

Bruce Prendergast, *CDIO Strategy Lead, HM Customs and Revenue*

In an ocean of literature championing why service design matters, the authors finally answers the ‹how›. Invaluable reading for practitioners who need the language to operate, influence, and make the case where it counts.

Teddy Prosser, *Independent Service Designer*

SERVICE DESIGN
A practical guide to creating customer centric services

Debra Paul and Jonathan Hunsley

Published by BCS Learning and Development Ltd, a wholly owned subsidiary of BCS, The Chartered Institute for IT, 3 Newbridge Square, Swindon, SN1 1BY, UK.
bcs.org

EU GPSR Authorised Representative: LOGOS EUROPE, 9 Rue Nicolas Poussin, 17000 La Rochelle, France.

Contact@logoseurope.eu

Paperback ISBN: 978-1-78017-727-4
PDF ISBN-13: 978-1-78017-728-1
EPUB ISBN-13: 978-1-78017-729-8

British Cataloguing in Publication Data.
A CIP catalogue record for this book is available at the British Library.

Publisher's acknowledgements
Reviewers: Katie Walsh, Daniele Gianni, Tim Manning
Publisher: Ian Borthwick
Commissioning editor: Heather Wood
Production manager: Florence Leroy
Project manager: Rachel Cook
Copy-editor: Rachel Cook
Proofreader: Jeanne Washington
Indexer: Ozgur Pala
Cover design: Alex Wright
Cover image: istock/Wirestock
Typeset by Deanta Global Publishing Services, Chennai, India
Printed in the UK by Ashford Colour Ltd

CONTENTS

LIST OF TABLES

LIST OF FIGURES

ABOUT THE AUTHORS

Debra Paul is the Non-executive Chair of AssistKD, having been the CEO for many years. Debra co-founded the Business Analysis Conference Europe and the BA Manager Forum. She is a Visiting Fellow at Reading University (Henley Business School). Debra developed the BA Service Framework and is widely recognised as one of the leading authorities within the global business analysis profession.

Debra was the chief architect of the BCS Advanced International Diploma in Business Analysis and co-developer of the A4Q Certified Service Designer award. She is the co-author of numerous books including *Business Analysis* (4th edition), *Delivering Business Analysis: The BA Service Handbook* and *Business Architecture: A Comprehensive Guide.*

Jonathan Hunsley is the CEO of AssistKD and a founder of the Service Design Forum. He co-founded the IRM Service Design Conference Europe and is the Chief Architect of the A4Q Certified Service Designer award. Jonathan is also the Lead Assessor for the BCS Advanced Diploma in Business Analysis.

Jonathan has played a significant role in the development of professional standards and qualifications across business analysis and service design, helping organisations strengthen customer-centric transformation and professional capability development.

Jonathan is the co-author of *Business Architecture: A Comprehensive Guide* and *Business Analysis Techniques 123 Essential Tools for Success*. He is also a contributing author towards *Business Analysis* (4th edition).

FOREWORD

In December 2025, we facilitated a workshop at the Service Design Forum in London to explore the current state of service design within organisations and as a profession more widely. Participants were asked to consider the service design services offered within organisations, the practices, tools and techniques in use, and the state of the service designer role, profession and community. The findings from this workshop provided relevant insights into the state of the service design discipline.

Service design is being applied in many organisations to develop and improve services for both internal and external customers. However, the value offerings of service designers can vary widely between organisations and business contexts, and few participants felt that a clear or comprehensive portfolio of service design services had been established and articulated in their organisation.

Understanding customer experience is a key focus in most organisations. This work involves exploring customer needs and expectations, and analysing customer journeys. Some organisations are applying service design to investigate and define problems, using research and business acumen to clarify issues and enable a 'big-picture' view. Key services offered currently by service designers encompass service definition, experimentation and deployment. Service blueprinting is seen as a primary activity in the design of services, while experimentation is used to test rapidly, obtain feedback and iterate solution design.

Essentially, service design is seen as removing silos through the application of holistic approaches, with customer-centricity and a focus on outcomes over outputs being key. In some organisations, service design is recognised as bringing competitive advantage.

There is a general sense that there is a lack of understanding of service design within organisations, with some service designers feeling that they must continually 'pitch' their offerings to justify their role and existence. A lack of advocates and unclear role demarcations were identified as key obstacles. The location of service designers within an organisation is a key issue. For example, where service designers work within IT teams this limits the potential reach and scope of the role. While service design should help to address holistic business problems, too often, it is perceived as an IT-centric offering or as a business analysis service.

Language and terminology are barriers to understanding the role, resulting in limited time to conduct thorough service design. Service design is sometimes seen as too obvious or just common sense.

Multiple challenges are facing the service design profession. These challenges are all too familiar for those working in other change professions and attempting to engage with multiple stakeholders when conducting a specific role or service. Without such engagement, service design and other change professions struggle to work effectively and enable organisations to realise the available benefits. Too often, the trigger for a project determines its focus, and budgets constrain project scope and resource allocations. Similarly, the position and integration of service design within an organisation relative to the complementary and overlapping professions (such as business analysis, business architecture and user research) create both conflict and ambiguity and, consequently, impact the entire organisation. This is despite the practical benefit of shared perspectives and a largely analogous skillset. The absence of, or inconsistency in, management, development and recognition of service designers across organisations, industries and sectors are major contributory factors.

There is currently no recognised brand for the service design profession – a view that is validated by the implementation of service design within organisations, and the ambiguity between service design and other disciplines. In line with many associated change professions, service designers report that they are rarely assigned automatically to digital transformation projects, resulting in limited opportunities for the profession.

Senior sponsorship/leadership buy-in and a network of advocates are critical in addressing the challenges facing service designers, together with determined action by service design professionals to provide clarity regarding their role and its purpose and scope. Such action is needed to drive consistency in job descriptions and skills, competencies and certifications/qualifications.

The tools, techniques and practices currently in use reflect how service design is practised today. There are a range of industry and government standards and professional frameworks (for example, SFIA) into which service design activities need to adapt to fit, depending on the context of the organisation and project. However, it is vital that there is consistency of language, whatever the context, and personal skills, such as facilitation, collaboration and communication, are required throughout the design and implementation of services.

Despite the challenges of aligning service design-specific activities within the available frameworks, a wide range of tools and techniques are in use, some directly linked with service design and others more broadly associated with overlapping and neighbouring professions. Service blueprints are particularly in demand, but there is frustration that some organisations limit their view of the profession to the creation of such documents. There is similar frustration about the prominence of customer journey mapping being viewed as an output rather than a technique to inform an outcome. Service designers feel they have to demonstrate continuously the value of their work, justify their role and assert that services need to evolve continually to meet the needs of the customers rather than just being the focus of a one-off design activity.

These challenges constrain the potential of the profession to contribute towards strategic change programmes in organisations, and need to be addressed if the profession is to mature and gain credibility.

The Service Design Forum discussion reveals a picture of the profession as currently operating at a low level of maturity, although some organisations are clearly committed to the approach and displaying characteristics of higher maturity. Key findings are:

- Individuals are applying a service design approach, and undertaking service design activities, on an ad-hoc basis in their own sphere of influence, or their immediate domain or project environment. Some are embracing service design as part of change management activities, which is pushing their organisation's maturity forward. Where sporadic service design activity is being undertaken, technology and tools ordinarily used by related professions are commonly adapted and re-purposed to suit these service design activities.
- Organisational knowledge of service design tools and techniques is limited to a few individuals, who apply them in discrete tasks. Coordinating these activities with other project and change professions, and establishing repeatable approaches and processes, has started to increase the maturity in some organisations particularly where skilled and experienced service designers are present.
- Service design activities and skills may form part of job descriptions and/or person specifications. In more mature organisations, individuals with these roles are working in or alongside established change functions that have senior level knowledge and sponsorship.
- Organisations are not routinely analysing data through a service lens or evaluating service design activities to inform strategy, initiatives or decision-making; smaller scale data collection and analysis are being undertaken as part of specific projects.

The lack of a recognised brand for service design is exacerbating the lack of wider awareness and understanding, and addressing this is critical to driving the profession forwards. The Service Design Forum was established for this purpose and is keen to increase the visibility and credibility of the profession.

The key to unlocking greater organisational maturity lies in raising leadership awareness and understanding of service design and its value proposition, earning service designers a voice at a strategic level.

The following actions have been identified as critical activities required to increase the influence of the profession:

- Organisations should be supported to embrace service-centred thinking. They should establish routines for gathering and analysing data about their services, make information available through a service-focused lens and actively seek a service design perspective in decision-making.
- A defined, formal approach to service design should be developed, with a clear statement of the scope and purpose of service design, the portfolio of services

  and policies and processes that are explicitly and intrinsically linked to wider business design and change processes.
- Organisations should be encouraged to invest in employing skilled and experienced service designers and the technology to support service design activities.

The findings from the Service Design Forum highlight the need for the establishment and communication of service design standards. We are sure that this book will provide a major step forward in defining a holistic view of service design, identifying where the disciplines overlap with other related professions such as Business Analysis and Business Architecture, and providing an extensive toolkit to enable effective service design practice.

Stuart Mullinger, AssistKD
Pip Hall, Telent

ACKNOWLEDGEMENTS

The decision to write this book, and the ideas and content, have resulted from more than a decade of research, application and discussion. Throughout this time, there have been many organisations that have provided us with customer experiences that have varied from positive, indifferent to negative (sadly, too often!). Each of these organisations has contributed to the motivation and analysis of situations that have been vital to the development of this book.

We have had the support of many AssistKD customers and colleagues and wish to thank them for their support provided during the writing and production process. Their insights have helped significantly as we have sought to extend and deepen our understanding of this important topic.

In particular, we would like to thank the following individuals:

- Dr Yin Leng Tan for her guidance regarding Service Science research, which has proved so invaluable;
- Ian Borthwick and Heather Wood from the BCS Publishing team for their encouragement and guidance;
- Bruce Prendergast and Michael Greenhalgh for providing such insightful and relevant service design implementation case studies;
- Debbie Archer from iSQI, Geertje Appel from Ilionix and Milena Mileva from PMBA for believing in our Service Design work from the outset and providing ongoing support;
- Shane McGlynn and Lesley Cook from IRM for collaborating to establish the Service Design Conference Europe;
- James Paul, Kiara De Silva, Catriona Paul and Tim Clarke for offering so many examples of service experiences and discussing the service issues they have encountered.
- Bertie Hunsley and Sienna Hunsley for contributing their service experiences and extending our service understanding.

We would also like to thank the co-founders and members of the Service Design Forum and the members of the Business Analysis Manager Forum. The sharing of knowledge, insights and practical tips through these forums has been invaluable.

Finally, we would like to thank our friends and families for their continued support and encouragement. Special thanks are reserved for Alan Paul and Mary Hunsley – this book would not have been possible without you.

PREFACE

Service Design is a rapidly growing discipline that has the potential to transform organisations and the experiences encountered by their customers. The standard of service that we have experienced, and have discussed with so many people, is often inadequate, if not poor. Examples abound, including the marketing company that declared that they weren't interested in feedback, but just wanted customers to agree to provide a 'five-star rating', and the courier company that declared that parcels are sometimes delivered to the wrong addresses but are usually to be found in the local neighbourhood, so can easily be located. Add to this the numerous organisations that demonstrate a determination to avoid customers and their issues. We often ask ourselves when a 'waiting time' of thirty minutes became acceptable – particularly while being assured that our call is very important.

However, at a time of global uncertainty in a world still recovering from the economic cost of the Covid pandemic, can organisations afford to be so complacent and dismissive of feedback regarding customers' experiences? How many organisations have been diminished by such complacency, sometimes to the point of failure? Why do so many organisations feel it essential to assure the world that they are 'delivering value' and make promises that inevitably they fail to keep?

The concept of service is one that all organisations need to understand and embed into their strategic vision and day-to-day operations. While competing on price is a valid strategy, the balance with the expected level of service has to be struck. In so many cases, there are straightforward solutions to address a fundamental service issue. For example, training front-line staff to listen to customers rather than reading a script or, even worse, dismissing concerns.

This book is intended to support all professionals working to improve their organisation's services and the capabilities that ensure their effective delivery. Our audience is primarily the digital transformation specialists working as service designers, business architects and business analysts. However, we firmly believe that understanding the nature of service is beneficial to anyone seeking to develop their organisation, and this includes those in general executive positions.

Given the breadth of our intended audience, we have incorporated many frameworks and techniques that originated from various change professional disciplines. Our objectives in doing this are to enable collaboration between those undertaking such roles and to ensure that a holistic approach to the analysis and design of services is deployed. Key examples of such frameworks and techniques are:

- Service Design Service Framework;
- Value Co-Creation Model;
- Feedback Engagement Matrix;
- Service Definition Canvas;
- Service Design Gaps Model.

We decided to write about Service Design because of our deeply held beliefs regarding the importance of service and our increasing frustration with the service we and many others experience all too regularly. The book content reflects our extensive experience in analysing business problems and evaluating and implementing solutions, coupled with our aim to extend the service design toolkit. Having led a service-focused organisation for many years, we believe that understanding service and applying design principles to define solutions offers a way forward that has the potential to benefit all organisations and, ultimately, their employees and customers.

Debra Paul
Jonathan Hunsley
June 2026

1 THE SERVICE DESIGN MINDSET

INTRODUCTION

Everyone has been a customer of an organisation, whether purchasing a tangible 'product' or an intangible 'service'. When engaging with an organisation, all customers have expectations regarding the way in which this engagement is conducted and how they will feel as a result. They may expect to receive transactional elements such as efficiency and accuracy and to have the required features provided. Depending on the context, they may prefer to engage with an organisation by email, telephone online platforms or in person, or by using a combination of channels. Where contact with a person is required, customers may feel that the organisation should meet behavioural expectations, such as offering warmth and understanding alongside delivering the transactional elements of the product or service. Should an organisation fail to meet such expectations, the nature of the encounter with the organisation – the standard of `service' – can result in customer dissatisfaction, frustration or even distress.

Concerns regarding the standard of 'service' encountered by customers have been recognised and highlighted as an issue by organisations such as Which?, the UK consumer organisation (www.which.co.uk), and the Institute of Customer Service (www.instituteofcustomerservice.com).

A report by Which? (December 2023) states:

> Too many people are experiencing shockingly poor customer service – whether that means struggling to get through at all, deficient chatbots or poorly trained staff that only seem to make the problem worse.
>
> Rocio Concha, Which? Director of Policy and Advocacy

The Institute of Customer Service January 2025 UK Customer Satisfaction Index survey indicates that 64% of employees spend 4 days per month (on average) dealing with service failures (www.instituteofcustomerservice.com, 2025). When extrapolated, the Institute of Customer Service suggests that problems with service failures cost UK organisations £7.3 billion per month.

Organisations across different countries and sectors are grappling with the impact of service failure and the costs associated with resolving the issues this raises. They are also operating within increasingly complex environments resulting from factors such as intensive competition, political instability and rapid technological advancements.

Organisations often attempt to address these challenges by reducing costs, which inevitably diminishes the service quality and, where a formal contract exists, risks failing to achieve defined service level agreements. However, customers recognise poor service quality and take their business elsewhere where they don't feel they have received the service they expect and deserve. Given this, reducing service standards is a risky approach.

An alternative path involves reviewing the service offered to customers. Analysis of the customer experience offered by an organisation can uncover where improvements may be made, often without requiring significant investment. For example, by streamlining processes, training front-line staff or adopting advances in technology. This analysis may also identify where a delivered product or service may be enhanced, perhaps to extend the features provided or to enrich the user experience.

Many organisations are seeking innovative solutions to the challenges they face and, increasingly, are introducing service design into their transformational change activities. Service design is an emerging professional discipline within the digital change industry that has the potential to revolutionise the service quality, the products and the services offered by organisations. While 'design' has a long history across a wide variety of applications, 'service design' combines the skills of effective design within a service context. This context encompasses aspects such as analysing and defining the service rationale, organisational positioning and value propositions. It is customer-centric, so it places the consumer audience and their requirements at the heart of the service design work.

Proficiency in service design requires more than an ability to design a delivered product or service. Instead, it needs the skills that enable innovation and offers creativity to address both organisational and customer service needs. This moves service design beyond product or service delivery to encompass the principles and philosophy regarding the nature of 'service' in line with the organisation's vision regarding its target market and world view. Accordingly, proficient service design is able to offer an innovative approach to service, including a basis for engaging and empathising with customers.

Service designers offer their organisations a portfolio of services that have the potential to transform the products and services offered to customers and the service experience they receive. Chapter 2 explores the service designer role and defines the suite of services within the Service Design Service Framework (SDSF). Each of these services requires service designers to utilise a wide range of skills, in particular the ability to select and apply relevant tools and techniques. A core service design toolkit that highlights the techniques that are particularly relevant to an individual service is described in Chapters 3–8. This toolkit is supplemented by the stakeholder engagement and generic investigation skills described in Chapters 9–11.

Understanding the services offered by service designers, and possessing the service design skill set and toolkit, is not sufficient to ensure successful service design; a service design mindset is also required.

This chapter introduces the four thinking approaches that, collectively, underlie the service design mindset and provide a foundation for successful service design.

The four thinking approaches are:

- systems thinking;
- service thinking;
- design thinking;
- lean thinking.

Figure 1.1 summarises the primary focus of each thinking approach.

Figure 1.1 The four thinking approaches

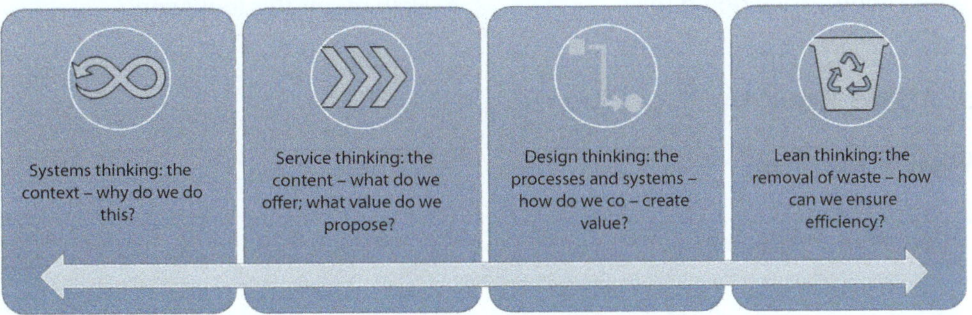

Service design should begin by investigating and understanding the underlying rationale for a particular service. Simon Sinek (2009) urged business leaders to 'start with why' and this remains relevant when engaging in service development or improvement. Systems thinking helps to uncover stakeholder perspectives and ensure a holistic understanding of a service. Service thinking helps to explore the value proposition to be offered and the desired outcomes from the service. These thinking approaches set the scene for effective service design. Design thinking focuses on the detail of the actual product or service and the service quality within which delivery should take place. Lean thinking enables efficiency and removal of waste during the delivery process.

RELATIONSHIPS BETWEEN THE THINKING APPROACHES

The four thinking approaches align as shown in Figure 1.2. Systems thinking provides a context for service thinking; the services are then explored for design innovation using design thinking; the designed services are explored for efficiency improvement using lean thinking.

Figure 1.2 The relationships between the four thinking approaches

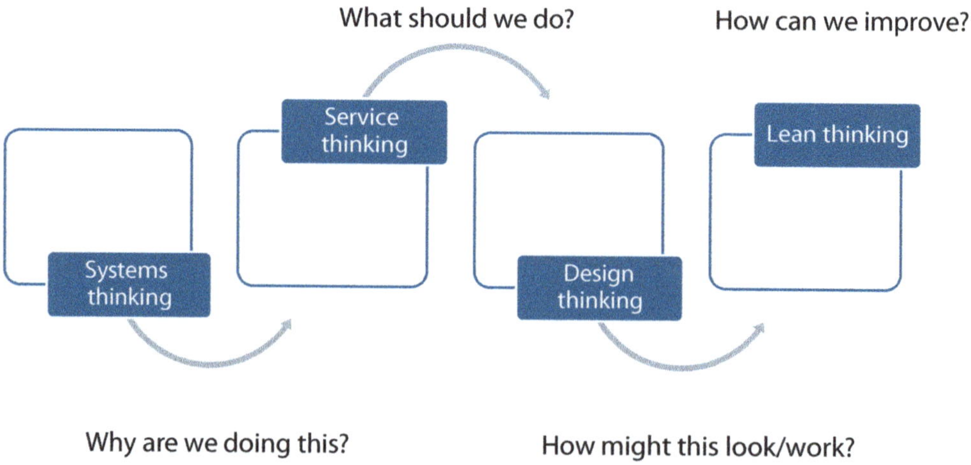

SYSTEMS THINKING

What is a system?

Definition of a system

The holistic organisational configuration of people, processes and technology to define value propositions and deliver offerings made possible by the capabilities of digital technologies.

Ross et al., 2019

A set of two or more interrelated elements of any kind.

Ackoff, 2016

A discipline for seeing wholes and a framework for seeing interrelationships rather than things, for seeing patterns of change rather than static snapshots.

Senge, 1990

What is systems thinking?

Systems thinking encourages a perspective whereby each ecosystem, enterprise or business area is viewed through a systems lens, perceiving that they are systems that consist of systems. In other words, the systems world view is of a system of systems. This is represented in Figure 1.3.

Figure 1.3 The system of systems

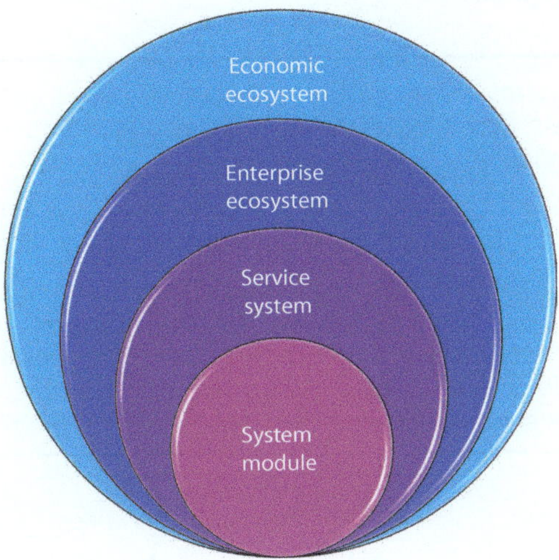

Each of these systems carries out activities to achieve a particular goal or outcome that is based upon a particular belief or viewpoint.

Systems thinking is concerned with taking a holistic, systemic view of situations, services, products or items, viewing each as a system with the following key elements:

- the underlying rationale and target audience (the customers);
- the elements that interact to conduct the work of the system (the systems within the system);
- the properties that emerge from the interaction of those elements.

These elements are represented in Figure 1.4 and described in Table 1.1.

Figure 1.4 The key elements of a system

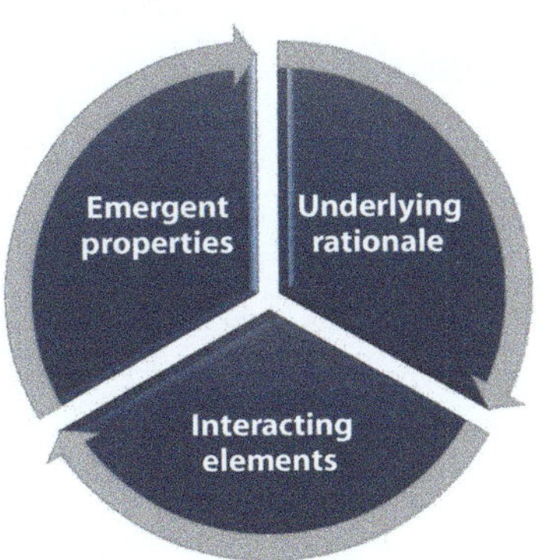

Table 1.1 The underlying principles of a system

System element	Description
Underlying rationale	A system has an underpinning set of values and beliefs that explain why it exists, what it is designed to do and who the target audience is.
Interacting elements	A system consists of several component systems that work together to deliver the required product, service or outcome.
Emergent properties	The properties or outcomes that result from a system as a whole. For example, a vehicle provides the emergent property of transportation. This property cannot be obtained from the individual elements of the system (for example the engine, wheels, chassis) on their own.

Types of system

Checkland (1981) defines four types of system. These are represented in Figure 1.5 and described in Table 1.2.

Figure 1.5 Checkland's four types of system

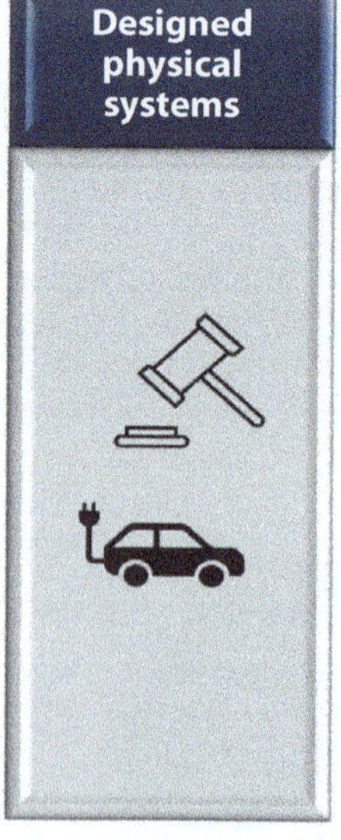

Table 1.2 Checkland's four types of system

Type of system	Description
Natural systems	Systems that are not made or controlled by humans but originate from the natural world. Examples include: systems such as an 'elephant' or 'coral reef'.
Designed physical systems	Systems that are physical artefacts created by humans as a result of conscious design. Examples include: a 'clock', 'bicycle' and 'smart phone'.
Designed abstract systems	Systems created by humans that are not physical artefacts and express ordered conscious thinking. Examples include: systems such as the 'Fibonacci sequence' (0, 1, 1, 1, 2, 3, 5, 8, 13, 21, 34...) or the 'Dewey Decimal' system (a classification index used by libraries).
Human activity systems	Systems that support a goal or purposeful human activity found in the real world. Human activity systems employ natural systems, designed physical systems and designed abstract systems. Examples include: a 'car cleaning' system or a medicine prescription system. Each such human activity system combines people carrying out the work, equipment, processes and pricing tariffs, thereby encompassing all four types of systems.

The term 'work system' is sometimes used to identify a type of human activity system.

Definition of a work system

A work system is a system in which human participants or machines perform work using information, technology, and other resources to produce products and services for internal or external customers.

Alter, 2008

This definition clarifies the need to view a system holistically and focus on the recipients of the outputs from the system. While this is a helpful clarification, the underlying rationale for the system also needs to be considered, as this provides a view about the desired outcomes in addition to the system outputs. This distinction enables a greater understanding of the nature of the service, and the associated level of service quality, to be offered by a system.

A system may be 'closed' so that it is unable to respond to influences or changes within its environment; a physical designed system (using Checkland's categories) such as a hammer is an example of a closed system. Alternatively, a system may be 'open' and have the ability to respond to changes; an open system is sometimes known as an adaptive system.

Definition of an adaptive system

A system that adapts to changes in its environment.

Examples include: a thermostat that adjusts the heating level in order to achieve a specified temperature.

Systems thinking approaches

Traditional management thinkers such as F. W. Taylor (1911) recommended a reductionist view of systems, breaking them down into component parts and working to optimise them at this level. However, this approach risks adopting a fragmented view where improvements to individual elements may not result in an overall improvement to the entire system. Systems thinking encourages a holistic perspective for investigating and addressing the complex problems typically found within organisations.

Checkland's Soft Systems Methodology (SSM) (1981) proposes a framework and techniques that may be used to apply systems thinking to change initiatives and projects. A systems thinking change process, developed using the principles within the SSM, is shown in Figure 1.6. SSM is discussed further in Chapter 12.

The systems thinking approach guides service designers towards consideration of perspective, rationale and purpose. The perspectives, at a minimum, should concern the organisation's vision and the customer expectations, which may or may not be in alignment. Once the perspectives are understood, the rationale for the system and the overriding purpose should be evident. This provides a firm basis for understanding 'why' and progressing to the definition of 'what' services may be offered.

Figure 1.6 Systems thinking change process

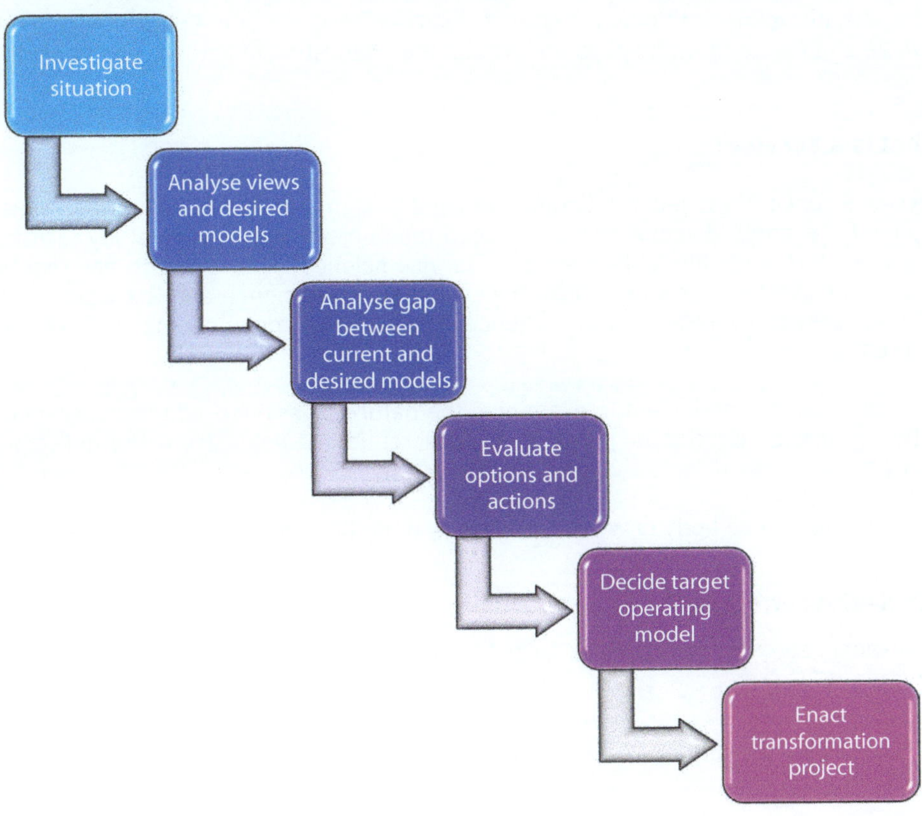

SERVICE THINKING

What is service thinking?

Service thinking applies a mindset that is focused on understanding the customer community, meeting the customers' needs and helping customers to realise the beneficial outcomes they require from engaging with an organisation. Service thinking aims to improve and innovate the business systems that deliver an organisation's service to its customers. Such improvements require an appreciation of what an organisation wishes to offer to its customers and how those customers are engaged in realising the value from that offering. Therefore, the service thinking mindset has to be balanced with the organisational view regarding the service characteristics. These characteristics are defined in a value proposition (see Glossary of Terms and Techniques).

Definition of service thinking

An interdisciplinary thinking approach focused on understanding the nature of value and the co-creation of value through the integration of actors' resources.

What is a service?

Service Science, Management, Engineering and Design (SSMED) is an interdisciplinary academic research discipline that has been the subject of extensive study for many years. SSMED is usually abbreviated to 'service science'. The research has resulted in an extensive body of knowledge concerning service science and the work undertaken by service systems. Service science is sometimes known as the study of value co-creation.

Service science is dedicated to examining the nature of 'service' and the interactions between service entities engaged in the co-creation of value from the delivery of service.

The service science body of work offers many definitions of the term 'service'.

Definitions of 'service'

The application of competences for the benefit of another.

Vargo and Akaka, 2009

The process of using one's resources to create value with and for the benefit of another actor.

Wieland et al., 2012

Typically, the term 'service' is used to refer to the delivery of an intangible item such as an entertainment or medical service. However, in contrast, these definitions establish that 'service' is concerned with outcomes and the co-creation of value. Understanding value and the importance of value co-creation is a fundamental element of a service approach.

Service is sometimes referred to as a 'meta concept' in that the 'delivery' of an item is viewed within a broader context that encompasses not just the delivered item but the entire customer experience and the outcomes realised from that experience.

In addition to the service (and services) provided to external customers, the concept of 'service' can also be applied to internal services provided to internal customers. Examples include services offered by internal departments such as digital transformation, business strategy, human resources and finance.

Core service thinking principles

Service thinking is based on core principles and encompasses distinct characteristics. Four service thinking principles are shown in Figure 1.7.

Figure 1.7 Service thinking principles

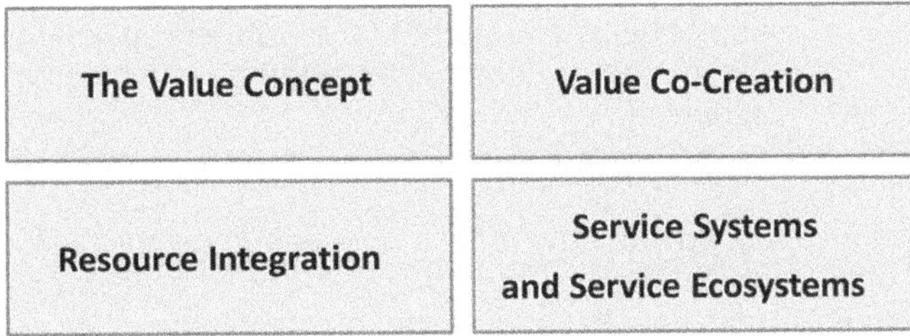

The value concept

The term value is typically used to describe the monetary worth of something. The term is also used to describe the 'relative worth, utility or importance' or 'to consider or rate highly' (merriam-webster.com). It may also be used when considering the experience and beneficial outcomes offered by a product or service and determined by a customer.

Value is defined as:

> Value concerns the utility, experience and beneficial outcomes offered by a product or service and determined by the customer.

Service thinking supports the view that value is determined by the recipient. Within the change profession this may include the delivery of solutions that provide great features, are used easily, are delivered in the required timescale and offer the potential for benefit realisation. These characteristics may also be relevant for other products or services.

Service science research distinguishes between the more traditional approach to understanding value – 'goods-dominant logic' – and the more contemporary approach known as 'service dominant logic' (Vargo and Lusch, 2008).

These terms are defined in Table 1.3.

Table 1.3 Two types of logic regarding value

Type of logic	Definition
Goods-dominant logic (G-DL)	A world view that proposes that value is delivered through the exchange of goods (products) or services for money.
Service-dominant logic (S-DL)	A world view that proposes that value is co-created with customers through the integration of resources and that value is realised in use. S-DL states that organisations do not deliver value but offer value propositions and that the customer determines whether or not value has been achieved.

G-DL reflects the product world view where it is assumed that value ensues from the acceptance of a product. This assumes that value is inherent within the delivered product. However, S-DL clarifies that a delivered product may not be used, resulting in no value being realised. This is summarised in Figure 1.8.

Figure 1.8 Two different forms of value-based logic

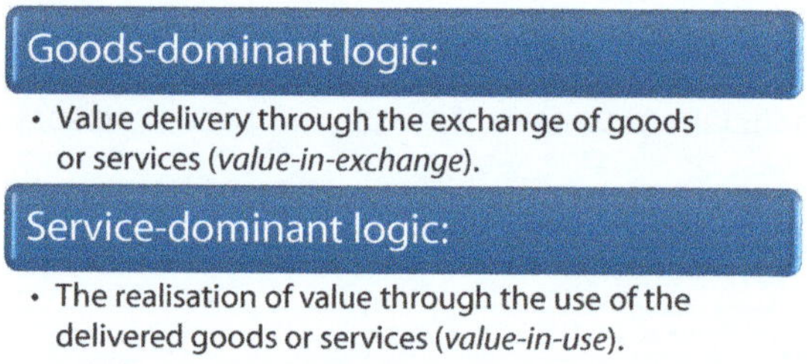

Goods-dominant logic:

- Value delivery through the exchange of goods or services (*value-in-exchange*).

Service-dominant logic:

- The realisation of value through the use of the delivered goods or services (*value-in-use*).

An example of this distinction is as follows:

- G-DL: A software product is purchased but not used. The potential value is not realised although the software manufacturer may believe that the value is inherent in the features offered by the product.
- S-DL: A software product is purchased and the functionality is explored and used to improve an organisation's business processes. The customer has engaged with the product to co-create value and ensure it is realised.

Statements about 'value' are often made by organisations and individuals that reflect the G-DL world view that value can be delivered. It is often the case that these claims are offered with conviction and a confidence that does not bear scrutiny. Table 1.4 identifies statements that are often made regarding value and clarifies where there are issues with such statements.

Table 1.4 Value statements from G-DL and S-DL perspectives

G-DL statement	S-DL perspective
Our solutions deliver value	Solutions, much like products, do not on their own deliver value. Customers must use the solution in order to realise the potential value. A more accurate statement would be 'our solutions include features that, when used, may realise value'. However, this is likely to be much less appealing from a sales or marketing perspective.
We deliver value	It is possible to deliver a product or service but not value. Value is determined and co-created by the recipient.
Our team adds value	A team must co-create value with its customers for value to be realised.
We provide early delivery of value	This is not possible given that value has to be realised through use and must be perceived by the customer. The timescale for value realisation must also be determined by the customer although the supplier may be able to contribute to this through collaboration and value co-creation.

Value co-creation

Research into service and value states that value is not delivered but must be co-created. The term 'value co-creation' is defined as:

> The application and integration of resources to propose and realise value.

The value co-creation model shown in Figure 1.9 sets out three activities that are essential for value to be realised.

Figure 1.9 The value co-creation model (Paul, 2018)

These activities are described in Table 1.5.

Table 1.5 The value co-creation model stages

Value co-creation stage	Description
Stage 1: Collaborating to identify where value might be achieved	This stage requires investigation of a proposed product or service to understand the customer needs, the features that may be provided and the beneficial outcomes these features can offer. Collaboration is key to ensure that the issues, challenges and requirements are understood so that the potential for value is clearly defined.
Stage 2: Collaborating to develop a solution that offers value	Organisations sometimes embark on product or service development because they have the capability to do so or because they believe there is a need. This isn't necessarily the case and can result in products and services offering new features that are not needed or are even disruptive. Where it has been established that a solution may enable the realisation of value, collaboration with customers when developing the solution is needed to fulfil this potential. This collaboration may involve demonstrating prototypes, and responding requesting feedback.
Stage 3: Collaborating to ensure that value is realised	Even where it has been established that a product or service is required and that customer collaboration has been part of the development process, there remains a need to realise the potential value through use. There are many examples of excellent products or services failing to result in beneficial outcomes because the customers did not engage with them. Therefore, this stage is essential to highlight the need for collaboration and accordingly realise value through the use of the product or service. Ultimately, stakeholders should be supported once a solution has been deployed in order to ensure the solution is used effectively and the value offered has been realised.

Value co-creation requires collaboration with stakeholders in order to understand their wants and needs. This requires the service designer to build rapport and demonstrate empathy, transparency, active listening and trust.

Resource integration

Resources, and the integration of resources, are a key element of SD-logic (Vargo and Lusch, 2016) and, accordingly, service thinking. The POPIT™ (Paul and Cadle, 2020) model offers a view of the resource categories that may be required to provide the capabilities needed to deliver a service; these are the people, organisation, processes, information and technology.

Collaboration is achieved through the integration of resources possessed by different stakeholders. Actors, including organisational entities, integrate their skills and capabilities to develop products and services that offer value to stakeholders.

Definition of resource integration

The application and integration of capabilities and competencies to co-create value.

Research has identified that co-creation of value occurs through integrating two distinct types of resource; the 'operand' and 'operant' (actor) resources (Edvardsson et al., 2010). Operand resources are tangible, static resources such as raw materials or physical products. These are acted upon by the dynamic and intangible operant resources, which include human skills, organisational routines and information.

Customers are deemed operant resources as they provide skill, experience and knowledge during the co-creation process. Customers engage in co-creation to enable both service innovation and value realisation. Therefore, service designers are skilled, operant resources that utilise operand resources, such as digital support tools, and collaborate with other skilled operant resources (the customers) to co-create value.

Service systems and service ecosystems

Service systems interact with other service systems to deliver an organisation's products and services. A service system may be an individual or an organisation, and the suite of service systems required to deliver a service form a service ecosystem.

Definition of a service system

A system where actors collaborate and integrate resources to deliver service, offer value and enable value co-creation.

Definition of a service ecosystem

An integrated group of service systems, all of which are required to deliver a service.

A relatively self-contained, self-adjusting system of resource-integrating actors connected by shared institutional arrangements and mutual value creation through service exchange.

Vargo and Lusch, 2016

Analysing a service ecosystem helps to clarify the areas of responsibility, the communication channels and the service offered by the different service systems. Each service system within the ecosystem contributes to the product or service delivered to customers. An example service ecosystem is shown in Figure 1.10.

Figure 1.10 Example ecosystem for a cosmetics company

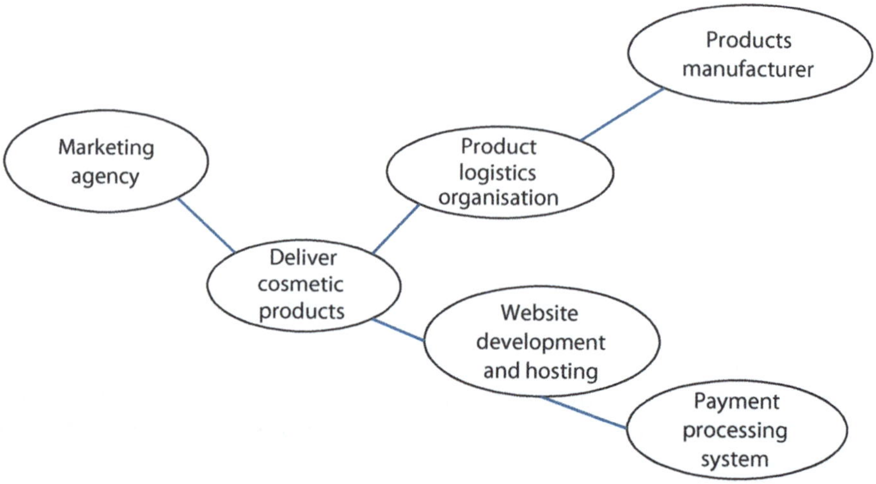

The diagram shown in Figure 1.10 represents the external service ecosystem for a cosmetics organisation. There are several external service systems involved in engaging with customers to deliver the service, including the marketing agency, the logistics company and the payment processing system.

The service mindset is focused on understanding the context for the service, the value proposition determined by the organisation, and the target audience and their value expectations. Applying the service mindset ensures a holistic approach that is customer centric. It also focuses on collaboration to co-create value through the integration of the customer engagement and the organisational capabilities.

DESIGN THINKING

What is design thinking?

Design thinking applies a creative and customer centric approach to product and service definition, development and deployment. It offers organisations a means of applying design principles to address the complexity faced within the global business environment. Collaboration and innovation are at the heart of design thinking.

Definition of design thinking

Design thinking is a human centric approach focused on innovative problem-solving and solution creation. It encompasses a process and set of techniques that encourage collaboration, ideation, and experimentation.

Brown, 2019

Core design thinking principles

The design thinking mindset is based upon the principles defined in Table 1.6.

Table 1.6 Principles of a design thinking mindset

Principle	Description
Collaboration	Working with colleagues and stakeholders to achieve the desired outcomes in a culture that values trust, respect and information sharing.
Outcome focus	Maintaining a focus on achieving the desired business outcomes.
Creativity	Applying a range of techniques and skills to generate new ideas and solutions.
Experimentation	Testing ideas and options to gain feedback, increased understanding and insights.
Customer centricity	Ensuring that the customer requirements and expectations are understood and that value co-creation with customers is a key element of the solution development process.

Design thinking approaches

Two key proponents of design thinking are the British Design Council and the d.school at Stanford University in the US. These organisations have been at the forefront of design thinking and offer frameworks that enable proficient service design.

The Design Council

The Design Council is the 'UK's national champion for design' (designcouncil.org.uk), providing leadership and guidance on the latest thinking regarding design. The Design Council developed the key design thinking framework, the Double Diamond. This framework is in widespread use within service design communities as it offers a direction of travel for the design activities and encompasses the core principles that enable effective design. Figure 1.11 shows a representation of the Double Diamond design thinking process.

Figure 1.11 Design Council's Double Diamond (Source: www.designcouncil.org.uk/our-resources/the-double-diamond/)

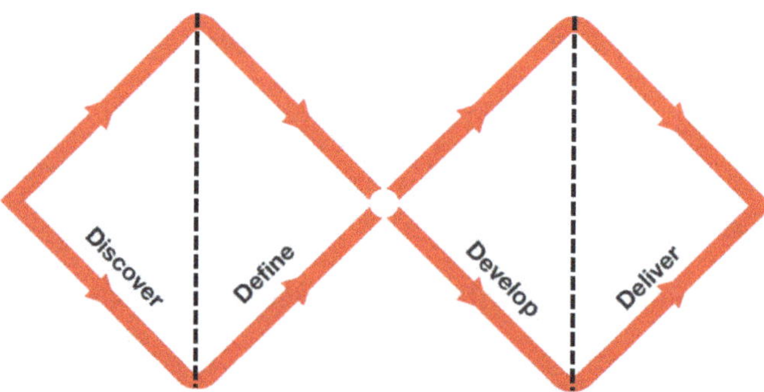

The structure of the Double Diamond encompasses four quadrants that are essential for effective design. These are described in Table 1.7.

Table 1.7 Description of the Double Diamond quadrants

Double Diamond quadrant	Description
Discover	This quadrant is concerned with the investigation of a situation to elicit information about the issues and challenges facing an organisation or business area. This may involve a problem or an opportunity facing an organisation. The investigative research is carried out to gain insight into the stated issue and consider where options for innovative change exist.
Define	This quadrant is concerned with evaluating and filtering the information elicited during the discovery research. The issues that have been uncovered are analysed and a clear problem definition is created.
Develop	This quadrant is concerned with identifying, prototyping and testing a variety of potential solutions. This is an iterative process where feedback from customers and other stakeholders is used to improve the proposed product/service design.
Deliver	This quadrant is concerned with launching a product or service into operation and seeking further feedback, which is used to refine further the product or service.

The Design Council design principles

The Design Council's framework for innovation includes the Double Diamond and four underlying design principles. These principles are described in Table 1.8.

Table 1.8 Design Council's framework for innovation principles

Principle	Description
Put people first	The customers for a product or service have requirements and expectations. Analysing the customer needs provides insight into why they wish to access an organisation's product or service and which outcomes they wish to achieve.
Communicate visually and inclusively	Communicating requirements, expectations and proposed solutions can be difficult and risk miscommunication. Visualisation and modelling techniques help to clarify information and ensure a shared understanding. They also promote inclusion and engagement.
Collaborate and co-create	Effective collaboration is essential to share requirements and gain feedback on proposed solutions. This enables value to be co-created and realised.
Iterate, iterate, iterate	Iteration provides a basis for exploring ideas, increasing understanding and allowing solutions to evolve.

Approaches to design thinking: the d.school model

The d.school at Stanford University has defined an approach to design thinking that comprises five stages. While the stages may be represented using an overall direction of travel, there is likely to be significant iteration. Figure 1.12 shows the d.school stages and the overall direction plus possible iterations.

Table 1.9 The five stages of the d.school approach

Stage	Description
Empathise	The empathise stage is concerned with understanding the intended audience for a product or service. Empathy results from engaging with customers, observing their behaviour and gaining understanding of their values, beliefs, priorities and concerns.
Define	The define stage is concerned with clarifying the needs of the customers and framing the problem or challenge to be addressed. The aim is to develop a clear problem statement that sets the foundation for the generation of ideas and development of possible solutions.

(Continued)

Table 1.9 (Continued)

Stage	Description
Ideate	The ideate stage is concerned with the generation of ideas and options for a new or improved product or service. The aim is to propose a high volume and wide variety of suggestions that may form the basis for developing prototypes during the next stage.
Prototype	The prototype stage is concerned with developing models and samples of proposed ideas. Initially, the prototypes may be low fidelity in order to explore possibilities at pace and with low costs. The aim is to learn from customer experiences and feedback.
Test	The test stage is concerned with using prototypes to gather feedback and refine solutions. This is done iteratively. The aim is to learn about the customers and their views regarding the proposed solution, and to identify where improvements might be made.

Figure 1.12 The d.school design thinking framework

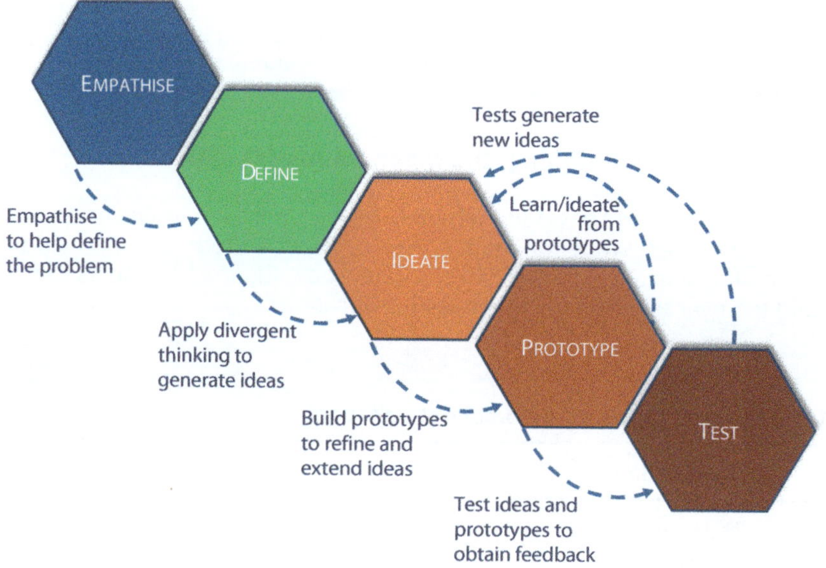

The stages defined by the d.school are summarised in Table 1.9.

There are a number of key design thinking practices that are applied when using frameworks such as the Double Diamond and d.school. The key design thinking practices are in Table 1.10.

Table 1.10 Definition of key design thinking practices

Practice	Definition
Empathy and perspective analysis	Engaging with customers and other stakeholders to understand and analyse their values, beliefs, concerns, requirements, priorities and motivations.
Research and investigation	Applying a range of techniques to uncover the issues and challenges regarding a situation and understand the perspectives of any involved individuals and organisations.
Divergent thinking	Thinking expansively and creatively about a situation or problem. Divergent thinking is used in many contexts and helps to identify challenges, issues, root causes of problems, risks, ideas and options.
Convergent thinking	Evaluating ideas and options to identify those that are most relevant and should be progressed or considered in greater depth.
Experimentation and prototyping	Building models and prototypes to explore ideas and possible solutions. The models and prototypes provide a basis for discussion with customers and other stakeholders. They may be built at different levels of functionality and fidelity and enable collaboration, testing and learning from feedback.
Visualisation	Using pictures and diagrammatic illustrations to represent ideas, processes, data and options.
Validation	Evaluating options by considering their desirability, viability and feasibility.
Assumption identification and testing	Probing information and assertions to uncover whether they are based on factual data or opinion/belief. Seeking evidence to confirm information or challenge inaccuracies.

LEAN THINKING

What is lean thinking?

Lean thinking applies a mindset that is concerned with ensuring process efficiency. The concept of lean (and lean thinking) has its origins in the Toyota Motor Company – and the work of Taiichi Ohno – where it involved an approach used to improve the car manufacturing processes through the elimination of unnecessary 'muda' or 'waste'.

In their seminal text, *Lean Thinking*, Womack and Jones attest that lean thinking is the 'powerful antidote' to waste and state the following:

> It provides a way to specify value, line up value-creating actions in the best sequence, conduct these activities without interruption whenever someone requests them and perform them more and more effectively.
>
> Lean thinking provides a way to do more and more with less and less – less human effort, less equipment, less time, and less space while coming closer and closer to providing customers with exactly what they want.
>
> Womack and Jones, 2003

Lean thinking principles

Womack and Jones (2003) advocate five summary principles of lean thinking. These principles are illustrated in Figure 1.13 and described in Table 1.11.

Figure 1.13 Womack and Jones lean thinking principles

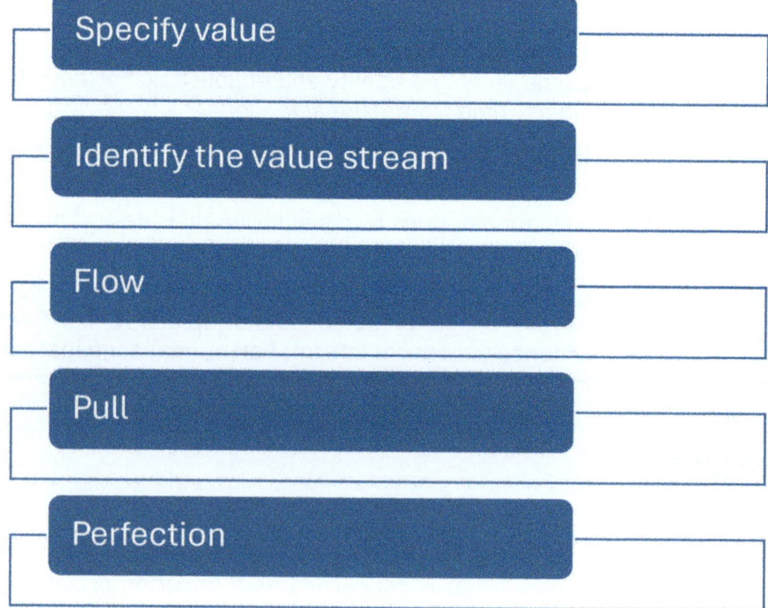

Table 1.11 Lean thinking principles

Principle	Description
Specify value from the point of view of the customer	Value can only be determined by the ultimate recipient or beneficiary of a product or service. It is a fallacy that an organisation can decide if it has delivered value to a customer and that a product or service is automatically imbued with value.
Identify the value stream	The value stream encompasses the activities that collectively create the product or service and offer value. These activities should be understood and represented sequentially. The value stream activities should be conducted efficiently and effectively when they are required.
Flow	Flow is concerned with organising the value stream so that there is a continuous flow of the activities that are undertaken in order to define, develop and deliver a product or service. Flow involves eliminating any internal barriers – such as those caused by departmental boundaries – and creating unnecessary batches of work. The aim is to reduce the time to provide a product or service.
Pull	Pull is concerned designing and creating what a customer wants when it is required. In other words, the customer 'pulls' the product or service from the organisation when needed. This contrasts with the situation where an organisation tries to 'push' the available products and services to the customer.
Perfection	Perfection is concerned with applying the other lean thinking principles to enable continuous improvement. When the value is understood, the value stream has been defined, and the principles of flow and pull are enacted, the potential for perfection with increasing removal of impediments, becomes more achievable.

The types of waste (muda)

Womack and Jones (2003) list seven types of waste plus an additional type that they defined later. These eight types of waste are described in Table 1.12 using the transport, inventory, motion, waiting, overproduction, overprocessing, defects and underutilisation of skills (TIMWOODS) structure.

Table 1.12 The TIMWOODS wastes

Transport	Moving people, parts, activities or information unnecessarily.
Inventory	Storing any parts, pieces or unfinished goods that are not required.
Motion	Engaging in unnecessary movement such as bending, turning or reaching.
Waiting	Failing to conduct activities in a timely manner causing delays in receiving parts, information, instructions, equipment and other resources.
Overproduction	Producing more items than are required.
Overprocessing	Producing items to higher quality standards than are required or justified.
Defects	Producing items that do not meet the customer requirements so require rework or removal.
Under-utilisation of skills	Failing to fully utilise the available skills.

Womack and Jones (2003) also state that 'value can only be defined by the ultimate customer', thereby aligning the lean view of value with that of service thinking (described earlier in this chapter).

Kaizen

Kaizen refers to 'continuous incremental improvement' and is a key aspect of lean thinking. It suggests that there should be a formal process that focuses on investigating, analysing and identifying where there are opportunities to improve aspects such as processes, procedures, products and services. The objective of Kaizen is to strive for perfection and thereby meet or exceed customer expectations.

Lean thinking lifecycles

Popular lifecycles used when applying lean thinking are:

- DMAIC;
- PDCA/PDSA.

These lifecycles are described below.

DMAIC

The Define, Measure, Analyse, Improve and Control (DMAIC) framework originates from the Six Sigma approach, which offers a set of techniques used in process improvement. This framework is often used by lean practitioners and the elements are defined in Table 1.13.

Table 1.13 DMAIC elements

Phase	Description
Define	The problem is investigated and defined and relevant process and customer data is obtained. The approach emphasises understanding customer expectations. As this is the initial phase of investigation this is typically where the charter for the problem solving initiative and associated plan are defined.
Measure	The measures used, the types of measurements and the areas they address are reviewed. The data used to facilitate measurement, plus the basis for collection and reporting that data, is investigated.
Analyse	The data is analysed to identify the root causes of errors, defects or problems. This provides a statistical basis for analysing and resolving issues.
Improve	The processes that develop the products and services are redesigned. Ideas are generated and evaluated to identify where they enable improvement. This is an iterative approach where ideas and improvement evolve.
Control	The redesigned processes are monitored to ensure that improvements are embedded and sustained.

PDCA/PDSA

The plan, do, check, act (PDCA) cycle is a continuous improvement method that was popularised in the 1950s, particularly within Japanese manufacturing. It was based on work by Walter Shewhart and W. Edwards Deming. The plan, do, study, act (PDSA) cycle was a further development by Deming, building on his earlier work and the PDCA cycle (The W. Edwards Deming Institute).

The cycles are described in Table 1.14.

Table 1.14 The PDCA and PDSA cycles

PDCA	PDSA
Plan. A problem is defined along with the possible causes and solutions.	**Plan.** The objective is established, the questions to be addressed, and the plan to conduct the work of the cycle is defined.
Do. A solution to the problem is developed and implemented.	**Do.** The plan is executed, and any challenges and concerns are recorded. The data is gathered for further analysis.
Check. The results of the solution are evaluated.	**Study.** The data is analysed to provide insights, areas for action and learning.
Act. Any further actions are identified and taken.	**Act.** The decisions regarding action are taken.

PDSA emphasises the need for learning and continuous improvement and the cycle representation illustrates that this should be ongoing.

Combining the four approaches

It is essential that anyone wishing to be a proficient service designer applies the four thinking approaches – systems thinking, service thinking, design thinking and lean thinking. The service design process model shown in Figure 1.14 reflects how these four approaches are interrelated and are used to develop a service-focused mindset.

Figure 1.14 The service design process model

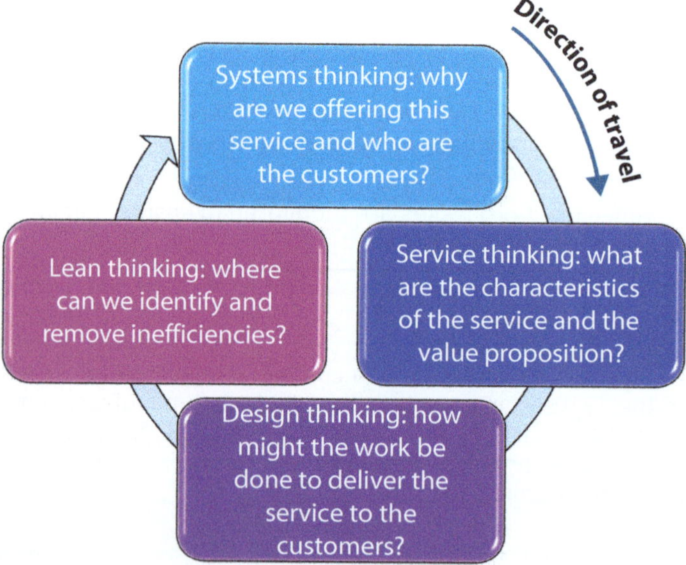

CONCLUSION

A service design mindset requires a world view that begins with understanding the underlying system rationale and context for a service. This understanding needs to encompass a focus on the customer and the value proposition offered by each service. Only then can design begin in earnest, applying a design thinking mindset that embraces the customer focus and is open to divergent thinking to enable idea generation and innovation. The inclusion of lean thinking within the service design mindset adds a further dimension, ensuring the service designer curates the service design to remove waste and ensure efficiency.

2 THE SERVICE DESIGNER ROLE

This chapter covers the following topics:

- maturity of the service design role;
- rationale for the service system view of service design;
- Service Design Service Framework (SDSF);
- value streams for SDSF.

The chapter concludes with a case study describing the approach applied when introducing service design to an organisation. The case study has been provided by Michael Greenhalgh of Places for People (PfP).

INTRODUCTION

Demand for competent service design practitioners is growing as organisations recognise increasingly the need for a strategic, integrated approach that enhances customer and organisational outcomes. At the same time, the role of the service design practitioner is subject to much confusion and ambiguity. This is in part due to the relative immaturity of the discipline. Many service design practitioners operate independently and offer services that align with their individual background, training and world view. While this level of variation persists, the credibility and recognition of the service design profession will be constrained. If service designers cannot provide clarity on the services that they offer, how can they be expected to gain influence over the definition and design of the organisation's services?

An opportunity exists to create shared understanding of the service designer role. This can be used as a basis to promote understanding among colleagues and stakeholders, share knowledge and enable continuous improvement of the service design profession.

This chapter defines an approach for assessing the maturity of the service designer role and introduces the Service Design Service Framework (SDSF). Each service within the framework is explored in terms of its value proposition and supporting value stream. Chapters 3–8 provide further guidance regarding the individual techniques used when delivering these services.

MATURITY OF THE SERVICE DESIGNER ROLE

The demand for the service designer role varies between organisations. Some organisations seek to apply service design by default on all service improvement initiatives, while other organisations have yet to encounter or consider the role at all. In addition, the service designer role is subject to mixed understanding and confusion. For example, for those with a background in IT service management (ITSM) there is a risk that the role is perceived to be focused on the design, delivery and management of IT services. Aligned to this school of thought are stakeholders, practitioners and organisations that have studied or adopted practices aligned to the Information Technology Infrastructure Library (ITIL). While these perspectives and standards contain valuable content, their roots in the IT service management discipline limit the potential for adoption of service design as a discipline focused on the holistic and continuous improvement of business, as opposed to IT, services. This chapter takes a holistic and non-IT centric perspective of the service designer role.

The areas of responsibility and artefacts associated with service design have gained recognition as the maturity and understanding of service design has developed. This has led to the role becoming more clearly defined resulting in greater stakeholder awareness.

The Capability Maturity Model Integration (CMMI) offers a basis for assessing the maturity of service design within an organisation. The CMMI was developed originally by the Software Engineering Institute (SEI) at Carnegie Mellon University and offers a standard for benchmarking and improving organisational processes.

Figure 2.1 is an adaption of the CMMI model and defines the stages in the maturity evolution of the service design standards and practices applied within an organisation.

Figure 2.1 Maturity evolution of the service designer role (© Assist Knowledge Development Ltd)

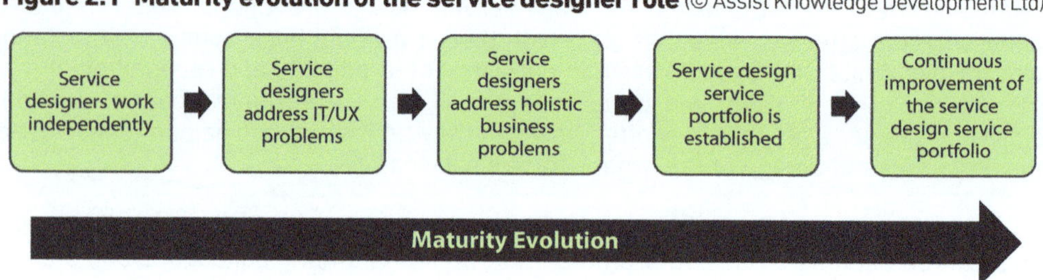

These stages are explained in Table 2.1.

Table 2.1 Maturity stages of the service designer role

Stage	Description
(1) Service designers work independently	Service design is a new discipline so lacks clarity of definition and output. Service designers work independently of each other and colleagues in related disciplines. Service design knowledge is not shared and few standards exist. Where defined, standards are rarely used. Service designers respond to requests in an ad hoc manner and are rarely proactive in supporting the organisation.
(2) Service designers address IT/user experience (UX) problems	Service design is recognised as a discipline focused on the enhancement and maintenance of IT and UX related to local service provision. Synergies across the service design community start to emerge leading to the adoption of standard approaches and artefacts. Service designers respond to requests and start to offer proactive support to the organisation.
(3) Service designers address holistic business problems	The service designer role focuses on addressing holistic business problems and opportunities. The service design community starts to be formalised leading to increased knowledge sharing, management and performance measurement and monitoring. Work is tailored to the improvement context. Service designers are proactive in identifying where they may support the organisation in enhancing individual business services.
(4) Service design service portfolio is established	Service designers apply a service mindset and consistent practices that are embedded across the organisation. They establish a portfolio based on the SDSF that is tailored to the needs of the organisation. Service designers work proactively to support and enable the execution of the organisation's strategy.
(5) Continuous improvement of the service design service portfolio	Service designers continually improve the design and execution of the service design service portfolio. Service designers are pivotal to the execution of the organisation's strategy.

Organisations working to establish a service design discipline need to clarify the role they expect their service designers to perform and define how this role relates to other relevant disciplines such as business analysis and business architecture. Without such clarification, there is likely to be role ambiguity and confusion among service design practitioners and their stakeholders. Role ambiguity raises the following issues:

- Those performing the role are not clear about their responsibilities, the standards they should apply and the outputs they should deliver. They are also unclear about the business outcomes their work supports and enables. Where service designers are unclear about their role, they may develop models and other artefacts without appreciating the strategic objectives and defined outcomes to be achieved.

- Those who are the recipients or 'customers' of the role outputs are unsure what to expect and how to best utilise the skills offered by the role. Where stakeholders are unclear about their expectations of the service designers, they are also unsure about how to apply any information or guidance provided, and may fail to request a service that a service designer can offer.

A service approach helps to ensure clarity of role definition by defining the portfolio of services offered by a role.

RATIONALE FOR THE SERVICE SYSTEM VIEW OF SERVICE DESIGN

The Business Analysis Service Framework (Paul, 2018) provided clarity on the services offered by business analysts. Additional service frameworks were developed and published within *Business Architecture* (Hunsley et al., 2025) for business architecture, service design, change management and project management.

A service framework is intended to establish the core services and value propositions offered by an individual role, and to provide a starting point for the development of shared understanding. An organisational service framework is a customised view of the standard service framework and defines the service portfolio offered by a role within that organisation. Service frameworks provide a foundation for discussion and agreement of the services offered by individual roles and as such provide a basis for the development of role clarity and shared understanding.

SERVICE DESIGN SERVICE FRAMEWORK (SDSF)

The SDSF defines a proposed portfolio of service design services. It has been developed to enable organisations to define the service designer role clearly and ensure it aligns with and supports the organisation's needs.

The SDSF shown in Figure 2.2 sets out a range of services that may be delivered by the service designers working within an organisation. This service framework offers a basis for consistency and role clarity within a community of service designers. The framework is intended to be customised so that it is relevant to a particular organisational context. It offers a basis for discussion with an organisation's stakeholders, enabling them to clarify what they require and which services should be offered by the service design practitioners.

Figure 2.2 The SDSF (Adapted from Hunsley et al., 2025)

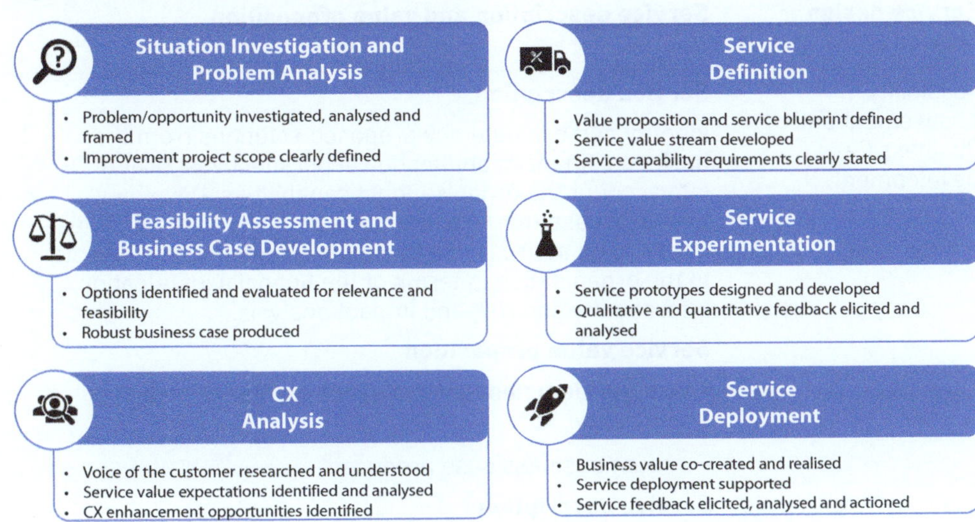

Each of the services shown within this SDSF is described in overview in Table 2.2.

Table 2.2 Service design service descriptions

Service design service	Service description and value proposition
Situation Investigation and Problem Analysis	**Service description** Investigate business situations that are problematic or where opportunities for service development or improvement are identified. Analyse the root causes of problems, and distinguish them from the manifest symptoms, or the potential opportunity. Frame the problem to be addressed or the opportunity to be grasped. Define the scope of the desired solution. **Service value proposition** • problem/opportunity investigated, analysed and framed; • improvement project scope clearly defined.

(Continued)

Table 2.2 (Continued)

Service design service	Service description and value proposition
Feasibility Assessment and Business Case Development	**Service description** Identify and evaluate any proposed solutions from the business, financial and technical perspectives, taking into account the organisational capabilities. Develop a business case that explains the situation and the business needs to be addressed and explores the options available to the organisation in terms of the financial justification, affordability and risk and impact analysis. **Service value proposition** • options identified and evaluated for relevance and feasibility; • robust business case produced.
Customer Experience (CX) Analysis	**Service description** Research, analyse and define the voice of the customer and service value expectations. Investigate and analyse both stated and implied customer wants and needs. **Service value proposition** • voice of the customer researched and understood; • service value expectations identified and analysed; • CX enhancement opportunities identified.
Service Definition	**Service description** Research, analyse and define current and proposed business services. **Service value proposition** • value proposition and service blueprint defined; • service value stream developed; • service capability requirements clearly stated.
Service Experimentation	**Service description** Support the design and development of service prototypes. Elicit and analyse feedback against prototypes to enable iteration and continuous improvement. **Service value proposition** • service prototypes designed and developed; • qualitative and quantitative feedback elicited and analysed.

(Continued)

Table 2.2 (Continued)

Service design service	Service description and value proposition
Service Deployment	**Service description** Support the deployment of new or enhanced services. Elicit and analyse feedback against services to enable continuous improvement. **Service value proposition** • business value co-created and realised; • Service Deployment supported; • service feedback elicited, analysed and actioned.

An auxiliary service – stakeholder engagement – is also provided by service designers when delivering each SDSF service.

The SDSF may be summarised to clarify the service designer role as follows:

The service designer role collaborates with stakeholders to co-create value for organisations through offering the following services:

- Situation Investigation and Problem Analysis;
- Feasibility Assessment and Business Case Development;
- CX Analysis;
- Service Definition;
- Service Experimentation;
- Service Deployment.

VALUE STREAMS FOR SDSF

Situation Investigation and Problem Analysis

This service is required when a business situation has been identified as problematic, requiring improvement or offering a service opportunity. The service aligns with the discovery phase of the Double Diamond covered in Chapter 1. The service designer collaborates with other change professionals to investigate any issues, identify problems and their root causes and define the scope and shape of the required change.

Stakeholders often highlight the problems they have observed within their business area and may identify how they feel these problems should be resolved. However, it is often the case that the 'problems' are the symptoms experienced rather than the deeper problems – the root causes. It is incumbent upon the service designer to challenge any assumptions made about the situation, ask questions of the stakeholders and review the available information objectively, to ensure the actual problems are uncovered. The investigation should also consider the impact of the problems on the delivered service, strategic goals, business outcomes and customer experiences.

Service designers collaborate with the stakeholders involved in the business situation to elicit and investigate the issues. This may require them to review various aspects of the situation, such as the processes and information, to identify where problems originate and which elements of the service need to be reviewed and improved.

Stakeholder engagement is key to the success of this service. Different stakeholders are able to offer their views and experiences about the issues and analysing these different perspectives provides a holistic view and helps to enrich the service designers' understanding.

The value proposition offered by the Situation Investigation and Problem Analysis service is that the business area is investigated and analysed with care to provide:

- a clear statement of the business problem to be addressed;
- a definition of the scope of the improvement project that is required to resolve the problem.

The activities required to carry out the Situation Investigation and Problem Analysis service are shown in the value stream diagram in Figure 2.3.

Figure 2.3 Value stream: Situation Investigation and Problem Analysis service
(Adapted from Hunsley et al., 2025)

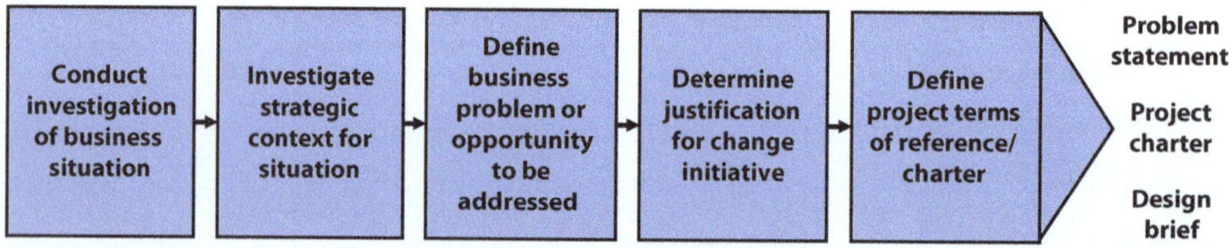

The context for this service is often unclear, with significant ambiguity regarding the issues affecting the situation and the ways in which they might be addressed. Accordingly, service designers need to possess a toolkit of techniques that enable them to contend with the ambiguity and work effectively with the stakeholders and their business change colleagues. Service designers require significant personal skills to enable them to discuss concerns at different levels within the organisation, manage expectations and navigate conflicting views.

The core techniques used in support of this service are explored in Chapter 3.

Feasibility Assessment and Business Case Development

This service is concerned with identifying the options that are available to improve a business situation and evaluating which option offers the best way forward. Each option should be considered from the three feasibility perspectives: business, financial and technical feasibility. Aspects to consider for these three perspectives are shown in Figure 2.4.

Figure 2.4 Three dimensions for feasibility assessment (Adapted from Paul and Cadle, 2020)

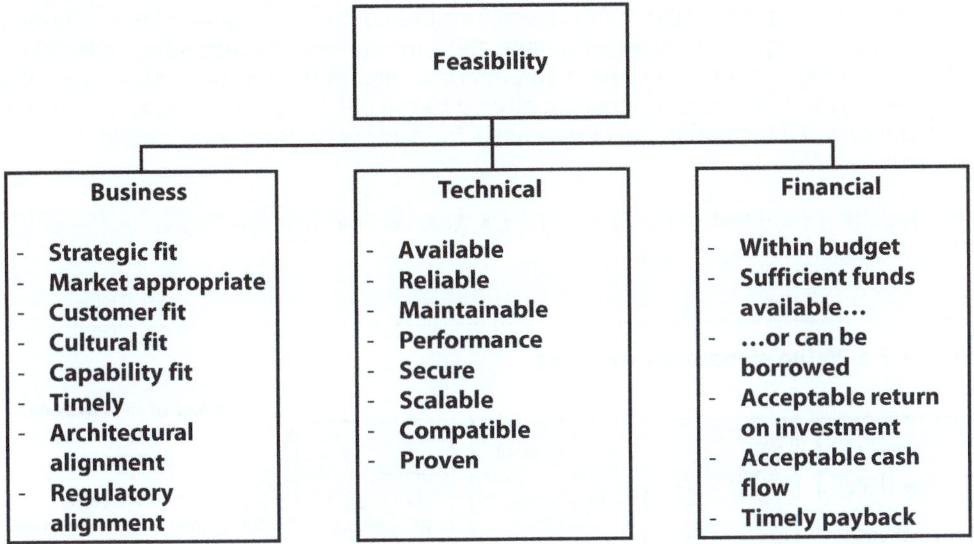

The activities required to carry out the Feasibility Assessment and Business Case Development service are shown in the value stream diagram in Figure 2.5.

Figure 2.5 Value stream: Feasibility Assessment and Business Case Development service (Adapted from Hunsley et al., 2025)

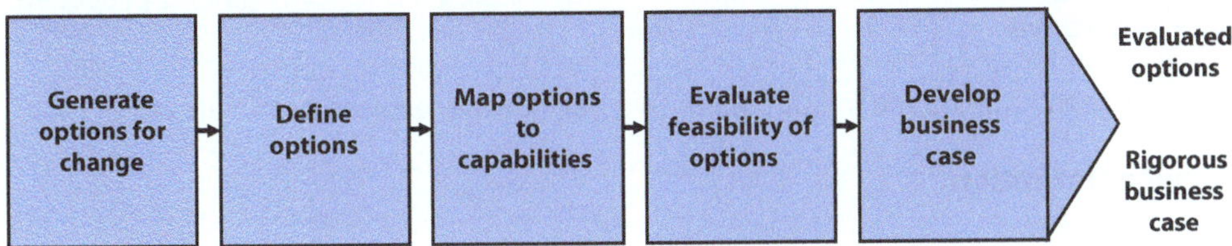

Assessing the business feasibility focuses on the alignment of an option with the organisational context. This may require the service designer to consider aspects such as the values and core purpose of the organisation, the organisational strategy and whether the option would be likely to succeed given this context.

The core techniques used in support of this service are explored in Chapter 4.

CX Analysis

This service is concerned with analysing and improving the customer experience encountered during the customer journeys undertaken when accessing an organisation's products or services. The delivery of this service enables service designers to offer a considered view of a customer journey that helps identify opportunities to improve the experience encountered by customers.

The service designer researches the voice of the customer to gain information and insights regarding customer expectations and experiences. The activities undertaken when providing this service require an understanding of the strategic context for the organisation and the value proposition offered by the particular products and services. This contextual information provides a basis for comparison with the voice of the customer research.

The activities required to carry out the CX Analysis service are shown in the value stream diagram in Figure 2.6.

Figure 2.6 Value stream: CX Analysis

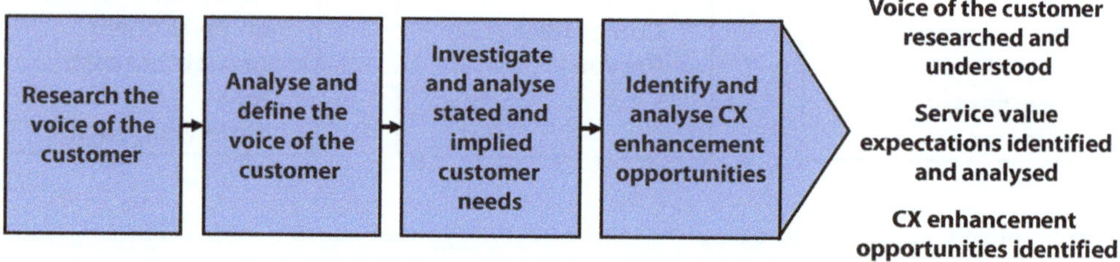

The strategic context for the organisation is subject to change. In addition, customer expectations can also change. If an organisation is to successfully adapt and deploy products and services that align with the value expectations of customers, the continued execution of this service in alignment with strategic decision-making processes is an imperative.

The core techniques used in support of this service are explored in Chapter 5.

Service Definition

This service is concerned with researching, analysing and defining both current and proposed business services. It includes defining the service value proposition, activities and features, and developing the service blueprint. The service blueprint should clarify the service value stream and the enabling capability requirements.

Some stakeholders perceive this service to be the only service offered by service design professionals. Mistakenly, they assume that the service blueprint is the only output used to define a service. While service blueprinting is a fundamental component of a Service Definition, the value proposition, value stream activities and enabling capabilities must also be documented. The extended Service Definition provides a basis for defining any capability gaps that need to be addressed.

These outputs ensure the service designer considers the following perspectives:

- who (the proposed beneficiary);
- why (service value proposition);
- what (service value stream);
- how (service blueprint and service capability requirements).

The activities required to carry out the Service Definition service are shown in the value stream diagram in Figure 2.7.

Figure 2.7 Value stream: Service Definition

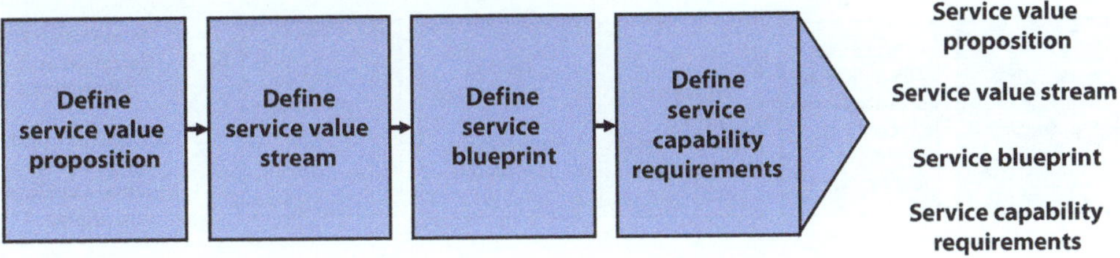

The application of the techniques identified in Service Definition provides the opportunity for shared understanding of the service with other change professionals such as business architects and business analysts. This is a prerequisite for value co-creation.

The core techniques used in support of this service are explored in Chapter 6.

Service Experimentation

This service is concerned with ideating and prototyping a range of potential solutions and using experimentation, testing and customer feedback to define desired ways forward.

Initially, divergent thinking is required to identify a range of potential solutions. Each should be considered as a hypothesis (or idea) for a proposed change that aims to solve an identified problem or opportunity.

It is not possible to test every single idea unless time and resources are unlimited. Convergent thinking is applied to sift the ideas and identify which proposed solutions can be prioritised for prototype development. Prototypes are used to experiment with ideas and demonstrate proposed solutions in order to obtain feedback and develop understanding. Each prototype also helps with the validation of any assumptions made by the service designers and their stakeholders, and clarifies where there are risks in adopting a particular approach.

Learning from testing a prototype and gaining feedback enables a decision to be made about the next steps, including:

- repeating the previous steps of the value stream;
- conducting further investigation into the business situation or voice of the customer;
- ceasing Service Experimentation work;
- accepting a proposed solution and progressing to Service Deployment.

The activities required to carry out the Service Experimentation service are shown in the value stream diagram in Figure 2.8.

Figure 2.8 Value stream: Service Experimentation

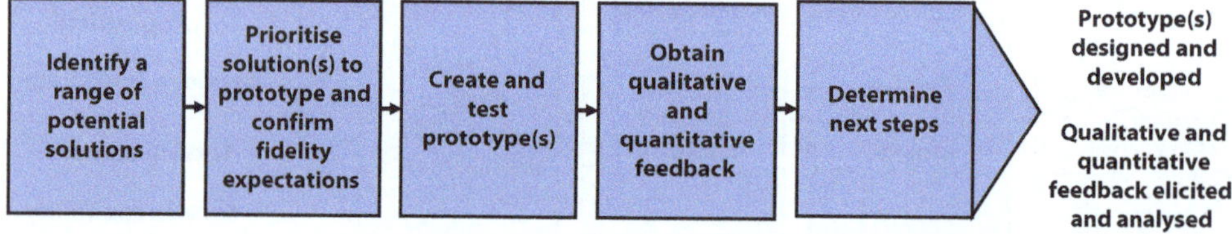

The core techniques used in support of this service are explored in Chapter 7.

Service Deployment

This service is concerned with the deployment of a product or service into operation. The execution of this service is often conducted alongside other change professionals such as change managers, project managers and business analysts.

Initially, this service involves assessing business readiness to adopt the new product or service. Business readiness assessment provides a basis for understanding the transition requirements (including communication of changes to stakeholders and addressing any training needs). Once identified, the service designer supports the development of necessary outputs and importantly the adoption of the service change itself. Once the service is deployed, the service designer should seek objective feedback. Where necessary, this can lead to the prioritisation and completion of actions required to enhance the service.

The activities required to carry out the Service Experimentation service are shown in the value stream diagram in Figure 2.9.

Figure 2.9 Value stream: Service Deployment

Assess business readiness	→	Identify transition requirements	→	Support adoption of service changes	→	Obtain qualitative and quantitative feedback	→	Prioritise and action feedback	Service deployment supported Value co-created Service feedback elicited, analysed and actioned

The core techniques used in support of this service are explored in Chapter 8.

Stakeholder engagement

The stakeholder engagement service is not included in the SDSF because it is an auxiliary service that must be applied when conducting any of the core services. This is the case for all of the business change professions, where stakeholder engagement is a relevant service irrespective of the particular role.

Stakeholders are affected by every business change initiative. However, the impact on individual stakeholders or stakeholder groups varies depending upon their position in the organisation's ecosystem. For example, some stakeholders may be affected directly by the changes while there may be a minimal, indirect impact on others. Some stakeholders may have specific perspectives about the business problems or opportunities and the nature of relevant solutions, while others may disagree or be indifferent. Customers are key stakeholders as their engagement with a product or service is essential if value is to be co-created.

It is the responsibility of the service designers and other change professionals to engage with the stakeholders and understand the rationale for their perspectives. Without this understanding, there is a risk of stakeholder resistance or even opposition.

The stakeholder engagement service offers the following value proposition:

> To support the achievement of business change success through effective stakeholder relationship management and communication.

The activities required to carry out the stakeholder engagement service are varied. Some are proactive, while others are responses to events, but this is rarely a service where a linear process may be followed. Figure 2.10 sets out the range of activities within the stakeholder engagement service.

Figure 2.10 Stakeholder engagement activities (Source: Hunsley et al., 2025)

Chapter 9 describes techniques that can be used in support of stakeholder engagement.

CASE STUDY: SERVICE DESIGN AT PFP

Michael Greenhalgh explains the introduction and application of service design within the social enterprise, PfP.

The context: where PfP started with business architecture and service design

PfP is a large and complex social enterprise with more than 262,000 homes across all tenures, over 100 leisure centres, almost a million customers across the UK, and more than 20 complementary companies. The organisation focuses on creating and supporting thriving communities by building new homes, investing in homelessness prevention, supporting customers with their finances and welcoming millions of visitors to leisure centres across the country.

At PfP the Business Architecture team is part of the Strategy Office, which serves as the organisational anchor for aligning strategy with execution, ensuring all efforts are unified toward delivering an effortless customer experience. Through close collaboration with our colleagues within the Strategy Office, the Customer Research and Insight (CR&I) team, we advocate a structured, holistic approach to business architecture, while staying adaptive to evolving customer needs and market dynamics.

PfP Business Architecture sits outside the IT function, so has the opportunity to advocate for customer-centric design and demonstrate how working collaboratively with CR&I can remove service design gaps. We achieve this through co-creating reusable models, building credibility through practical use cases and leveraging our partnership.

As PfP doesn't have specific service design roles, we have needed to clarify where the available roles should work together when designing services and developing complementary deliverables. Figure 2.11 represents the PfP illustration of this approach.

Figure 2.11 PfP customer-centric role structure

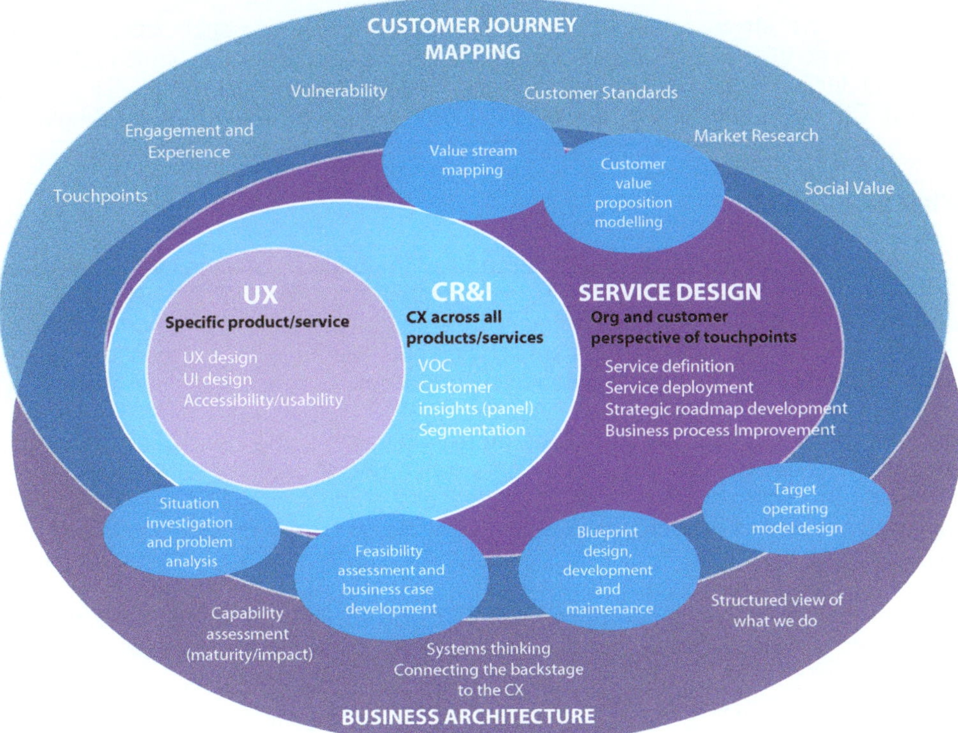

To aid with shared understanding, we need to recognise where there are overlaps in services offered by the various professional disciplines. Some overlaps between business architecture and service design are obvious (for example, with the business analysis services of 'Situation Investigation and Problem Analysis' and 'Feasibility Assessment and Business Case Development' identified within the Business Analysis Service Framework (Paul, 2018)), for other disciplines this overlap in services is less clear (for example, with risk or quality management).

Where service overlaps exist, the team needs to show how we offer additional value to engagements. Business architecture provides a structured approach to ensure the holistic consideration of POPIT™, connected through capability models. Value stream modelling (representing value stages, inputs, outputs and stakeholders) also aids in the development of a holistic and customer-centric view. Information regarding capability and value stream models is captured through workshops and process shadowing. This approach enables us to identify dependencies across teams. We also consider key performance indicators (KPIs), service level agreements (SLAs) and controls that affect services.

The Strategy Office teams emphasise a broader time horizon, focusing on strategic alignment, the to-be operational model and longer-term goals, innovation opportunities and future state vision. However, the business architecture team also provides support on projects focused on short-term deliverables and service enhancements.

As a team, we strive actively to demonstrate the value of collaboration and co-creation. To do this, we use various models and views that provide insights and enable informed decision-making. These structured models also enable greater visibility and control. Other benefits of the approach include a reduced volume of meetings and documentation, as well as streamlined reporting to support decision-making.

What went well?

A supportive senior leadership team recognised the benefits of aligning CR&I, service design and business architecture in a single strategic function at PfP. It was extremely beneficial to be part of the PfP Strategy Office and aligned to the director of strategy as there were significant complementary aspects. The alignment of business architecture with other domains was aided by a consistent approach and clear standards.

The concept of 'business services' was more familiar to some colleagues than 'business capabilities'. However, the focus on service design had the secondary benefit of helping to improve understanding of business architecture. The service-focused approach enabled us to capture valuable insights to add to our models and knowledge base.

A business architecture knowledge base is complex and there are many threads to maintain and decisions and impacts to track. It was important to show the value offered by the knowledge base at an early stage; contributing to service design proved an excellent way to achieve this.

Through collaborating, Business Architects can fast-track the knowledge base development, building on existing work and achieving some early wins. This also offers the opportunity to expand networks, opportunities, and business context knowledge, without having to establish the need or assume full responsibility for facilitation or outcomes.

Collaborations with others involved in service design (CX leads, business analysts, subject matter experts (SMEs)/business unit leaders) included target operating model design, strategic roadmap development, blueprint development and maintenance.

Due to an absence of dedicated service designers, business architects were able to help with Service Definition. The approach helped identify gaps, ensure connection between initiatives and encourage big picture thinking. Through taking an end-to-end analysis and design approach (supported by value stream and capability analysis), we have been able to define the service requirements and the capabilities needed to fulfil these requirements. Discussion regarding the value proposition has been added to discovery workshops to support the development of a holistic, informed and strategically aligned set of views/blueprints.

The PfP business architecture framework and supporting guidance make the approach clear and support improved clarity, alignment and constructive challenge. The framework defines the artefacts produced and the roles and responsibilities of those involved. Requesting and responding to stakeholder feedback, and subsequently adapting the framework to the context, enabled adoption. For example, clarifying what inputs and support business architects need, what they will provide and why helped encourage adoption. Through highlighting differences and complementary perspectives between roles, we were able to improve collaboration to achieve desired outcomes and increase advocacy.

Working closely with CR&I provided useful insights and established ongoing commitment to better understand complementary capabilities and the value of customer insight linked to holistic organisational models.

Practical application opportunities to collaborate helped to validate a joint approach to support service design and enabled us to demonstrate the value of business architecture and customer insight.

What did not go well?

Establishing the need for service design and demonstrating the value of business architecture at the same time has led to existing resources being stretched. Stakeholder engagement and time constraints are a constant challenge. While we have worked hard to establish the need and value this combined approach offers, there has been a strain on resource capacity.

Significant effort has been spent agreeing roles and responsibilities, particularly where role conflicts and overlaps need to be addressed. If not resolved, this issue can lead to wasteful duplication of work and the provision of contradictory advice. This can impact credibility negatively and cause significant rework.

Building capability in business architecture and CR&I, and ensuring effective collaboration, requires a team effort. It was challenging to secure time with partners across the business, given their competing business priorities and timescales. The complexity of the organisation has meant that significant time and effort have been needed to establish a common vocabulary and cross-organisational views.

Business architecture, CR&I and service design conduct complex work and are new disciplines to many PfP stakeholders. Therefore, thoughtful, clear communication that is delivered when needed is essential; trying to progress too quickly has sometimes caused setbacks.

What are the lessons learned?

Business architects are developing the baseline knowledge base while attempting to support service design. The content in the knowledge base becomes more useful once it reaches a critical mass but that takes time and effort. Cross-mapping business architecture artefacts with the application(s), data and technology architectures to ensure coherence across the enterprise landscape has not been possible to date, as enterprise architecture continues to gain maturity within PfP. However, plans are in place to build cross-mapping of relationships between applications and stakeholders, business units, value streams and business capabilities.

Our greatest successes have resulted from working with business units that were ready to engage with our approach, supporting programmes of work that were resourced and where business buy-in was assured through sponsorship. These successes provided a basis for progression and resulted in advocacy from stakeholders. This helped to illustrate the value realised from our approach and, as a result, gained the support from other areas of the business.

The PfP business architecture team had to be prepared to deal with imperfect circumstances, information and engagement. The team needed to be creative, using an iterative approach to enable models to evolve. The model in Figure 2.11 was used to illustrate the multiple overlapping roles, approaches and contributions, and provide a basis for shared understanding and the development of a responsible, accountable, consulted, informed (RACI) matrix.

CONCLUSION

The SDSF has been developed to offer a service view that clarifies the service designer role. This chapter has described the service design services and has provided a set of value stream activities that collectively fulfil a value proposition for each service. Chapters 3–8 describe the individual techniques used in support of these services and Chapter 9 describes the techniques that support the Stakeholder Engagement service. Chapters 10–11 describe generic techniques used in support of all services.

While the SDSF is intended to clarify the service designer role, it is anticipated that it will be subject to customisation by each organisation. The organisational context is key when defining roles, and the service designer role is no exception. Therefore, the framework provides a starting point from which an organisation can clarify the service design services offered and develop its service design capability.

3 SITUATION INVESTIGATION AND PROBLEM ANALYSIS

This chapter covers the work conducted by service designers during the Situation Investigation and Problem Analysis service. The key activities of this service and the techniques that may be applied to carry out these activities are described in this chapter. These techniques may be supplemented by other techniques, in particular those described in Chapters 10 and 11. The techniques described in Chapters 4–9 may also be applied to offer additional insights, particularly where relevant to a specific context.

INTRODUCTION

The importance of investigating a problematic business situation or an identified business opportunity cannot be overstated. Too often, this initial service is conducted in a limited manner or not conducted at all, leading to ill-defined projects and assignments, unpopular, fragmented changes and expensive failed initiatives. The aim of this service is to look beyond the obvious symptoms of problems to uncover where the root causes and underlying issues lie. It is not possible to frame a problem clearly – or scope an opportunity – if there is limited understanding of the legitimate issues.

THE SITUATION INVESTIGATION AND PROBLEM ANALYSIS SERVICE

This service includes the following service activities:

- Investigate business situations that are problematic or offer opportunities for improvement.
- Identify root causes of problems and distinguish them from the manifest symptoms.
- Analyse and define the problem to be addressed.
- Define the scope of the desired solution.

The service value items offered by the service concerns the following:

- problem/opportunity investigated, analysed and defined;
- improvement project scope clearly defined.

Figure 3.1 shows a value stream diagram for this service, including the deliverables provided.

Figure 3.1 Value stream: Situation Investigation and Problem Analysis service
(Adapted from Hunsley et al., 2025)

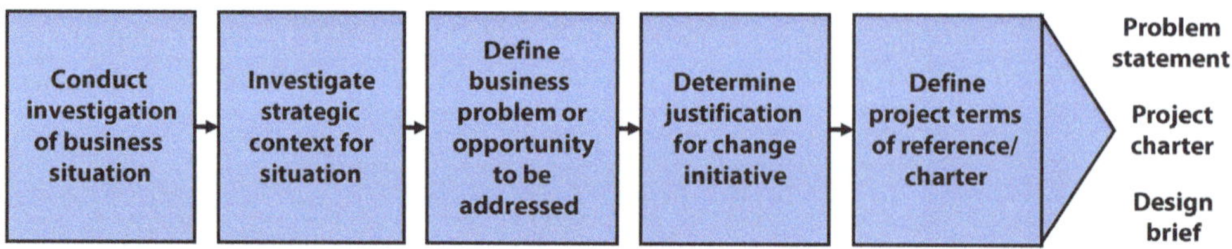

The nature of the problems to be investigated by service designers can vary considerably. Some may be localised and straightforward to define and resolve, while others may be more complex and have a broader, cross-functional impact. Where a problem is complex, service designers may need to apply a variety of techniques and use frameworks such as Soft Systems Methodology (see Chapter 12) to define the most relevant approach.

THE TECHNIQUES

The extensive service designer toolkit includes numerous techniques, many of which may be used to carry out the work of this service. A service designer required to conduct situation investigation should always consider which techniques may be relevant as the work progresses. The generic techniques used in investigation are described in Chapters 10 and 11. Service design techniques that are often beneficial when undertaking this service are:

- service safari;
- rich picture;
- fishbone diagram;
- empathy map;
- problem definition.

Service safari

Purpose

A service safari is used to enable service designers to gain personal experience of a service. The objective is to obtain detailed insights into the way in which a service is provided and the nature of the service.

Examples of services where a service safari would be insightful are:

- eating a meal in a restaurant;
- attending a training course;
- staying at a hotel;
- buying items in a shop;
- purchasing a flight.

Process

The process for conducting a service safari is shown in Figure 3.2.

Figure 3.2 Service safari process

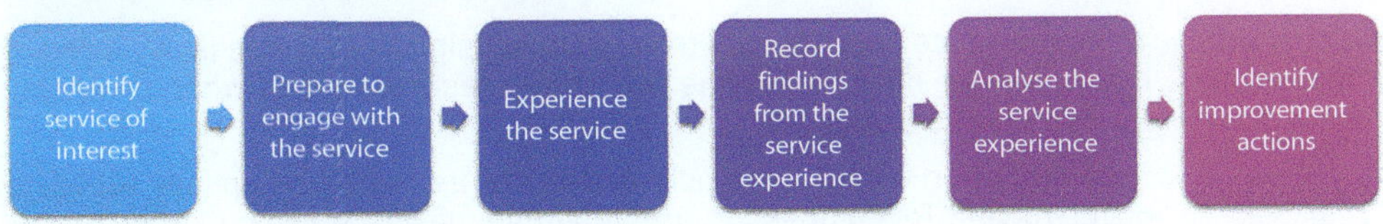

These stages are described in Table 3.1.

Table 3.1 The stages required to conduct a service safari

Stage	Description
Identify service of interest	The service designer needs to understand the services under investigation and identify those where a service safari would be beneficial.
Prepare to engage with the service	Services tend to be initiated by different business events each of which may require a particular scenario to be conducted. For example, a meal in a restaurant may be required because of a celebration (such as a birthday or anniversary), a desire to try a new restaurant or chef or may just be a regular social event with friends. Each of these events may result in different scenarios taking place within the restaurant. The service designer needs to identify the events and the possible scenarios and should decide which situation should be the focus of the service safari. The preparation should also include identifying any particular aspects for investigation. For example, if eating a meal in a restaurant, the following aspects are considered: • booking experience: the efficiency of the booking process; • serving experience: the efficiency of the meal ordering and delivery service; the helpfulness of the restaurant staff; • product experience: the quality of the food; • environment experience: the décor and general presentation of the restaurant. Frameworks such as the POPIT™ model and Feedback Capture Grid (see Glossary of Terms and Techniques) may be used to structure this part of the preparation activity. Preparation is essential for an effective service safari. Service designers should be clear about the reason for the service and the desired outcome if they are to evaluate the characteristics and effectiveness of the service.

(Continued)

Table 3.1 (Continued)

Stage	Description
Experience the service	The service designer engages with the organisation, applying the agreed scenario and adapting as necessary to the reality of the delivered service. Where possible, notes about the experience are made.
Record findings from the service experience	The experience encountered through accessing the service is recorded by the service designer, in line with the aspects identified when preparing for the service safari. Service design techniques such as a customer journey map (see Glossary of Terms and Techniques) or empathy map (described below) may be used to record different aspects of the service experience.
Analyse the service experience	The service experience is analysed using relevant service design techniques and frameworks. For example, where a customer journey map has been created, each activity or stage is analysed to identify any particular issues or highlights. These are then examined further to identify areas for improvement. Divergent thinking may be used to explore the various aspects of the service experience and identify a wide range of issues. Convergent thinking is then applied to clarify and define the problems to be addressed. Divergent/convergent thinking is described in Chapter 1.
Identify improvement actions	A service blueprint may evolve during the analysis of the service safari information, resulting in the identification of the 'back stage' areas where improvement is needed. Divergent thinking may be used to generate suggestions for improvement and to create innovative ways forward. This is followed by convergent thinking to synthesise and prioritise the actions to improve the service experience.

Benefits of a service safari

A service safari places the service designer within the delivered service, enabling them to gain personal experience of all aspects of the service. Figure 3.3 shows the benefits offered by this technique.

Figure 3.3 Service safari benefits

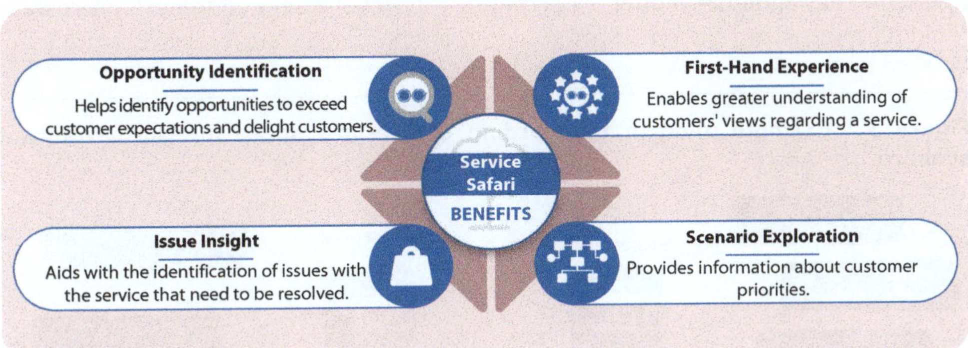

Example service safari

A service safari has been conducted to explore the service quality at a restaurant. The scenario enacted is described in Table 3.2.

Table 3.2 Example service safari scenario

Scenario element	Description
Context: why	A family of four wishing to celebrate a birthday. The family consists of two adults and two teenage children.
Content: what	A meal that meets the needs of all four family members. One of the family is vegetarian and another has a gluten intolerance.
Process: how	Booking made online. Family arrive on time at the restaurant. Drinks are ordered. Main meal only ordered. Dessert requested once main meal eaten. Payment made by credit card by one of the adult members of the party.
Outcome: how well	Consider the following: • ease and efficiency of booking; • welcome on arrival; efficiency of guiding to the table; • the environment for attractiveness and cleanliness; • speed of ordering and delivery of items; • quality of drinks and food; • speed of taking payment; • efficiency of ordering, delivery and payment systems; • availability of information regarding the menu.

The results of the service safari may be recorded in text or diagrammatically. A mind map can be a useful approach as it helps to structure the service report and can be adapted to any situation. Figure 3.4 provides a report of a service safari for a restaurant meal.

Figure 3.4 Example mind map recording the service safari for the restaurant scenario

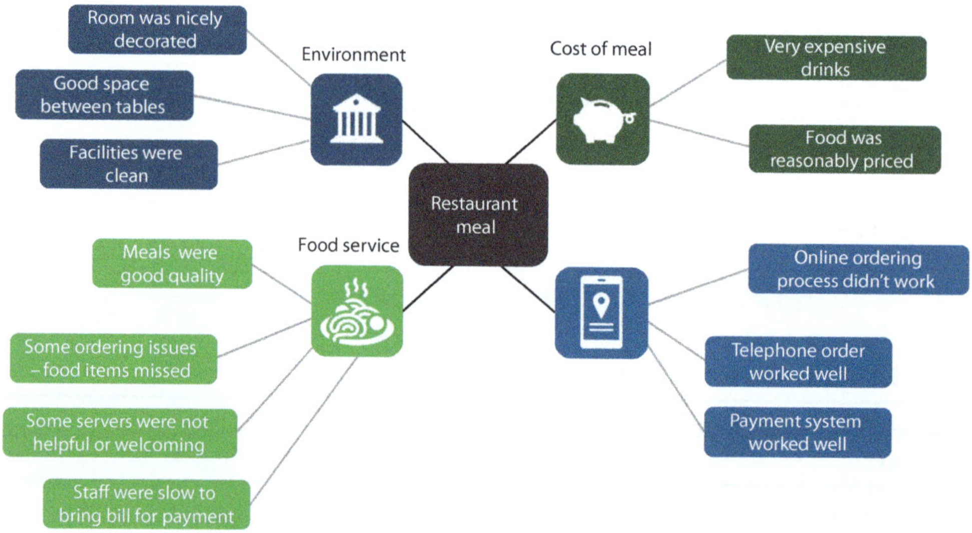

Service safari results can identify where service improvements are needed. They may also be used during voice of the customer analysis, possibly to augment a customer journey map and support service blueprint development.

Rich picture

Purpose

A rich picture is a free-format technique that is used to record information about a business situation (Checkland, 1981). Rich pictures are highly visual and do not apply formal modelling guidelines; instead, the service designer may use any symbols or images that they feel are relevant and helpful. Accordingly, they can accommodate any aspect relevant to the business situation under investigation, including relationships between people, different stakeholder perspectives on the situation and the organisational culture.

The objective of a rich picture is to enable anyone from a transformational change discipline, such as service design, to develop a mental map of the key challenges and risks inherent in a business situation.

Examples of business situations where a rich picture would support the service investigation are:

- A sales process where incorrect product orders have been recorded.
- A customer journey where several of the touchpoints indicate problems when engaging with customers.
- A café where the staff feel overworked and unable to deliver the level of service required by customers.

Process

The process to develop a rich picture is shown in Figure 3.5.

Figure 3.5 Process to develop a rich picture

Identify service situation to explore → Elicit information about the situation → Record the elicited information → Analyse the rich picture → Elicit further information → Enrichen the picture → Continue building the rich picture as required

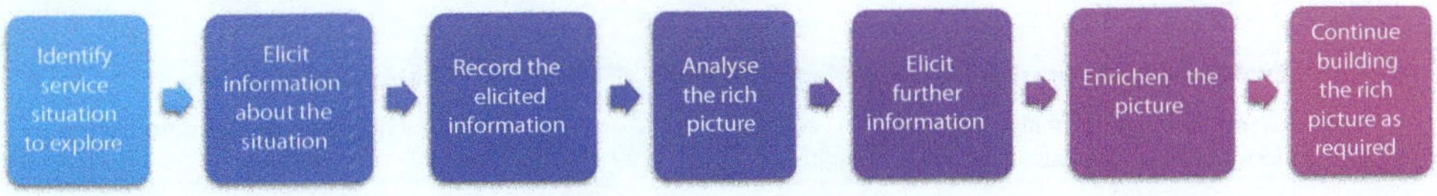

These stages are described in Table 3.3.

Table 3.3 The stages applied to develop a rich picture

Stage	Description
Identify service situation to explore	The area under investigation is identified and the scope to be explored is clarified. This may concern an entire business function, department, team or service.
Elicit information about the situation	Techniques to elicit information about the area are applied. At this initial stage, generic techniques such as interviews and workshops are used (see Glossary of Terms and Techniques).
Record the elicited information	The information elicited is recorded using any relevant images, symbols, notation or text. A rich picture is a visualisation that reflects personal or team understanding so should include imagery that is relevant to those responsible for its development.
Analyse the rich picture	The initial rich picture is analysed to identify where further investigation is needed. A key factor to consider is whether the information gained is based on authentic data or is an opinion. Where the latter is the case, it may be possible to validate the opinion by seeking confirmatory data.
Elicit further information	Additional techniques are applied to elicit further information. This stage may involve voice of the customer or design thinking techniques such as customer journey maps or empathy maps.
Enrich the picture	The rich picture should be enhanced, or enriched, with further imagery to represent the additional information.
Continue building the rich picture	This process continues until the rich picture is felt to provide a sufficiently detailed representation of the situation under investigation.

Benefits of a rich picture

A rich picture enables the service designer to represent a comprehensive view of the organisational, human and cultural aspects as well as the process and information flows related to a business situation or service. The unstructured nature of the technique allows the service designer significant freedom to document a wide variety of issues.

Figure 3.6 shows the benefits offered by a rich picture.

Figure 3.6 Rich picture benefits

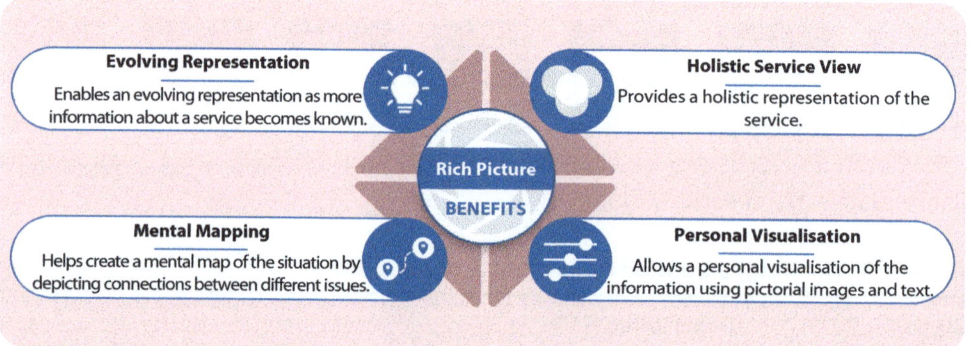

Example rich picture

Figure 3.7 shows a rich picture that summarises some of the key issues within the restaurant scenario.

Figure 3.7 Example rich picture for the restaurant scenario

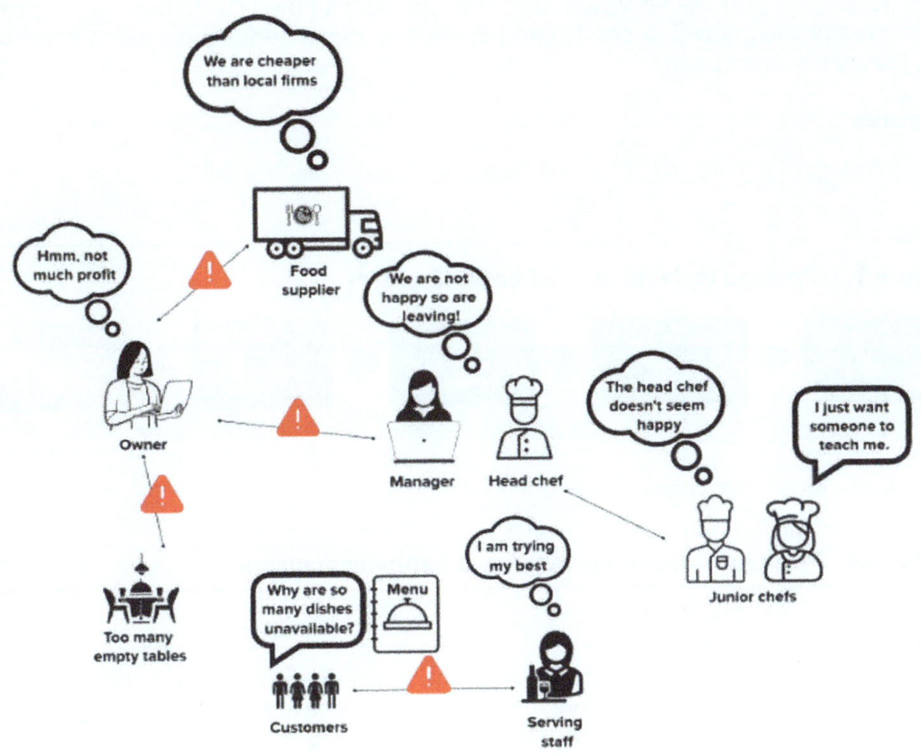

Fishbone diagram

Purpose

A fishbone, or Ishikawa, diagram is used to record structured information about a problematic service. It offers a means of investigating and analysing a problem using a selected framework. The framework helps to isolate different aspects relevant to the problem that may be explored in further detail.

Examples of the frameworks used are:

- The six Ps: people, processes, place, performance measures, physical evidence, product. Additional 'Ps', price and/or promotion, may also be included if relevant.
- The five Ss: systems, staff, skills, surroundings, suppliers. Additional 'Ss', such as shared values and/or strategy, may also be included to form 6 Ss or 7 Ss frameworks if relevant.
- The six Ms: machines, methods, manpower, materials, mindset, measures.
- The POPIT™ model.

A combination of these frameworks may also be used to construct the fishbone diagram.

The technique helps the service designer to understand the factors that may contribute to the problems with a service and to explore the underlying issues that are the root causes of a problem.

Process

The process to develop a fishbone diagram is shown in Figure 3.8.

Figure 3.8 Process to develop a fishbone diagram

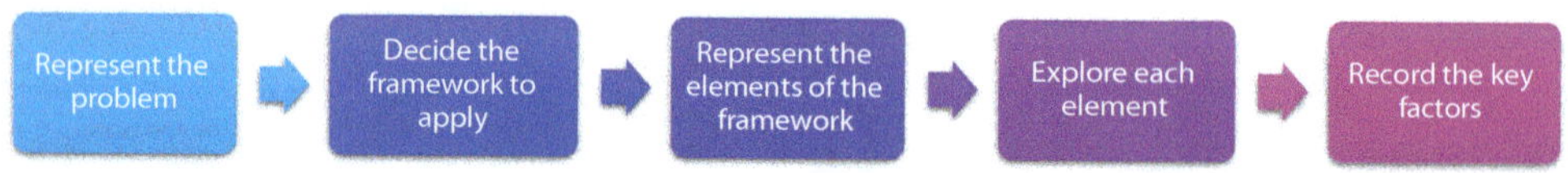

These stages are described in Table 3.4.

Table 3.4 The stages applied to develop a fishbone diagram

Stage	Description
Represent the problem	Draw a box to represent the 'head' of the 'fish'. State the problem succinctly within the box. Draw a central spine, emanating from the box representing the 'head'.
Decide the framework to apply	Review the available frameworks (see above) and decide which combination of elements would provide the most relevant structure for analysing the problem.
Represent the elements of the framework	Draw the 'spines' of the fish; one spine per element from the selected framework.
Explore each element	Analyse each element to identify the positive and negative factors that have an impact on the problem situation.
Record the key factors	Draw the key factors as smaller lines emerging from each spine. Draw positive factors in green with each line shown to the left of the spine. Draw negative factors in red with each line shown to the right of the spine. Further detailed points may be added as lines emerging from the corresponding positive or negative factor.

Benefits of a fishbone diagram

Figure 3.9 shows the benefits offered by the fishbone diagram technique.

Figure 3.9 Fishbone diagram benefits

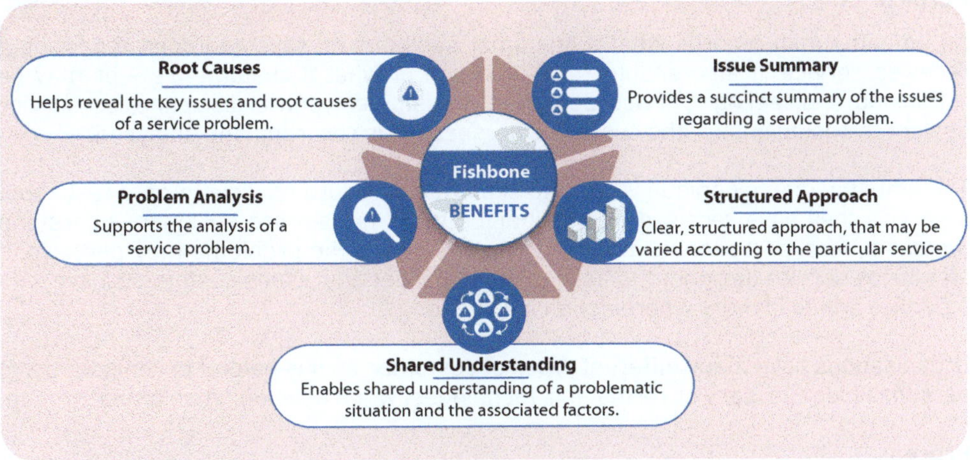

Root Causes
Helps reveal the key issues and root causes of a service problem.
Issue Summary
Provides a succinct summary of the issues regarding a service problem.
Fishbone
BENEFITS
Problem Analysis
Supports the analysis of a service problem.
Structured Approach
Clear, structured approach, that may be varied according to the particular service.
Shared Understanding
Enables shared understanding of a problematic situation and the associated factors.

Example fishbone diagram

Figure 3.10 is an example of a fishbone diagram for the restaurant scenario. This fishbone diagram uses a version of the 6 Ps framework as it provides a means of exploring the factors most relevant to the problem.

Figure 3.10 Example fishbone diagram for the restaurant scenario

People
Processes
Promotion
Keen junior chefs
Senior staff have left
Owner has clear vision
No central ordering system
Complex food supply processes
Fresh ingredients promised
Numerous complaints
Local food suppliers
Proximity to customers
New, cheaper suppliers
Required service times met
Many customer complaints about quality
Use of local ingredients
Menu too extensive
Place
Performance measures
Product

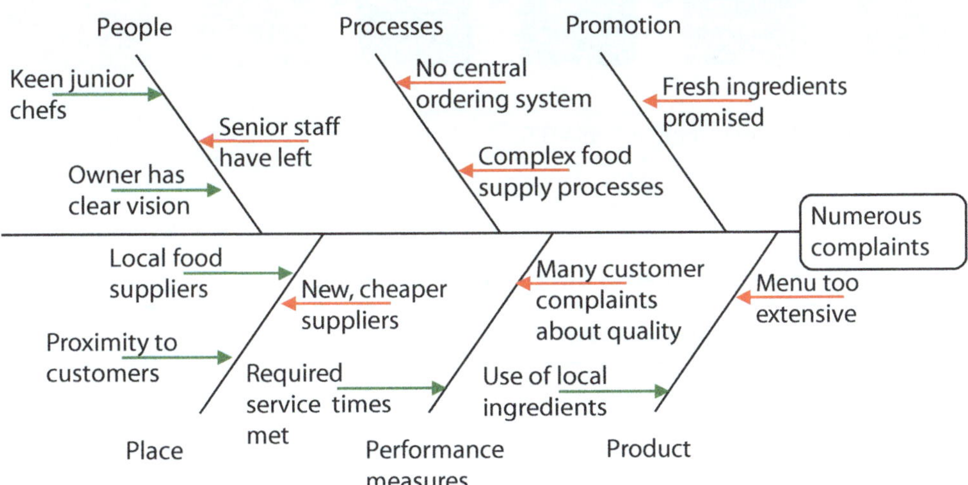

Empathy map

Purpose

An empathy map records what a customer sees, hears, says and does regarding a received service. It also enables consideration of what a customer is – or may be – thinking and feeling. Service design is a customer-centric discipline, so service designers should ensure the customer perspective is recorded and analysed.

The empathy map technique is used to explore and record how customers feel about a service they have received. The technique helps the service designer understand the customers' perspectives regarding a service and the problems they perceive. It also helps service designers to assess the impact of any issues customers have with a service and to identify where action is needed.

Organisations have many different types of customer, so it is helpful to consider using personas (see Glossary of Terms and Techniques) when developing an empathy map.

Process

The process applied to create an empathy map consists of the steps shown in Figure 3.11.

Figure 3.11 Process to develop an empathy map

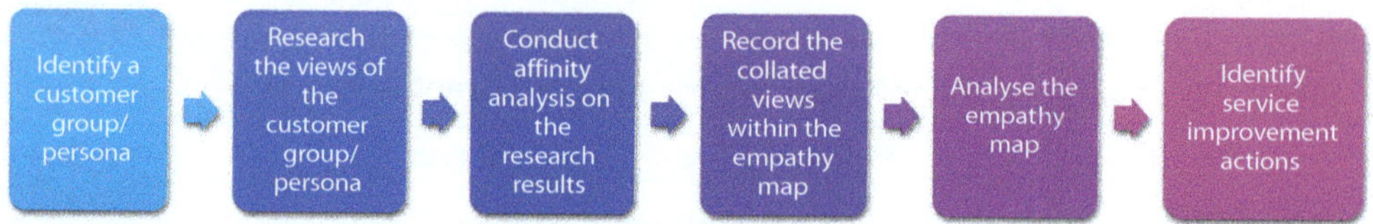

These stages are described in Table 3.5.

Table 3.5 The stages applied to develop an empathy map

Stage	Description
Identify a customer group/persona	Review the customers that engage with the organisation and the characteristics they demonstrate. Identify different customer groups using categorisation approaches such as: • market segments; • business sectors; • typical behaviours; • specific customer interests.

(Continued)

Table 3.5 (Continued)

Stage	Description
Decide the research approach	Evaluate the customer groups/personas identified and consider the various research techniques available (see Glossary of Terms and Techniques). Decide which research techniques would be most appropriate given the nature of the service offered and each individual customer group.
Research the views of the customer group/ persona	Apply the selected research approach to elicit the information required for the four quadrants of the empathy map. The information elicited from a particular customer group/persona should be collated using the empathy map structure.
Conduct affinity analysis on the research results	Review the information elicited for each empathy map quadrant. Apply affinity analysis to group comments deemed to be fundamentally aligned or overlapping.

Record the collated views within the empathy map	Create an empathy map for each customer group/ persona. The resultant empathy maps should state the following:
	• The name of the customer group/persona.
	• The specific characteristics relevant to the customer group/persona.
	• The analysed comments regarding:
	  • What the customer group/persona sees when experiencing the service.
	  • What the customer group/persona hears when experiencing the service.
	  • What the customer group/persona says regarding the service.
	  • What the customer group/persona does when experiencing or having experienced the service.

Identify service improvement actions	Analyse the service given the information recorded within each empathy map to consider what the customer group/ persona thinks or feels. Identify where action needs to be taken to improve the delivered service.

Benefits of an empathy map

Figure 3.12 shows the benefits offered by the empathy map technique.

Figure 3.12 Empathy map benefits

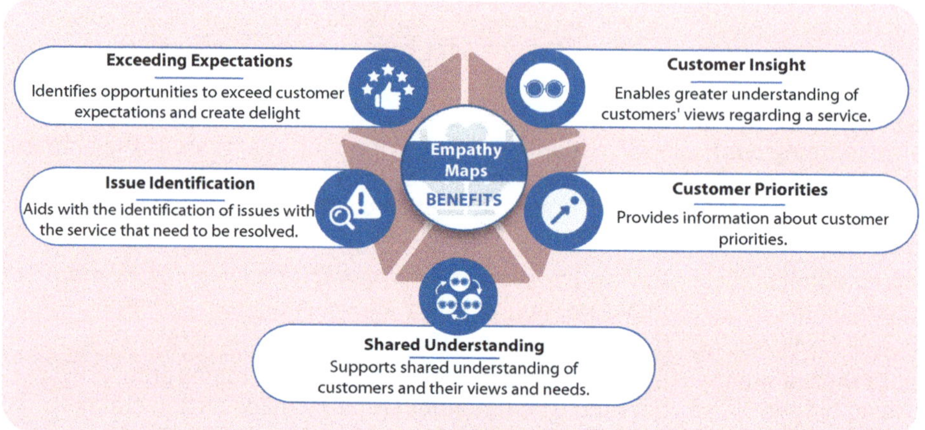

Example empathy map

Figure 3.13 shows an example empathy map that records the perspective of a special occasion diner in the restaurant scenario.

Figure 3.13 Example empathy map for the restaurant scenario

Service title: Order meal	**Persona name:** Special occasion diner
See: Recently refurbished dining room Clean environment Clear space between tables	***Hear:*** Laughter Conversation Some noisy groups
Think: the food was fine but the experience wasn't as good as I expected ***Feel:*** a little disappointed; not sure about celebrating here again	
"This isn't what I ordered" "We have waited a while for the bill" "The food was good overall" **Say:**	Look around impatiently Leave table to find a waiter Write mixed online review **Do:**

Problem definition

Purpose

Change professionals often encounter situations where a 'solution' has been identified without the fundamental issue or problem having been defined. Retrofitting a 'solution' to a business situation rarely works and usually leads to unnecessary expenditure, work disruption or both.

A clearly defined – or 'framed' – problem helps ensure that there is a shared understanding about the business issue to be resolved and that any recommended solution can be evaluated in the light of the defined problem. Change initiatives should always begin by answering the question: 'what problem are we trying to solve?'

Problem definition requires an initial investigation of a business situation; this was described in the earlier section about rich pictures.

Process

The process applied to create a problem definition consists of the steps shown in Figure 3.14.

Figure 3.14 Process to develop a problem definition

These stages are described in Table 3.6.

Table 3.6 The stages applied to develop a problem definition

Stage	Description
Identify the key stakeholders	Use the results that have emerged from investigating a business service to identify the stakeholders whose views are needed to establish the nature of the problem to be solved. Having investigated a service, the key stakeholders should be apparent. Where senior stakeholders have been interviewed, they may be able to identify other key stakeholders whose viewpoints are relevant. The Stakeholder Wheel (see Chapter 9) offers a formal structure that helps identify the range of potential stakeholders and ensures that none are overlooked.

(Continued)

Table 3.6 (Continued)

Stage	Description
Investigate the stakeholder problem perceptions	Apply research techniques to elicit each stakeholder's views about the service and the inherent problems that may be encountered. Each stakeholder has experienced the service from a particular viewpoint – such as the customer or supplier viewpoint – so may have different perceptions regarding the problem with the service.
Analyse the stakeholder perceptions	Evaluate the viewpoints of the different stakeholders and identify where there are patterns and trends regarding the problems encountered with the service. Distinguish between any symptoms of a problem and the genuine problem. Request or obtain data to support detailed understanding of the problem.
Define the underlying problem	Consider the following elements regarding the problem (adapted from the 5 Ws and 1 H (how) technique): • What are the issues identified with the service? • Why are these issues of concern and to whom? • When and where do the issues arise? • How might the organisation, service and stakeholders be impacted by the issues? A fishbone diagram using a formal structure, such as the 6 Ps or 5 Ss, offers an alternative approach. This technique may be used to clarify a problem and identify the root causes or to represent the problem and the corresponding issues.

Benefits of problem definition

A clear problem definition that is developed at an early stage in the service design process offers service designers the benefits shown in Figure 3.15.

Example of a problem definition

An example problem definition for the restaurant scenario is as follows:

> Customers are complaining about the quality of the meals served within the restaurant. The majority of the complaints relate to vegetable and salad ingredients. These ingredients are provided by three suppliers. Records show an average of 25 complaints over the last 3 months. Each complaint requires approximately 30 minutes to investigate and manage. In 15 cases, a discount has been given, reducing the price of each meal by 10%. This has had a significant impact on the profit level for the organisation, which has reduced by 4% over the last 6 months.

Figure 3.15 Problem definition benefits

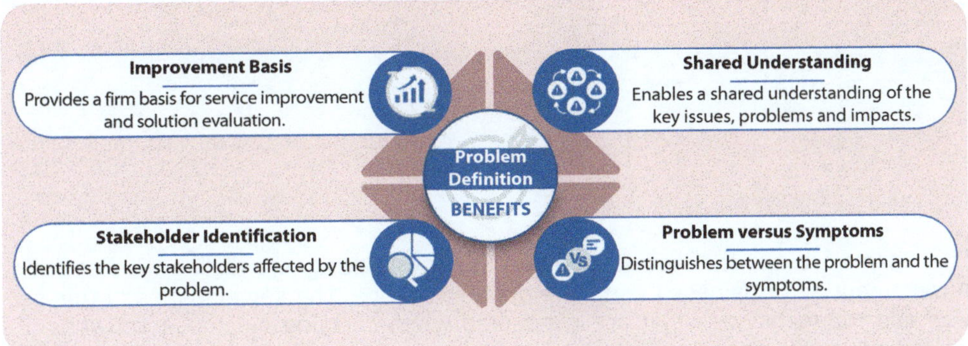

CONCLUSION

Early exploration of a situation or problem is essential whether developing a new service or improving an existing service. Where this service is omitted, the basis for the service design is likely to be flawed and may result in a less than optimal offering.

The value stream activities enacted to conduct this service ensure there is a clear definition of the problem to be addressed or opportunity to be grasped. The techniques described in this chapter support the service designer when carrying out these activities although they may be applied when conducting other service design services.

4 FEASIBILITY ASSESSMENT AND BUSINESS CASE DEVELOPMENT

This chapter covers the work conducted by service designers during the Feasibility Assessment and Business Case Development service. The key activities of this service and the techniques that are conducted when carrying out these activities are described in this chapter. These techniques may be supplemented by other techniques, in particular those described in Chapters 10 and 11. However, the techniques described in Chapters 3 and 5–9 may also offer additional insights.

INTRODUCTION

Service designers seek out innovative ideas when developing or improving a service. The expertise offered by service designers can provide significant innovations that are advantageous to organisations. While ideation is encouraged, a process of assessment and evaluation is needed to ensure commercial viability and organisational alignment. Therefore, service designers require both ideation and evaluation skills.

This chapter explores the activities performed to assess feasibility and develop a business case for change, and the techniques used in pursuit of these activities.

THE FEASIBILITY ASSESSMENT AND BUSINESS CASE DEVELOPMENT SERVICE

This service encompasses the following service activities:

- ideate options to address the business problem;
- define the selected shortlist of options;
- review the options in the light of the available capabilities;
- evaluate the feasibility of the defined options;
- develop the business case for change.

The service value items offered by the service are as follows:

- Change options are identified, defined and evaluated.
- Rigorous business case developed.

Figure 4.1 shows a value stream diagram for this service, including the deliverables provided.

Figure 4.1 Value stream: Feasibility Assessment and Business Case Development service (Adapted from Hunsley et al., 2025)

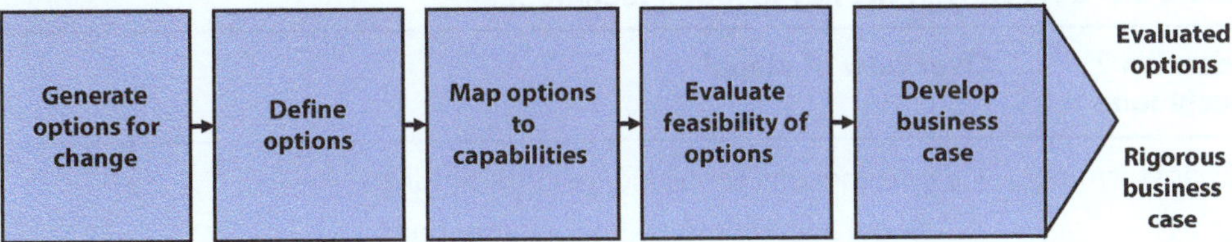

THE TECHNIQUES

Many techniques are used to carry out the work of this service. The generic techniques used in investigation are described in Chapters 10 and 11. The specific techniques relevant to this service are:

- ideation;
- affinity analysis;
- lotus blossom;
- investment appraisal.

Ideation

Purpose

Ideation is an essential element of service design and is a key stage when generating options for the Feasibility Assessment and Business Case Development service. The objective of an ideation exercise is to generate a range of ideas or insights that may be evaluated once the session has concluded.

Examples of business situations where an ideation session may be used to support the Feasibility Assessment and Business Case Development are:

- A problematic situation requiring insight from a variety of stakeholders.
- A focus group where the attendees do not know each other.
- A business function that has the opportunity to increase scale and ideas are needed to achieve this.

There are several techniques that may be used to elicit insights and ideas that lead to options, in particular:

- brainstorming;
- brainwriting;
- round robin;
- sticky note exercise.

These techniques are described in Table 4.1.

Table 4.1 Overview of the key ideation techniques

Ideation technique	Overview of steps
Brainstorming	• Pose concern requiring insights or ideas. • Ask participants to call out suggestions. • Record each suggestion made by participants. • Continue until there are no further suggestions made. • Evaluate suggestions.
Brainwriting	• Pose concern requiring insights or ideas. • Place sheets of paper in the centre of a table (if physical meeting); enable use of online collaborative notes (if virtual meeting). • Ask participants to record one suggestion per sheet/note. • Ask participants to add to a sheet where there is already a suggestion recorded. • Continue until there are no further suggestions made. • Evaluate suggestions.
Round robin	• Pose concern requiring insights or ideas. • Ask each participant in turn for a suggestion. • Record each suggestion. • Continue asking participants for suggestions until no more are forthcoming. • Evaluate suggestions.
Sticky note exercise	• Provide each participant with a set of sticky notes. • Pose concern requiring insights or ideas. • Ask participants to record one suggestion per sticky note. • Continue until participants have no further suggestions. • Ask participants in turn to share their suggestions (either on a wall or whiteboard surface (physical meeting) or online). • Suggest participants place each of their sticky notes with related suggestions made by other participants. • Evaluate suggestions.

Each of the techniques may be enhanced by the use of creative problem-solving approaches such as Assumption Reversal and Substitute, Combine, Adapt, Modify, Put to another use, Eliminate and Reverse (SCAMPER) (see Glossary of Terms and Techniques).

The ideation techniques apply the following key principles:

- Aim for quantity. Participants in an ideation session should be encouraged to contribute as many ideas as possible.
- Encourage participants to propose innovative and unconventional ideas, possibly stimulated by suggestions from others.
- Defer evaluation. Participants should be advised to focus on idea generation and defer judgement or evaluation of the ideas.

The techniques need to be considered to ensure those selected align with the needs of the participants. Brainstorming and round robin sessions can deter engagement from those who are hesitant about expressing ideas publicly. A high level of confidence is required to express ideas in a group, particularly where the group members do not know each other well. Tailoring the ideation techniques to fit the group helps to improve engagement and the resultant quantity of ideas. This is represented in Figure 4.2.

Figure 4.2 Confidence levels required for ideation techniques

While brainstorming and round robin require participants to be comfortable expressing ideas to the group, sticky note sessions and brainwriting tend to be more inclusive as they allow participants personal thinking time and idea expression. Brainwriting enables collaboration as it allows each individual to work at their own pace while also encouraging them to develop the insights and ideas provided by others.

Brainwriting provides a basis for all session participants to contribute and addresses the issues often associated with verbal contribution techniques, such as brainstorming and round robin exercises. Accordingly, it meets the needs of a variety of learning styles so ensures that all participants can support the objectives of the session, uncovering insights into situations and problems, and generating innovative ideas.

Process

The process to run a brainwriting ideation session is shown in Figure 4.3.

Figure 4.3 The brainwriting process

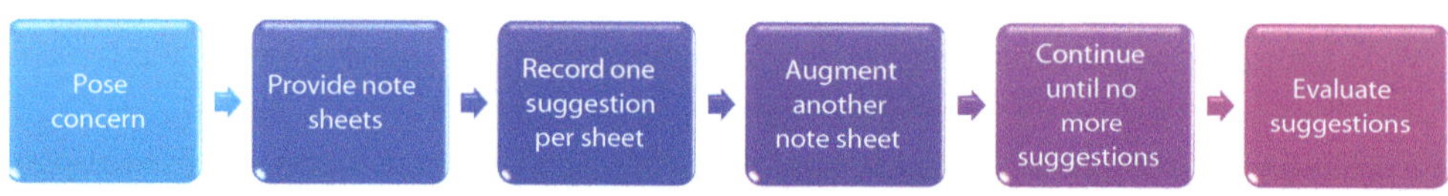

These stages are described in further detail in Table 4.2.

Table 4.2 The stages of the brainwriting process

Stage	Description
Pose concern	The situation requiring further information, insights or ideas for improvement is described to the participants.
Provide note sheets	A set of note sheets is provided for the group. These are placed in a central location where they may be accessed by all participants. This may be a physical pile of paper note sheets or a virtual set.
Record one suggestion per sheet	Each participant is asked to take a note sheet and write one suggestion on the sheet. Once they have done this, each sheet containing a suggestion should be returned to the central location where they can be accessed by the other participants.
Augment another note sheet	Each participant accesses a note sheet where another participant has already placed a suggestion and adds to the original item. This is an opportunity for the participant to develop further the original point made.
Continue until no more suggestions	The participants continue to access note sheets and add items to the other participants' suggestions. The exercise ends when the participants have no further items to add.
Evaluate suggestions	The note sheets are analysed and the ideas are evaluated. Typically, this requires the application of affinity analysis and feasibility assessment (described below).

Benefits of an ideation session

An ideation session where the key principles (described earlier) are applied offers a means of generating insights and ideas in a collaborative environment, without fear of criticism. Figure 4.4 sets out the benefits of an ideation session.

Figure 4.4 Benefits of an ideation session

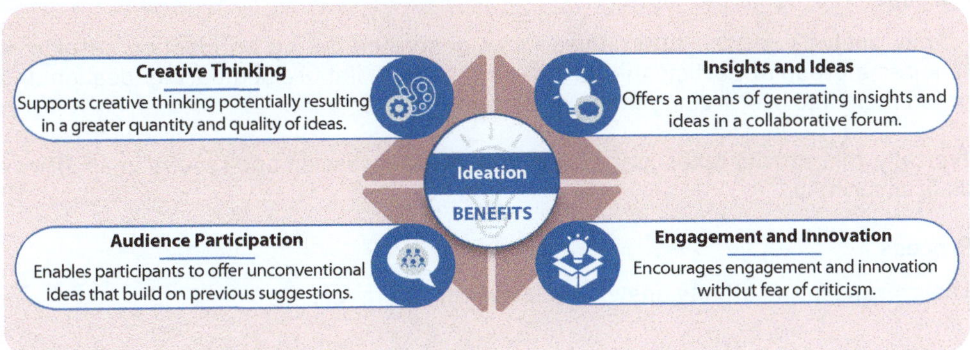

Example brainwriting results

The mind map shown in Figure 4.5 summarises the results of a brainwriting session to identify the issues with the restaurant's online booking system.

Figure 4.5 Mind map summarising a brainwriting session

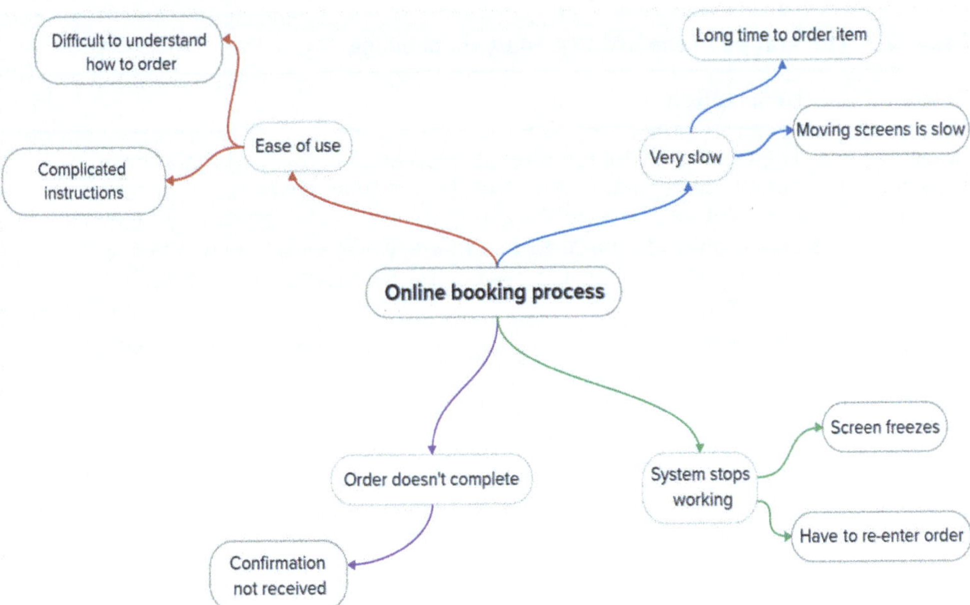

Affinity analysis

Purpose

Affinity analysis is used to organise ideas generated during an ideation session. It requires a group of participants to review a set of points raised during ideation and group them into overarching themes and patterns.

Typically, this activity takes place during an ideation session and results in an affinity diagram or map.

Process

The process for an affinity analysis is shown in Figure 4.6.

Figure 4.6 The affinity analysis process

These stages are described in further detail in Table 4.3.

Table 4.3 The stages of the affinity analysis process

Stage	Description
Review ideation session	The results of the ideation session are reviewed in the light of the stated concern and objective. This may involve reading through the points made with the group to ensure that all have an overview appreciation of the progress made. Reviewing the results may also initiate further discussion and the identification of further suggestions.
Consider notes	The notes are analysed in turn to identify where they are related or overlap. The analysis is conducted in discussion with participants, who are encouraged to contribute or contradict thoughts about correlations between the points raised.
Group notes	Any possible relationships between individual notes are indicated by grouping them together. Where sticky notes have been used for the session, they are moved to be placed together. Where points have been written on a whiteboard (physical or online) or on individual note sheets, they are rewritten on a central, visual board. The exercise to identify groupings continues until all notes have been analysed and the participants are content with the resultant affinity map.

(Continued)

Table 4.3 (Continued)

Stage	Description
Review emergent themes	The emergent themes are described and discussed with the participants. This discussion may result in the identification of additional relationships or themes. The review continues until there is consensus within the group that the themes represented on affinity map reflect the participants' ideas accurately.
Decide actions	The affinity map is used as a basis for identifying options and actions. The options are developed from the themes that have emerged from the grouped ideas. Once a set of viable options has been agreed, they are evaluated for feasibility and inclusion within a business case for change.

Benefits of affinity analysis

Figure 4.7 shows the benefits of an affinity analysis.

Figure 4.7 Benefits of affinity analysis

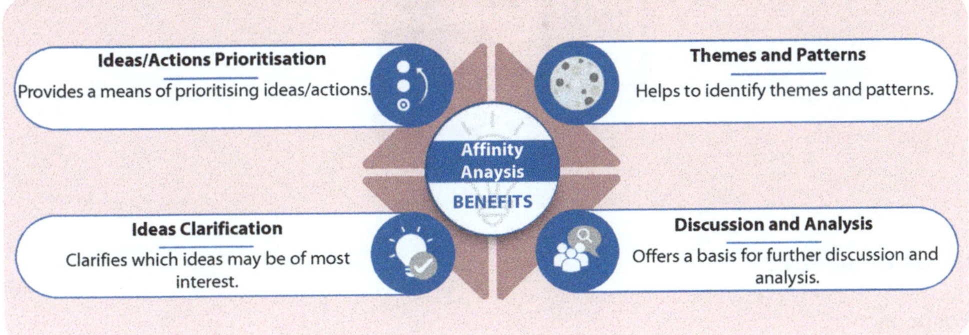

Example affinity analysis results

Figure 4.8 is an example of an affinity map for the restaurant scenario. The themes emerging from the affinity analysis are highlighted with the contributing ideas grouped underneath each theme.

Figure 4.8 Example affinity map for the restaurant scenario

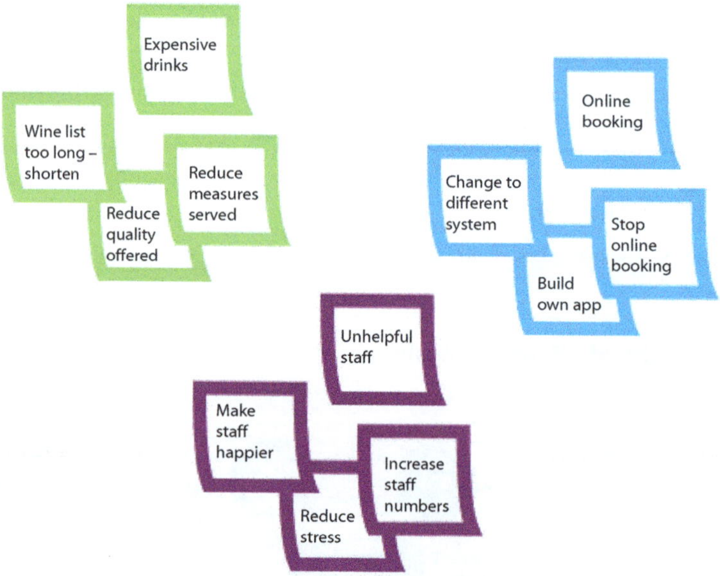

Lotus blossom

Purpose

The lotus blossom technique is used to structure a discussion about a business problem and offers a means of generating relevant ideas. The objective is to gain insights into the different aspects of a problem and consider how these aspects may be addressed.

This technique provides a clear structure for conducting an ideation exercise. An initial idea or problem is identified and used as the central concern for the exercise. This central concern is then discussed to identify associated ideas and themes.

Process

The process for developing a lotus blossom is shown in Figure 4.9.

Figure 4.9 Process for applying the lotus blossom technique

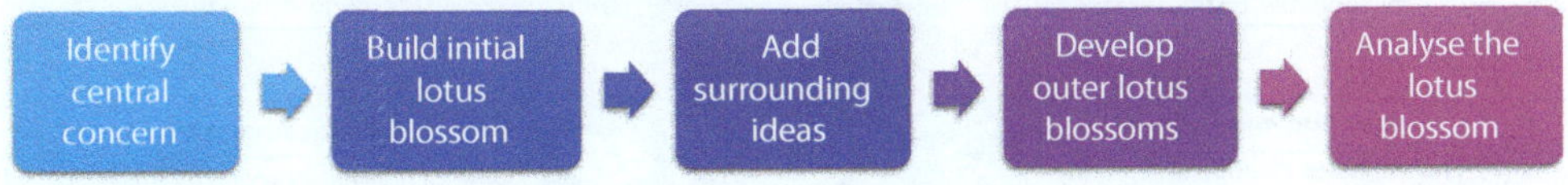

These stages are described in Table 4.4.

Table 4.4 The stages of the lotus blossom technique

Stage	Description
Identify central concern	The service designer identifies the central concern regarding the service under consideration. This central concern is explained to the group of participants.
Build initial lotus blossom	The lotus blossom is begun by placing a box containing the named concern at the centre of a grid. This is typically a 3 × 3 matrix.
Add surrounding ideas	Eight challenges related to the central concern are identified. These are arranged around the lotus blossom in the boxes adjacent to the box containing the central concern.
Develop outer lotus blossoms	The boxes surrounding the central concern offer a means of expanding and enhancing a discussion. A lotus blossom (3 × 3 matrix) is created for each challenge. Each challenge is discussed by the group to identify potential actions that may resolve or mitigate the challenge. The proposed actions are placed in the boxes surrounding a challenge.
Analyse the lotus blossom	The lotus blossom diagram is reviewed, the ideas suggested are considered and actions are proposed and agreed.

Benefits of a lotus blossom

A lotus blossom offers a structure for problem analysis and ideation. It works well with other ideation techniques such as brainstorming and round robin. The benefits of a lotus blossom are shown in Figure 4.10.

Figure 4.10 Benefits of a lotus blossom

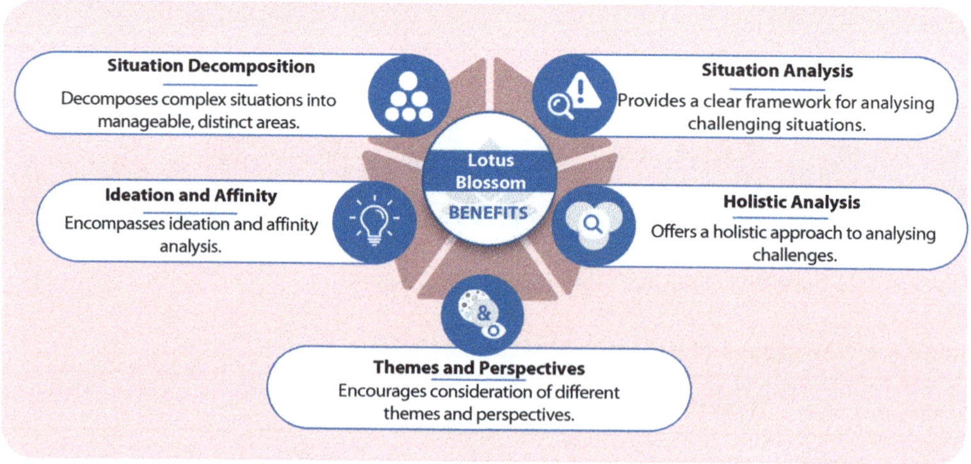

Example lotus blossom

A lotus blossom has been conducted to explore the service quality of the restaurant scenario. It has been noted that the serving staff often make errors when taking orders from customers, and this has resulted in negative comments, some posted online. The example shown in Figure 4.11 is a partial lotus blossom diagram that identifies the following:

- the key challenges related to the central concern;
- the ideas generated to address the issues regarding recruitment.

Investment appraisal

Purpose

An investment appraisal is used to analyse the costs, benefits, risks and impacts of an improvement option. This approach is concerned with evaluating each option in order to ensure that it is desirable from an organisational perspective, technically feasible and financially viable. This helps to confirm the business relevance and acceptability of an option before it is presented to an organisation's decision makers.

There are three aspects evaluated regarding each option:

(1) Financial viability: The costs and benefits associated with an option are defined, quantified where possible and subject to financial analysis.
(2) Technical feasibility: The technical requirements of the proposed option are defined and evaluated in the light of the organisation's technical strategy and infrastructure.
(3) Business desirability: The alignment of the option with the organisation's strategic objectives, culture, operating model and market position is analysed and evaluated.

Figure 4.11 Example lotus blossom for the restaurant scenario

	Staff training			Technology			Menu changes	
Require experience	Test skills	Apply probation period	Staff training	Technology	Menu changes			
Rewrite job description	Recruitment	Create induction plan	Recruitment	**How can we reduce ordering errors?**	Rewards		Rewards	
Request certificates	Use agency	Check references	Targets	Processes	Guidance			
	Targets			Processes			Guidance	

It is often assumed that investment appraisal focuses on the financial viability of an option. However, a holistic approach whereby all three aspects are evaluated is required as any technical and business feasibility issues have the potential to disrupt the success of an option if not considered.

Process

The process applied to create an investment appraisal consists of the steps shown in Figure 4.12.

Figure 4.12 Process to develop an investment appraisal

These stages are described in Table 4.5.

Table 4.5 The stages applied to develop an investment appraisal

Stage	Description
Analyse costs	The costs for a selected option are identified and categorised. The categories are shown in Figure 4.13. The tangible costs are quantified so that, for each cost, the associated financial values and timings are identified. Where a cost is deemed to be intangible, it is analysed to determine if there are elements that may be quantified. For example, while the cost of staff acquiring the ability to apply a new process is considered intangible, it may be possible to calculate the cost associated with providing a training session to introduce the process.
Analyse benefits	The benefits for a selected option are identified and categorised. The categories are shown in Figure 4.13. The tangible benefits are quantified so that, for each benefit, the associated financial values and timings are identified. Where a benefit is deemed to be intangible, it is analysed to determine if there are elements that may be quantified. A further benefits categorisation is shown in Table 4.6. This categorisation is adapted from Ward and Daniel (2012) and distinguishes between benefits that can be quantified financially and those that can be quantified using an alternative measurement. The categories also distinguish between benefits that may be quantified in advance of introducing an enhanced or new service and those that can only be quantified once the new service is in operation.

(Continued)

Table 4.5 (Continued)

Stage	Description
Analyse risks	Inevitably, each option attracts risks. These may be risks to the project to develop an enhanced or new service, or may be risks associated with the operation of the service. For example, there may be a project risk regarding the scope definition resulting in 'scope creep'; there may be a business (operational) risk associated with software failures or security. All risks should be analysed to determine the significance of the risk, where action is needed to manage the risk and the available risk responses. A risk heat map may be used to determine where action is needed, the degree of urgency, and the level of required investment. An example risk heat map is shown in Figure 4.14. The risk response categories are shown in Table 4.7.
Analyse impacts	The introduction of an enhanced or new service is likely to impact the organisation. Evaluating these impacts involves considering whether or not they raise any technical or business issues. The categories of impacts are shown in Table 4.8.
Apply investment appraisal calculation	The investment appraisal calculation provides a means of assuring the financial viability of an option. The quantified costs and benefits, plus any additional costs associated with taking action to address risks or impacts, are analysed using investment appraisal techniques such as payback (cash flow) or discounted cash flow/net present value calculation. These techniques are described below. The investment appraisal analyses the costs to be accrued from an option and the benefits/savings that will result. The calculation applies the values over a forward period and assesses the extent of the financial return for the organisation.

Figure 4.13 shows how both costs and benefits may be categorised according to the following:

- Are they tangible such that a financial value can be calculated during the feasibility assessment? Where this is not the case, the costs and benefits are deemed to be intangible.
- Are they incurred (costs) or accrued (benefits) immediately or do they arise over the longer term? Many costs are incurred during the work to develop a new/enhanced service, so they are immediate within the context of the investment appraisal calculation. However, many benefit savings do not accrue until the new service has been in operation for a while, and the calculation should reflect this timing. Typically, this means that many costs occur at the outset of the project or service deployment, while the benefits reduce the total outgoings over an

extended period. An exception concerns avoided costs, where payments required to operate an existing service may cease once the new service begins operation. Software licences typically fall into this category.

Figure 4.13 The categories of costs and benefits

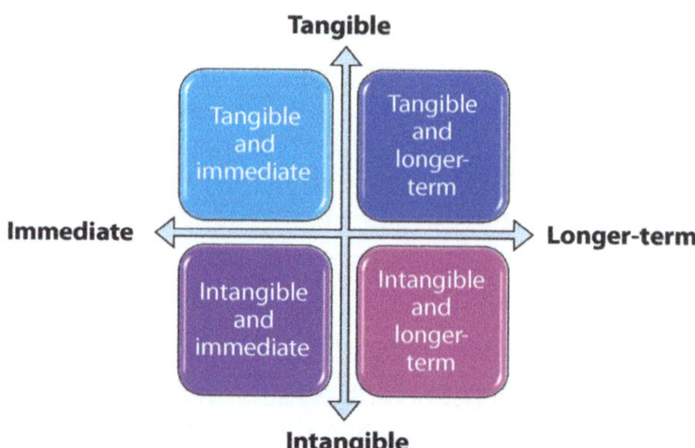

Ward and Daniel (2012) provided a more detailed benefits categorisation. Table 4.6 describes these categories.

Table 4.6 Ward and Daniel's four categories of benefits (adapted from Ward and Daniel, 2012)

Type of benefit	Description
Financial	A financial value can be obtained or calculated for a benefit. For example, the amount paid to maintain a piece of equipment that is not required once a new service is in operation; the fee paid to an organisation for work that is no longer required.
Quantifiable	It is possible to calculate units of savings but not to place a financial value on them. For example, a decrease in injuries resulting from the introduction of changes to working practices.
Measurable	A financial value can be calculated by comparing the situation before the change with the situation once it has been implemented. It is not possible to forecast measurable benefits but they can be calculated with confidence once the new/enhanced service is in operation. For example, the increase in sales turnover or profit resulting from an improved service.
Observable	A general improvement can be perceived but it is not possible to place a value on this, either before or following the introduction of a new/enhanced service. For example, improved morale within a team.

Understanding benefits in greater depth rather than just categorising them as tangible or intangible can help to quantify benefits and improve the investment appraisal for an option. It is sometimes possible to decompose a benefit and identify an element that may be quantified financially. For example, a quantifiable benefit has been identified for the restaurant scenario:

- The restaurant service is to be improved by the introduction of an online payment facility. Customers will be able to scan a QR code to access their bills and make payments.
- One of the quantifiable benefits is the reduction in the number of people who complain about the delay encountered when wishing to pay for their meals. This has been a key issue for the restaurant for several months.
- The benefit has been decomposed to identify elements that may be quantified financially.
- One element of this benefit is the discount offered to customers who had a long (over 30 minutes) wait for their bill. Further investigation has averaged the cost incurred by the restaurant due to these discounts over the previous six months.
- This average amount has been used to determine a monthly figure that may be deemed a saving once the change has been introduced. This figure may be used within the financial cost/benefit analysis.
- Other elements of the original benefit have not been financially quantifiable.

A risk heat map uses the red, amber, green (RAG) rating approach to highlight which risks require most urgent attention. Each risk is evaluated according to two factors:

1. The likelihood of the risk occurring.
2. The degree of impact should the risk occur.

Figure 4.14 shows an example risk heat map for the restaurant scenario (partial).

The risk heat map calculates the severity of each risk by multiplying the probability and impact. The resultant RAG rating is determined by the following algorithm:

- severity 1–4: green rating;
- severity 5–8: amber rating;
- severity 9–12: red rating.

This is an example approach; typically, the algorithm used within an organisation is determined by the particular organisational standard.

The risk responses shown in Figure 4.14 concern different types of risk mitigation. Table 4.7 describes the key types of risk response applied during product or service development.

Figure 4.14 Example risk heat map for the restaurant scenario

ID	Date Raised	Risk Owner	Risk Description	Probability	Impact	Severity	Risk response
1	05/12/2025	CIO	Cyber Attack	2	3	6	Investment in security controls. Regular staff training and awareness sessions. Formal testing for cybersecurity certifications. Business continuity simulations.
2	05/12/2025	CEO	Restaurant market slowdown	3	3	9	Government policy changes. Global economic situation. International conflict.
3	05/12/2025	COO	Lack of cooking staff	1	2	2	Staffing levels forecasting. Staff development/ succession planning.

Table 4.7 Descriptions of risk responses

Risk response	Description
Avoidance	Changing the business operations or project plan to eliminate the risk.
Mitigation	Taking action to reduce the likelihood or impact of a risk.
Transfer	Moving the impact of a risk to a third party.
Acceptance	Recording that a risk exists but deciding to accept it without taking action.
Sharing	Working with another organisation to determine where the impact from the risk might be borne and agreeing to share this impact.

The impacts from a service change proposal can be extensive. They may be identified within the business areas identified in Table 4.8. Example impacts, structured using the POPIT™ model, are described within Table 4.8.

CPPOLDAT is an alternative framework for identifying and evaluating impacts of a proposed service change. The elements within this framework and example questions they may raise are shown in Table 4.9 (adapted from Paul and Cadle, 2020).

Table 4.8 Example service change impacts using POPIT™ model

Area	Example impacts
Processes	The new service may impact current business processes and working practices.
Organisation	The new service may disrupt current business structures, roles and line management. A new service may also change the ways in which the organisation engages with customers or works collaboratively as a team; this may require cultural change.
People	The new service may require the organisation's employees to assume additional or different responsibilities, and acquire new skills.
Information	The new service may require the organisation to obtain, record and access additional information. This may increase the data protection and security requirements imposed upon the organisation.
Technology	The new service may impact the current technology and communications infrastructure used within the organisation.

Table 4.9 Example questions related to the CPPOLDAT framework

CPPOLDAT element	Description
Customer	Have the different customer groups been identified and are customers aware of the forthcoming changes? Is there a need for further communication with customers? Do some customers need training in the new service, processes and systems? Is there any resistance to the changes that needs to be addressed?
Product	Are the products used to provide the service ready for deployment? Will the deployment be incremental? Are there any known risks or issues with the product? Is documentation available that describes the product?
Process	Do the service changes align with the process architecture? Have the new processes been designed and communicated?
Organisation	Are any role or management structure changes needed?
Location	Have any changes to offices or venues been analysed and agreed?
Data	Do the changes align with the data architecture? Is the data in a fit state for migration and conversion? Are there any security concerns related to the service and the required data?
Application	Do the changes align with the applications architecture? Are any new or enhanced applications in place or planned for implementation?
Technology	Do the changes align with the infrastructure architecture? Is any required technology available?

This technique is particularly helpful when assessing business readiness (discussed in Chapter 8).

The analysis of the costs, benefits, risks and impact associated with an option provides a basis for evaluating the feasibility from the financial, technical and business perspectives. The financial investment appraisal encompasses all the quantified costs associated with the development and deployment of the new service, the countermeasure responses to the risks and the actions to manage the organisational impacts. The standard techniques used to conduct the financial investment appraisal are described in Table 4.10. Each of these investment appraisal techniques may be used to compare the different options available.

Table 4.10 Descriptions of investment appraisal techniques

Technique	Explanation
Payback calculation	A 'payback' calculation applies cash flow forecasting to a project to develop a new or enhanced service. It considers the cost of the initial and ongoing investment and calculates the point at which the savings accrued from the benefits cover these costs and a return on investment is achieved.
Discounted cash flow/net present value (DCF/NPV)	A DCF/NPV calculation takes account of the 'time value of money'. This reflects that a financial amount available today would have lower purchasing power over time. Rather than applying a cumulative approach, this calculation considers each year individually. A 'discount' is applied to the result of the net amount (costs minus savings) achieved in each year following the initial year of investment (year 0). The period of the calculation has to be decided at the outset. Once all the annual discounted amounts have been calculated, they are totalled to produce a net present value.
Internal rate of return (IRR)	The IRR is the percentage return on investment from a new service. This is used to compare options against the organisation's minimum level of return; this is sometimes called the 'hurdle rate'. IRR is calculated by reversing the NPV calculation. It is concerned with identifying the percentage discount rate that results in a net present value of zero after a specified number of years.
Return on investment (ROI)	The ROI is used to evaluate the profitability of an investment in a new service. It is calculated by dividing the net profit (total revenue generated minus total costs) by the initial amount invested in developing and deploying the new service.

Benefits of investment appraisal

Investment appraisal supports decision-making and clarifies which options offer benefits to the organisation. Figure 4.15 shows the benefits of an investment appraisal.

Figure 4.15 Benefits of investment appraisal

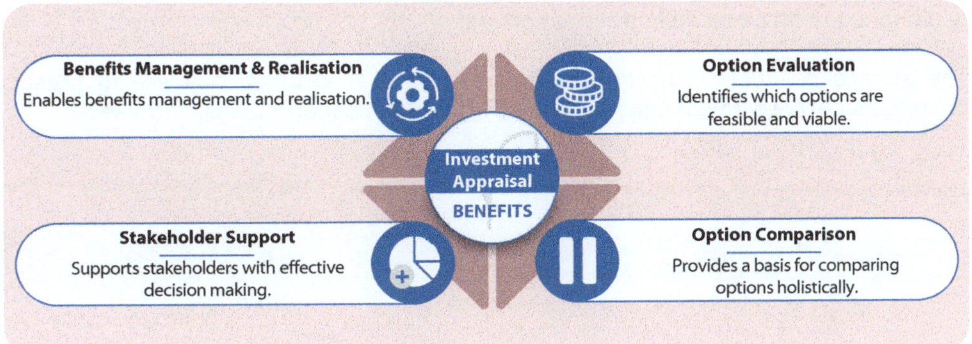

Example of an investment appraisal

An example investment appraisal for the restaurant scenario using a payback calculation is shown in Table 4.11. This investment appraisal concerns service improvements that require the purchase and setup of additional equipment, a new software platform and software licences. Table 4.11 shows that payback occurs in Year 3.

Table 4.11 Example payback calculation

Item	Year 0	Year 1	Year 2	Year 3
Brought forward		–75,000	–40,000	-5,000
Equipment	40,000			
Software platform set up	60,000			
Software licences	15,000	15,000	15,000	15,000
Effort savings	40,000	50,000	50,000	50,000
Cumulative cash-flow (savings less costs)	–75,000	–40,000	–5,000	30,000

CONCLUSION

Organisations have many options when introducing new services or enhancing the current services offered. Service designers use ideation techniques to gain insights into issues and themes and to generate ideas for service improvement options.

Having identified a range of possible options, service designers need to ensure that the options are viable before presenting them within a business case. The feasibility evaluation has to be holistic and must consider technical and business feasibility in addition to the financial investment appraisal.

The service designer requires investment appraisal skills if they are to present options that are worthy of consideration by the organisation's decision makers.

5 CX ANALYSIS

This chapter covers the work conducted by service designers during the CX Analysis service. The key activities of this service and the techniques that are conducted when carrying out these activities are described in this chapter. These techniques may be supplemented by other techniques, in particular those described in Chapters 10 and 11. The techniques described in Chapters 3–4 and 6–9 also offer service designers additional approaches to help gain further ideas and insights.

INTRODUCTION

Techniques to analyse customer needs, feelings and priorities are invaluable when conducting service design. The experience customers encounter when engaging with organisations often guides their future decision-making. These decisions may concern whether to purchase products or services, explore possible accesses to services, provide constructive feedback or, ultimately, look for organisations offering alternative or substitute products and services.

Figure 5.1 represents key customer opinions expressed in response to different customer experiences and levels of product or service quality.

Figure 5.1 The Feedback Engagement matrix (© Assist Knowledge Development)

The four quadrants are described in Table 5.1.

Table 5.1 Description of the Feedback Engagement matrix quadrants (© Assist Knowledge Development)

Engagement quadrant	Description
Good experience/ product or service meets requirements	I'll be back: Customers are happy with the organisation's value proposition and are likely to return, engage further and/or purchase other products or services.
Poor experience/ product or service meets requirements	Listen to my feedback – please!: Customers are pleased with the delivered product or service but have not been happy with the customer experience encountered. They provide feedback and are keen that it is considered and changes made. However, the poor experience may indicate that customers are not listened to and this may deter them from returning if a required product or service is available elsewhere.
Good experience/product or service doesn't meet requirements	Not for me but thanks for trying: Customers are happy with the experience provided by the organisation but are disappointed with the delivered product or service. There are many reasons why this may be the case and, as customers feel that the organisation has tried to meet their needs, they are likely to return where they require a different product or service.
Poor experience/product or service doesn't meet requirements	Never again: Customers are unhappy with both the experience encountered and the delivered product or service. This is likely to deter them from engaging further or purchasing other products or services, switching to a different organisation where possible.

Investigating and analysing the voice of the customer helps organisations to make effective decisions regarding the products, services and experience offered. Failing to undertake this service designer service can result in poor product and marketing strategies that fail to enable the organisation to succeed.

This chapter explores the activities performed to analyse the voice of the customer and determine the customer experience needs. The chapter provides guidance regarding the techniques used in pursuit of these activities.

THE CX ANALYSIS SERVICE

Service description

This service encompasses the following service activities:

- Research, analyse and define the voice of the customer.
- Research, analyse and define the service value expectations.
- Investigate and analyse both stated and implied customer wants and needs.

Service value proposition

The service value items offered by this service are as follows:

- The voice of the customer is researched and understood.
- The service value expectations are identified and analysed.
- CX enhancement opportunities are identified.

Figure 5.2 shows a value stream diagram for this service, including the deliverables produced.

Figure 5.2 Value stream: CX Analysis service (Adapted from Hunsley et al., 2025)

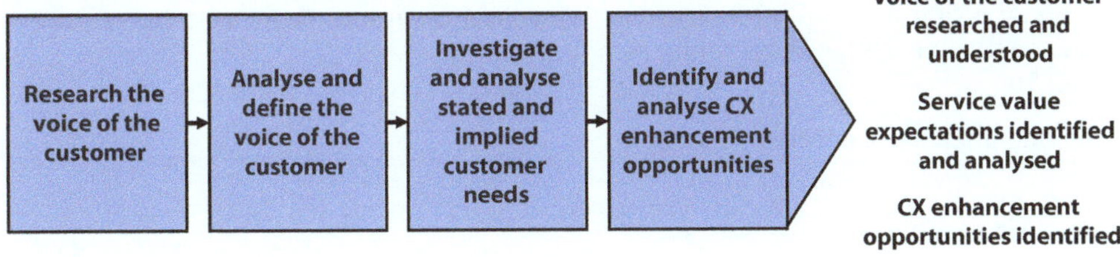

THE TECHNIQUES

There is a wide range of techniques used to carry out the work of this service, including several described in earlier chapters. The generic techniques used to research the voice of the customer and the value expectations are described in Chapters 10 and 11. The following techniques are particularly relevant to this service and are described in this chapter:

- user role and persona analysis;
- customer journey map;
- usability and accessibility analysis;
- Kano analysis;
- navigation path analysis.

The techniques explore the voice of the customer from several different perspectives. Applying each technique enables service designers to obtain qualitative and quantitative data, which may be used to ensure that any service development or improvements meet customer needs. These techniques are also relevant to other roles engaged in understanding the customer perspective, in particular user researchers and business analysts.

User role and persona analysis

Purpose

User role and persona analysis is an essential element of the CX Analysis service.

This area of analysis is key to understanding the variety of customers engaging with the organisation, their characteristics and the expected customer experience. The term 'user' is often subject to debate about whether it applies to an entire service or the software products supporting the service. In this book, the term user role refers to a service user so encompasses the entire service.

The objective of user role and persona analysis is to provide a means of understanding different service perspectives, enabling in-depth analysis of the customer expectations and requirements.

A service user role is defined as follows:

> **Service user role**
>
> A generic title for a role taken by an individual or group of actors who require access to a particular set of features offered by a service.

User role analysis is defined as follows:

> **User role analysis**
>
> A technique used to identify and understand the service user roles that interact with and access a service offered by an organisation.

Individuals adopt a 'user role' when interacting with an organisation, service or system. The user role carries out tasks and accesses features and information related to those tasks. A user role is identified through grouping tasks and accesses to similar features. This may be done at a workshop or focus group, using ideation techniques such as brainwriting or round robin (see Chapter 4). A more analytical approach involves reviewing the work to be undertaken by different service users and forming logical groups of tasks.

An individual service user may adopt more than one role where they wish to undertake two distinct sets of tasks. For example, within the restaurant scenario, an individual may attend the restaurant as a customer and may also be a food supplier. Therefore, this individual would have two user roles: customer and supplier. People management (human resources) offers further examples where an individual may adopt more than one user role. An individual may be:

- an 'employee', requiring access to services related to their personal details and situation;
- a 'manager', requiring access to services related to their responsibilities regarding line management of staff.

A persona is a representation of a user role, aggregating users with common characteristics, behaviour, attitudes and needs.

Persona analysis helps build a shared, more detailed understanding within the service design team of the personalities that embody a user role. The technique helps to determine ideas and evaluate options to address the needs of the user group represented by the persona.

Each user role should be analysed to determine if it encompasses groups of individuals with identifiable shared characteristics, behaviours, preferences and requirements. For example, in the restaurant scenario, there may be personas that represent customers with particular food or drink preferences. Analysing such preferences enables the restaurant to ensure that the preferences and requirements are understood and accommodated.

Figure 5.3 illustrates the relationship between user roles and personas. This structure includes user role subcategories where a user role would benefit from being decomposed further. For example, the 'employee' user role may benefit from being decomposed into subcategories such as 'sales employee', 'HR employee' or 'senior manager'. This level of decomposition is not necessarily required as it depends upon whether it is needed to enable detailed analysis of a particular user role.

Figure 5.3 A user role and persona analysis structure (including user role subcategories)

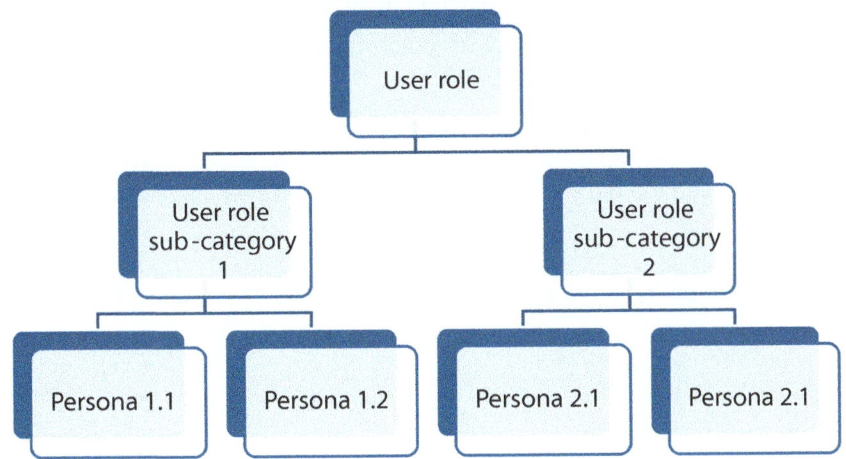

There are two types of persona:

- A validated persona is based on data, typically obtained from market or customer research.
- A proto persona is derived from the observations and insights of the service designers or close colleagues such as business analysts.

Where a proto persona has been identified, research may be conducted to clarify the defined characteristics and the basis in reality.

These personas are typically developed from observations of the staff working within an organisation. This information helps when designing processes and services to ensure that they meet the needs of the personas who wish to access them. Personas can also be useful when analysing users of the business system who have particular accessibility requirements. For example, a persona representing customers who have a specific disability might be defined in order that their accessibility requirements may be fully explored and understood.

It is often tempting for organisations to believe that the internal viewpoint encompasses the external customer view. However, this risks ignoring any disconnect between these two perspectives and allowing organisational wants and needs to hold sway over those held by customers.

Examples of business situations where persona and user role analysis is needed to support CX Analysis are:

- Insights are needed into the different customer groups that share requirements and encounter similar scenarios.
- A service has been proposed that is intended to offer a value proposition to a specific group of customers.
- Analysis of the customers who may be interested in engaging with the organisation is needed to help define a new service.
- The potential to improve a service has been identified.
- Complaints have been received from some customers and in-depth understanding of their perspectives is desired.

A customer journey map begins with an understanding of the user role accessing the service. This understanding can be enhanced if the user role is analysed to reveal variants of the role and the personas that conduct the tasks associated with each variant.

Process

The process to identify user roles and personas is shown in Figure 5.4.

Figure 5.4 The user role and persona analysis process

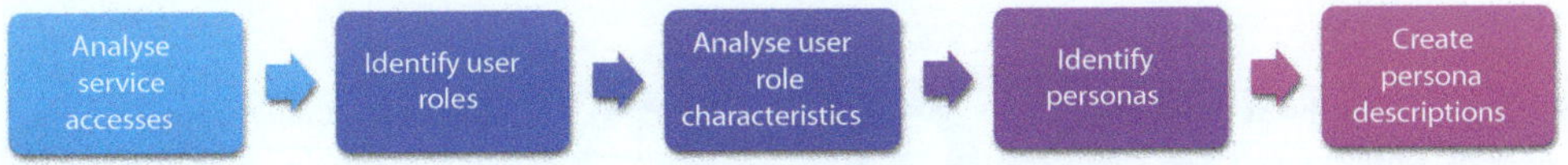

The stages shown in Figure 5.4 are described in Table 5.2.

Table 5.2 The stages of user role and persona analysis

Stage	Description
Analyse service accesses	The service or system accesses are identified and analysed to determine where a particular group of users require access to overlapping/duplicate tasks or information.
Identify user roles	Each grouping of accesses is analysed to determine if a particular user role is evident.
Analyse user role characteristics	The characteristics associated with each user role are analysed and the user role is named and described in overview. The name should reflect the work of the user role. The analysis may lead to the identification of subcategories for the user role, each of which is also named. The set of tasks and information accesses are defined for each user role and, where relevant, each subcategory.
Identify personas	Each user role/subcategory is analysed to determine if there are particular user personality types evident. This analysis may be based on market and customer research or on observations made by the service designers. The personality types concern the behavioural characteristics, requirements and expectations demonstrated by those conducting the user role tasks. Personas are identified that reflect the groups of individuals demonstrating the behaviours and characteristics.
Create persona descriptions	Persona descriptions are created that state the behavioural characteristics, requirements and expectations for each persona.

Benefits of user role and persona analysis

Figure 5.5 shows the benefits of user role and persona analysis.

Figure 5.5 Benefits of user role and persona analysis

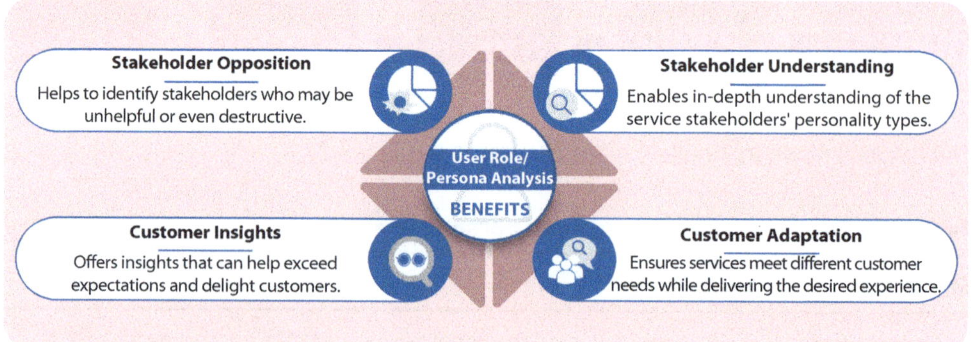

Example user role and persona descriptions

There is a risk that user role analysis is based on assumptions and results in broad categories that do not reflect the characteristics associated with a particular role. Persona analysis can address this risk as it is based on a more detailed analysis of the customers within a user role group. For example, in the restaurant scenario, the user role 'employee' may be decomposed into the following subcategories:

- server;
- cook;
- receptionist;
- manager.

Some of these subcategories, such as 'server', may also be subject to persona analysis.

Table 5.3 describes the diner user role for the restaurant scenario and three alternative personas.

Table 5.3 A set of personas for the 'diner' user role for the restaurant scenario

User role name: diner

User role description: An individual who is a customer who dines at the restaurant.

Persona name	Persona description
Susan	Susan is a regular customer of the restaurant. She requires vegetarian meal options and is content with a limited menu. She eats a broad range of vegetarian meals so can adapt easily to a changing menu.
Chris	Chris is a discerning diner. He appreciates high quality produce and will complain if a meal does not meet the standards he requires. He has very few food preferences, eating a wide range of ingredients.
Julia	Julia is an infrequent diner. She lives locally so will book a table on occasion. She has several food preferences so has only limited choices available within the standard menu.

Customer journey mapping

Purpose

A customer journey map is a key service design artefact and may be used by service designers when carrying out several of the service design services. However, it is particularly relevant when conducting the CX Analysis service. It is used to represent the following elements of a customer journey:

- The user role and the specific persona that wishes to access a service offered by an organisation.
- The touchpoints, where the persona engages – or attempts to engage – with an organisation when accessing a service.
- The tasks conducted by the persona during each touchpoint.
- The emotions experienced by the persona during each touchpoint.

These elements ensure that a customer journey map provides a visual, holistic view of the service encountered by a persona and highlights where improvements need to be considered.

The customer journey map also provides a basis for the following:

- developing the service blueprint for a new or enhanced service;
- enabling effective customer journey management.

Process

The process for developing a customer journey map is shown in Figure 5.6.

Figure 5.6 The process to develop and analyse a customer journey map

These stages are described in further detail in Table 5.4.

Table 5.4 The stages of the customer journey mapping process

Stage	Description
Identify type of customer	The customers are analysed to identify the user roles and personas. A particular user role/persona is identified as the basis for the customer journey likely to be conducted.
Define touchpoints	The stages within the customer journey are identified. Each stage is a 'touchpoint' where the user role/persona engages with the organisation in order to access the service. The touchpoints are explored in detail and the steps conducted are defined.
Analyse customer perceptions	The defined touchpoints are analysed to uncover the customer perceptions at each stage. The perceptions depend upon the experiences encountered and how they align with what is needed and expected.
Model emotions	Each touchpoint and the corresponding perception are evaluated to determine the user role/persona's emotional response. A rating is applied based on the extent to which the emotional response is negative, neutral or positive. A RAG rating may be applied or the emotions may be shown on a scored grid.
Identify possible improvements	The customer journey map is analysed to identify where improvement is needed and to prioritise the improvements. Actions are identified that will facilitate improvement. These may be to isolated elements such as a process change or system update, or may require more fundamental changes, possibly to the entire POPIT™ for a touchpoint.

Benefits of customer journey mapping

Modelling the customer journey for a service offers the service designer the opportunity to visualise the entire set of experiences encountered by a particular customer group – the selected 'persona'. It also provides a means of exploring how the organisation engages with a persona and identifying which touchpoints may be particularly problematic.

Figure 5.7 shows the benefits of customer journey maps.

Figure 5.7 Benefits of customer journey maps

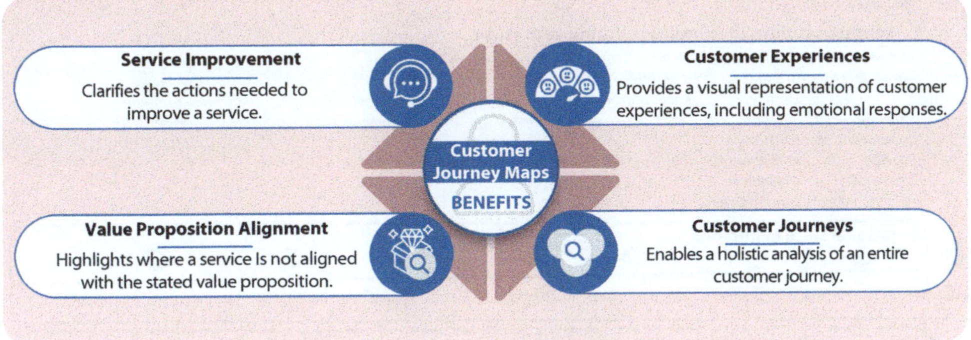

Example customer journey map

Figure 5.8 is an example of a customer journey map for the restaurant scenario.

Figure 5.8 Example customer journey map for the restaurant scenario

User role: Diner; **Persona:** Discerning Diner
Goal: Enjoy meal in a high -quality restaurant

	Book table	Arrive at restaurant	Order meal	Dine	Make payment	Leave restaurant	Provide feedback
Persona activities	Access restaurant website Review menus Enter booking details Receive booking confirmation	Travel to restaurant Enter restaurant Advise staff of arrival Walk to table	Review menu Order drinks Query ingredients Order meal	Receive drinks Receive meal Eat meal Order additional items	Ask for bill Pay amount due Receive receipt	Exit restaurant Travel home	Receive feedback request Provide feedback on restaurant visit
Persona perceptions of experience during each stage	*Nice website* *Menus easy to find* *Straightforward booking process* *Booking confirmation received quickly*	*Easy location to find* *Entrance a little obscured* *Staff not immediately available to lead to table*	*Menus brought promptly* *Knowledgeable staff*	*Drinks served promptly* *Delay for meal to be served* *Long delay before dishes were cleared*	*Staff not available to provide bill* *Slow payment process*	*Staff friendly during exit*	*Feedback provided* *No response needed from restaurant*

Emotional state of persona

Opportunities for improvement

- Improve entrance signs?
- Increase number of staff on reception?

- Improve meal production processes?
- Improve serving/clearing processes?

- Update payment process?
- Introduce new payment system?
- Train staff?

Usability and accessibility analysis

Purpose

Usability and accessibility analysis is concerned with understanding different personas and the factors that enable them to engage with an organisation, service, process or system effectively.

Usability is defined as follows:

Usability

Usability concerns the ease with which users are able to interact with services, processes and systems, and achieve their goals.

Neilsen defined five usability 'quality components' (www.nngroup.com). These are described in Table 5.5. The term 'service' is used in these descriptions to refer to an

Table 5.5 Neilsen's usability 'quality components'

Quality component title	Quality component description
Learnability	This component concerns how easily users are able to undertake tasks when accessing the service for the first time.
Efficiency	This component concerns how quickly users who are familiar with the service are able to undertake tasks.
Memorability	This component concerns how easily users accessing the service following a period where they have not used it, are able to become proficient in its use.
Errors	This component concerns the volume of errors made by users when using the service, the severity of impact of these errors, and the ease with which it is possible to recover from an error.
Satisfaction	This component concerns how enjoyable the user finds using the service.

entire service or a product, process or system that contributes to the delivery of the service.

Neilsen also defined 'utility' as a key quality attribute. This is concerned with the features offered by the service and how well they address the users' needs.

Usability analysis is concerned with defining the service requirements and evaluating the designed service to determine the extent to which the quality components are achieved.

Nielsen also defined 10 principles that should be considered when undertaking interaction design. These principles are called 'usability heuristics' because they are intended to be used as broad rules of thumb rather than specific rules. The principles may be perceived as relating purely to software interaction design but they are beneficial when applied to the customer interactions with an entire service.

The 10 principles as applied to a service (rather than just a software product) are described in Table 5.6 (adapted from Thompson, 2025).

Table 5.6 Neilsen's usability heuristics (adapted to the service context)

Heuristic	Explanation
(1) Visibility of service status	Customers should be kept informed about what is happening regarding the service at all times.
(2) Match between the service and the real world	The language, concepts and actions within a service should mirror a customer's mental model and real-world expectations. The use of familiar terminology and representations helps to minimise cognitive load.
(3) Customer control and freedom	Customers should have the ability to undo actions and easily navigate the service.
(4) Consistency and standards	Customers should be able to apply established conventions and standards as part of a consistent service interface.
(5) Error prevention	The service should be designed to prevent errors wherever possible.
(6) Recognition rather than recall	The service information should be visible and easily retrievable.
(7) Flexibility and efficiency of use	The service design should encompass both novice and expert service users.
(8) Aesthetic and minimalist design	The service design should be clean and minimalist, avoiding unnecessary information and distractions. An aesthetically pleasing design contributes to a positive customer experience.
(9) Help customers recognise, diagnose and recover from errors	Errors made by service users when accessing a service should be communicated clearly, providing constructive guidance on how to fix the issue. Customers should be helped to understand the problem and guided towards a solution.
(10) Help and documentation	The means of accessing a service should be self-explanatory and intuitive across the customer journey. Where required, easily accessible, concise and task-focused documented guidance should be available.

Accessibility is defined as follows:

Accessibility

Accessibility concerns ensuring that all users, regardless of disabilities, are able to access services, products or systems.

The Web Content Accessibility Guidelines (WCAG) were developed by the World Wide Web Consortium (W3C) and provide internationally recognised recommendations to help improve web accessibility. There are four principles that are fundamental to WCAG; these are described in Table 5.7.

Table 5.7 The four principles that underlie WCAG

Principle	Description
Perceivable	Those using a digital service must be able to use only one of their senses to understand the web content.
Operable	Those using a digital service must be able to interact with and navigate all elements on a particular web page.
Understandable	Those using a digital service must be able to understand the information provided by a digital service.
Robust	A digital service must communicate information effectively to all users, including those using assistive technologies. The digital service must also continue to be compatible with evolving technologies and user needs.

Services should be analysed to ensure they are designed to be accessible to all, including those with the following impairments:

- vision;
- hearing;
- mobility;
- thinking and understanding.

Accessibility also needs to be considered where there are temporary impairments. For example, where an individual has been in an accident and is temporarily physically impaired.

Accessibility analysis may identify the need for adjustments or accommodations to the service design. For example, these adjustments or accommodations may include:

- making changes to the physical environment, such as heights of counters or tables;
- ensuring the service design is consistent and predictable;
- providing guidance that enables customers to provide the correct information;
- ensuring the service design allows for the use of assistive technology (where access to software products is needed).

Service designers should apply a range of techniques, in particular those described in this chapter, to understand the usability and accessibility requirements that any delivered service or product must fulfil.

Process

The process for usability and accessibility analysis is shown in Figure 5.9.

Figure 5.9 Process for applying usability and accessibility analysis

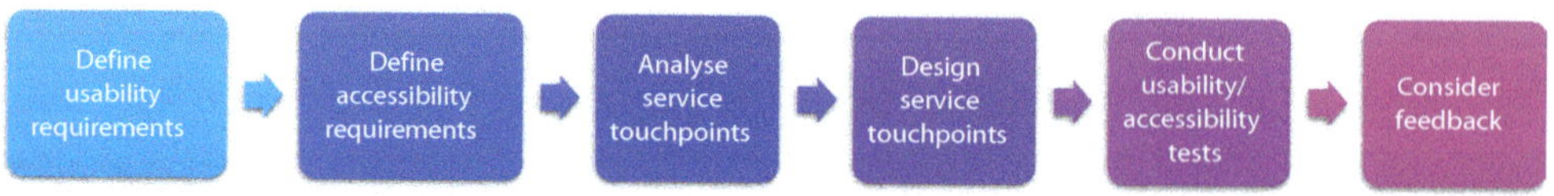

These stages are described in Table 5.8.

Table 5.8 The stages of usability and accessibility analysis

Stage	Description
Define usability requirements	The service designer investigates the product or service, the customer user roles/personas and the customer journey. Quality components, such as those described in Tables 5.5 and 5.6, are used to investigate and analyse the usability requirements The usability requirements are elicited, analysed and defined. Requirements definition techniques, such as those used when conducting requirements engineering (Paul and Cadle, 2020), are applied to ensure the usability requirements are clearly understood and documented.
Define accessibility requirements	The service designer investigates the product or service, the customer user roles/personas and the customer journey. Frameworks such as WCAG are used to guide the investigation and analysis of the accessibility requirements. Requirements definition techniques, such as those used when conducting requirements engineering (Paul and Cadle, 2020), are applied to ensure the accessibility requirements are clearly understood and documented.
Analyse service touchpoints	Each of the service touchpoints is explored to determine where usability or accessibility requirements should be considered and any additional support may be needed.
Design service touchpoints	The options for meeting usability and accessibility requirements are identified and evaluated to determine how the service may be designed to meet the requirements. Services typically require environmental, personal or technological support that is tailored to each particular touchpoint. For example, an examination service may offer personal support with listening or reading; a physical counter service may require height adjustments; an online ordering service may require the use of assistive technology. The service design has to consider the objectives of the service, the requirements to be met, the options available and the customer viewpoints.

(Continued)

Table 5.8 (Continued)

Stage	Description
Conduct usability/ accessibility tests	The service must be tested to ensure the usability and accessibility needs are met by the service design. The service designer should collaborate with colleagues relevant to the context and customer requirements, to develop and conduct the tests. Scenario analysis is a technique used to identify different events, their objectives and the steps conducted to use a service. This technique may be used to identify where different customer personas need to navigate relevant scenarios. These scenarios may then be used as a basis for designing the usability/accessibility tests.
Consider feedback	Service design is an iterative process. Usability and accessibility testing results in test outcomes and feedback. These are analysed to identify where improvements are needed to a service and to support further design and testing.

Benefits of usability and accessibility analysis

Usability and accessibility analysis is applied to define the requirements that must be fulfilled if customers are to be able to use a product or service effectively. The benefits of usability and accessibility analysis are shown in Figure 5.10.

Figure 5.10 Benefits of usability and accessibility analysis

Usability and Accessibility
BENEFITS
Customer Needs Analysis
Provides a clear understanding of customers and their needs when using a product or service.
Early Problem Recognition
Enables early recognition of product or service usage difficulties that need to be addressed.
Regulatory Compliance
Assists organisations to comply with regulatory requirements.
Enhanced Experience
Enhances the customer experience when accessing a product or service.
Wider Audience Reach
Extends the customer audience for a product or service.

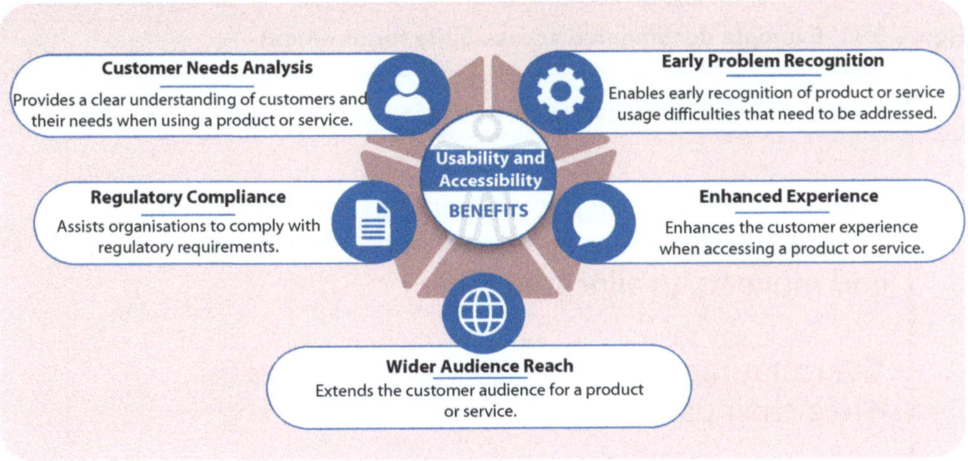

Example usability and accessibility requirements

Table 5.9 contains a documented usability requirement using an extract from the Requirements Catalogue standard (Paul and Cadle, 2020).

Table 5.9 Example documented usability requirement

Requirement identifier	UR01
Requirement name	Website usability
Requirement description	This requirement applies to the restaurant website. The website shall have the following usability features: • The website shall be usable by all service customers without any prior experience of using the website. • The website shall be navigable by all service customers without any training or guidance. • The website shall include features that enable service customers to avoid making errors. • The website shall respond to customer data inputs within two seconds.
Source	Restaurant owner

Figure 5.11 shows a documented accessibility requirement for a diner who is a wheelchair user.

Figure 5.11 Example documented accessibility requirement

User role: Diner with wheelchair

The restaurant shall provide access to wheelchair users allowing them to enter via the main entrance and move to an allocated table.

The restaurant shall provide toilet facilities for wheelchair users.

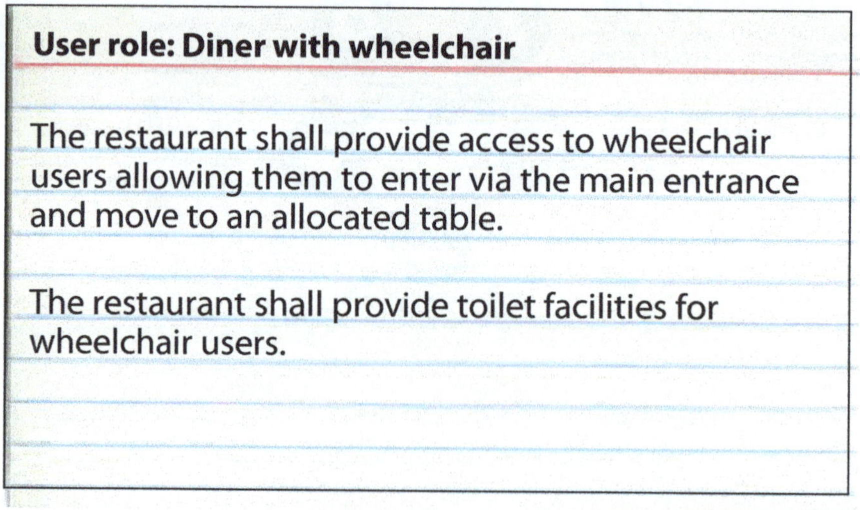

Kano analysis

Purpose

The Kano model was developed by Noriaki Kano in 1984 to provide a basis for prioritising customer needs and offer a guide to the features that should be included when developing a product. Within service design, the Kano model also offers a means of analysing the customer experience requirements to be achieved when delivering a service. It helps clarify customer priorities regarding the experiential features offered by a particular service. Kano can provide a basis for understanding where customers' priorities lie with regard to the elements of an organisation's value proposition. For example, a priority may be placed on a particular brand or the timescale for delivery.

Kano offers a means of determining which customer experience requirements should be prioritised. While other prioritisation techniques, such as MoSCoW, are effective when prioritising functional and non-functional features provided by a product (see Glossary of Terms and Techniques), Kano analysis is particularly suited to the analysis and prioritisation of customer service needs. This is because the focus in a Kano analysis is on understanding customer expectations and the priorities that impact customer satisfaction.

There are several versions of the Kano model. An adapted version, highlighting the three key priority levels and their link to customer satisfaction, is shown in Figure 5.12.

Figure 5.12 Kano model (After Kano et al., 1984)

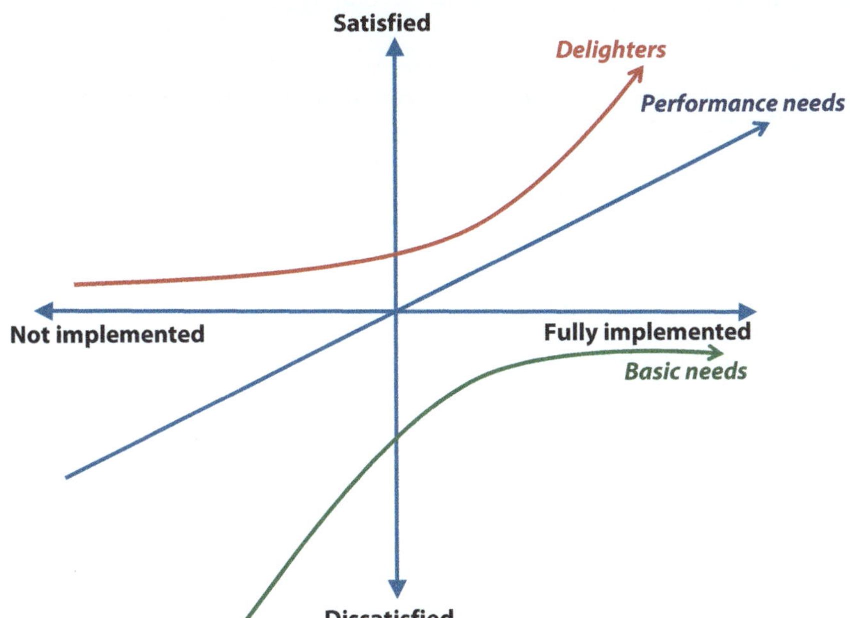

This technique applies three levels of priority; these are described in Table 5.10.

Table 5.10 Three Kano priority levels

Kano priority level	Description
Basic or essential features	These are the key product or service features that are expected by customers. They may not be suggested by customers initially, requiring discussion and probing for them to emerge. It is usually assumed by customers that these features will be provided so dissatisfaction can result if this is not the case. Tacit knowledge, where information is assumed or taken for granted, can be an issue when eliciting requirements regarding basic features. Techniques that help uncover tacit knowledge, such as scenario analysis and prototyping (see Glossary of Terms and Techniques), are invaluable when identifying basic feature requirements.
Performance features	These are the product or service features that customers are likely to raise as particular requirements they wish to receive. Typically, customer satisfaction increases where such features are provided and decreases where this is not the case.
Excitement (delighter) features	These are the product or service features that are unexpected but customers perceive as valuable. These are the additional features that delight customers so delivering them can enhance the customer experience encountered and increase satisfaction significantly.

The Kano model shown in Figure 5.12 highlights the following:

- A service or product that provides merely the basic features does not ensure significant customer satisfaction. However, where they are not delivered, there is likely to be significant customer dissatisfaction.
- A service or product that does not meet the performance needs will result in customer dissatisfaction. However, where a service or product meets the performance needs, increased customer satisfaction is likely.
- A service or product that offers the delighter features will result in very high customer satisfaction. However, if these features are not provided, they do not cause customers to be dissatisfied, largely because they are unexpected and their absence may not be recognised.

The delighter features can create a sense of customer engagement and a desire to ensure an excellent customer experience so are extremely powerful. They can enhance an organisation's value proposition for a particular service or product and can provide competitive advantage. However, over time, the impact of performance and delighter features is likely to diminish as they become expected and possibly taken for granted. The performance features become basic features, and the delighters become performance features. This requires service designers to be innovating regularly, identifying customer expectations, behavioural trends, changing demographics and recognising where technological advances can enhance services or products.

Process

The process for conducting a Kano analysis is shown in Figure 5.13.

Figure 5.13 Process for conducting Kano analysis

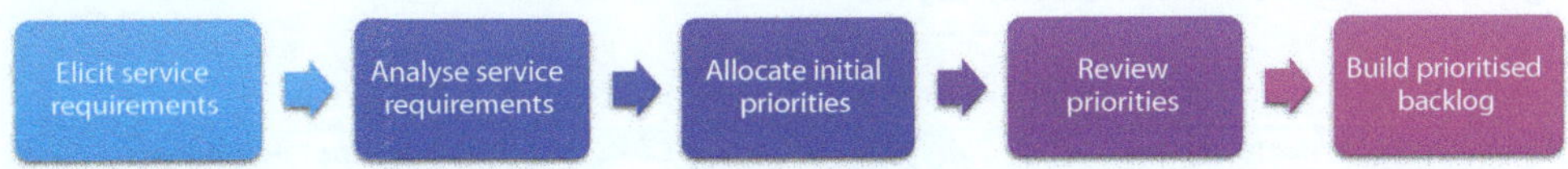

These stages are described in Table 5.11.

Table 5.11 The stages of Kano analysis

Stage	Description
Elicit service requirements	The service designer engages with customers to uncover their requirements for the service and product, including the customer experience requirements. Requirements elicitation techniques such as interviews, observation and storytelling, surveys, focus groups and workshops (see Glossary of Terms and Techniques), should be used to ensure the requirements are elicited effectively and comprehensively. Engagement with other stakeholders may elicit additional requirements. For example, the value proposition defined for a product or service or technological developments may generate requirements that are not identified by customers.
Analyse service requirements	The service designer reviews the elicited requirements to identify and resolve any duplication, overlapping requirements, inconsistencies and conflicts. Stakeholder engagement techniques such as the stakeholder wheel, perspective analysis and principled negotiation (see Glossary of Terms and Techniques) may be used to help resolve some requirement issues.
Allocate initial priorities	The service designer works with customers and other stakeholders to categorise the requirements as basic, performance or delighter features. The delighter features may be those identified due to the value proposition and the need to demonstrate an enhanced product or service beyond that offered by competitors.
Review priorities	The service designer reviews the initial priorities with representatives of stakeholder groups, including customers, product developers, customer service functions and executive management.
Build prioritised backlog	The service designer defines the prioritised backlog of service and product requirements.

Benefits of using Kano analysis

The Kano model offers the benefits shown in Figure 5.14 when analysing service or product features.

Figure 5.14 Benefits of Kano analysis

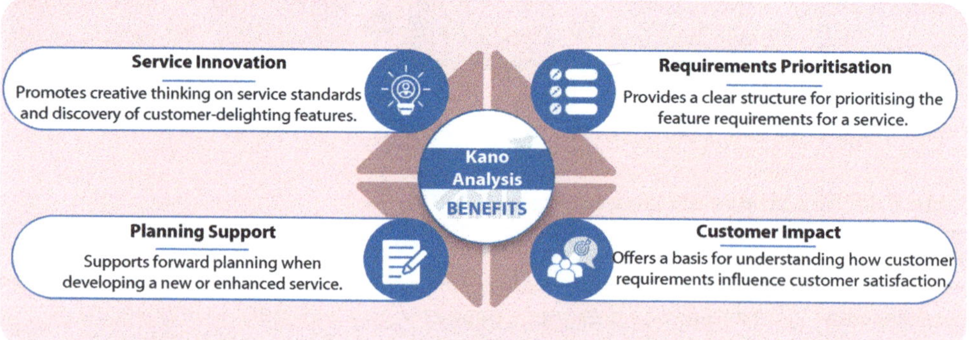

Example Kano analysis

Figure 5.15 provides a Kano analysis for three requirements relevant to the restaurant scenario.

Figure 5.15 Example Kano analysis for three restaurant service requirements

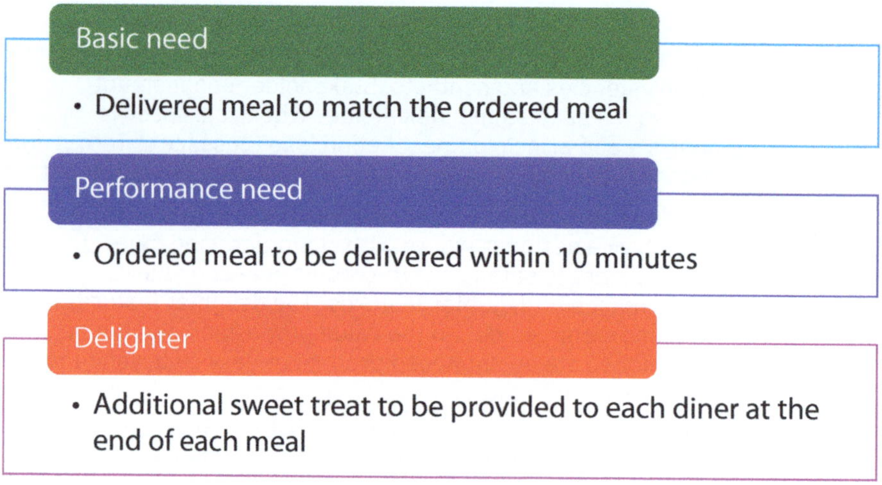

Basic need

- Delivered meal to match the ordered meal

Performance need

- Ordered meal to be delivered within 10 minutes

Delighter

- Additional sweet treat to be provided to each diner at the end of each meal

Navigation path analysis

Purpose

Navigation path analysis is used to identify the navigation paths used by customers when accessing products or services. This technique is used primarily for products and services that are delivered online. However, it may also be applied to investigate the navigation paths used to access physical products and services.

This technique is used for the following reasons:

- to validate that the navigation paths offered are clear and usable;
- to identify where alternative navigation paths are used and determine their usability and accessibility;
- to highlight aspects of a product or service that are unpopular with customers;
- to identify where navigation issues are encountered and clarify the required improvements.

Online navigation path analysis may be enabled using tracking software. Physical navigation path analysis requires the use of techniques such as shadowing or observation (see Glossary of Terms and Techniques).

Process

The process applied to navigation path analysis consists of the stages shown in Figure 5.16.

Figure 5.16 The navigation path analysis process

These stages are described in Table 5.12.

Table 5.12 The stages applied during navigation path analysis

Stage	Description
Identify personas	The customer personas required to test a navigation path are identified.
Define scenario	The scenario to be accessed and the goal to be achieved are defined. The steps in the scenario are defined in outline, enabling the persona to determine how to navigate the service in order to achieve the stated goal.

Table 5.12 (Continued)

Stage	Description
Track access pathway	The pathway navigated by the persona is tracked and an audit trail is recorded. This may be achieved using tracking software where the service is conducted online. Where service touchpoints are navigated in person, a record of the pathway and approach taken by the customer must be kept.
Analyse results	The navigation paths taken by each customer are reviewed and the following aspects are analysed: • the speed of access, navigation and response; • the ease of access and navigation; • unexpected ways of accessing the service; • issues encountered; • pathway consistencies and inconsistencies; • misunderstandings and errors; • customer feedback; • the need for guidance to continue accessing the service.
Determine actions	The navigation path analysis results are used to identify where the service design needs to be amended or may be enhanced. The potential actions are evaluated, prioritised and undertaken where appropriate.

Benefits of navigation path analysis

Navigation path analysis provides detailed insights into how customer personas access and navigate a service to achieve a predetermined goal. The benefits of navigation path analysis analysis are shown in Figure 5.17.

Figure 5.17 Benefits of navigation path analysis

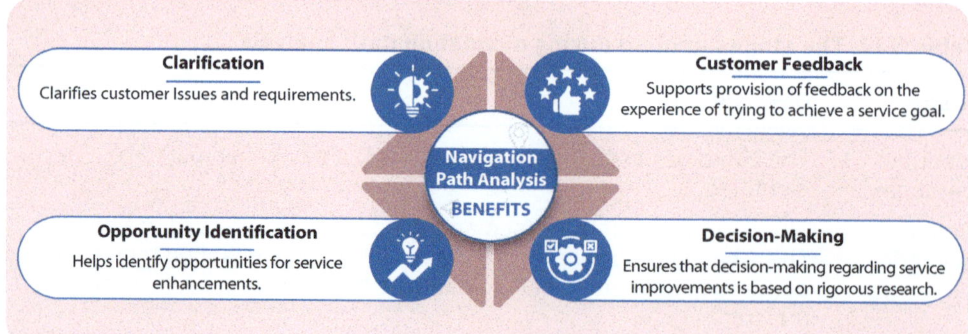

Example of a navigation path analysis

An example set of navigation path analysis results is shown in Table 5.13.

Table 5.13 Example navigation path analysis results

Navigation pathway analysis for restaurant scenario: goal – book table in restaurant

	Description	Steps	Comments
Customer A	Online booking for four people Table required for evening meal	(1) Use browser search for restaurant. (2) Access restaurant website. (3) Select book table (from home page). (4) Enter date/time required; number of diners. (5) Enter booker details. (6) Confirm booking. (7) Receive confirmation.	Website easy to use. Navigation straightforward and intuitive. Confirmation was clear and received promptly.
Customer B	Dinner booking for eight people Table required for evening meal	(1) Use browser search for restaurant. (2) Access restaurant website. (3) Select book table (from home page). (4) Enter date/time required; number of diners. (5) Advised table for more than six diners needs telephone booking. (6) Telephone restaurant to book table.	Frustrating experience. Website easy to use. Navigation to book table straightforward. Needed to enter date/time before advised eight exceeded diner limit. Called twice before anyone answered the phone. Person who answered phone was helpful and efficient. Restaurant is not open on Mondays and Tuesdays. No one to answer phone (not explained on website).

(Continued)

Table 5.13 (Continued)

Navigation pathway analysis for restaurant scenario: goal – book table in restaurant

	Description	Steps	Comments
Customer C	Lunch booking for two people Table required for lunch	(1) Use browser search for restaurant. (2) Access restaurant website. (3) Select book table (from home page). (4) Enter date/time required; number of diners. (5) Enter booker details. (6) Confirm booking. (7) Receive confirmation.	Very frustrating experience! Navigation to book table function straightforward. Unable to book table for 12.00 p.m. – only 11.30 a.m. and 1.00 p.m. allowed Unavailability not due to table bookings. Appears to be due to menu change after 11.30 a.m. (brunch to lunch). Eventually booked for brunch at 11.30 a.m.

CONCLUSION

The experience encountered by customers when accessing a service can determine whether or not they are likely to continue engaging with the organisation. A poor experience may deter customers from returning and convince them to change service provider. They may be prepared to try another service before moving to an alternative service provider that offers a similar service. However, where a customer becomes aware that the organisation does not offer the required customer experience, and that this is an endemic issue rather than related to a particular service, they are likely to switch.

Alternatively, a positive experience can create a sense of trust in the provider and build loyalty. Therefore, the customer experience both across the customer journey and at each individual touchpoint is an opportunity for a service provider to demonstrate the level of quality offered and build a positive relationship with customers.

The techniques described in this chapter are used to analyse the voice of the customer, and enable service designers to ensure that the customer experience offered by an organisation meets customer requirements. The Kano model also highlights the potential for delivering 'delighter' features to increase customer satisfaction and build customer loyalty.

6 SERVICE DEFINITION

This chapter covers the work conducted by service designers when offering the Service Definition service. The key activities of this service, and the techniques that may be applied to carry out these activities, are described in this chapter. These techniques may be supplemented by other techniques, in particular those described in Chapters 10 and 11. The techniques described in Chapters 3–5 and 8–9 may also offer additional insights.

This chapter concludes with a case study describing the approach applied to embed a service mindset within an organisation. This case study has been provided by Bruce Prendergast of His Majesty's Revenue and Customs (HMRC).

INTRODUCTION

The elements required to enable effective end-to-end business service provision, within the context of an ecosystem, must be defined with accuracy. A lack of clarity regarding these elements can raise the risk of critical aspects necessary for effective service provision being overlooked. All too often, ineffective Service Definition or design leads to products or services failing to meet customer or other stakeholder expectations. Failing to define the elements needed can also lead to significant waste for the organisation and its suppliers and partners. In addition, ineffective Service Definition can raise regulatory and compliance risks for the organisation.

In contrast, effective Service Definition provides a foundation for services to be developed in a way that:

- meets and potentially exceeds customer expectations;
- minimises waste for the organisation and its suppliers;
- maximises the leveraging of the organisation's capabilities;
- mitigates regulatory and compliance risks.

THE SERVICE DEFINITION SERVICE

This service includes the following service activities:

- Research, analyse and define current and proposed business services.

The service value items offered by the service concerns the following:

- service value proposition defined;
- service value stream developed;
- service blueprint defined;
- service capability requirements clearly stated.

Figure 6.1 shows a value stream diagram for this service, including the deliverables produced.

Figure 6.1 Value stream: Service Definition

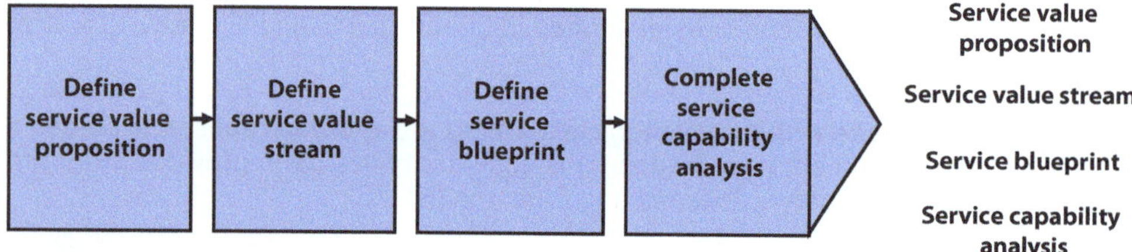

THE TECHNIQUES

Many techniques are used to carry out the work of this service. The generic techniques used in support of Service Definition work are described in Chapters 10 and 11. The specific techniques relevant to this service are:

- value proposition analysis;
- value stream analysis;
- service blueprint;
- service definition canvas;
- service capability analysis.

Value proposition analysis

Purpose

A value proposition for a service:

- clarifies the beneficial outcomes that an organisation offers from delivering a product or service;
- demonstrates to customers that the organisation's service offers what they desire or need;
- differentiates the organisation's service from the services offered by competitors.

The objective of applying this technique is to obtain clarity and shared understanding of the 'why' for the service. The technique also provides a basis for defining the 'what' for the service (see value stream analysis) and the 'how' (see service blueprint and service definition canvas).

When analysing the performance of deployed services (see Glossary of Terms and Techniques), the value proposition can be used to determine any gaps between customer expectations and experiences versus the promises made by the organisation.

The value proposition technique can also be used to analyse the value offered by an entire organisation or division; in this context, the technique is referred to as a strategic value proposition.

Process

The process for the analysis, development and validation of a value proposition is shown in Figure 6.2.

Figure 6.2 Value proposition analysis process

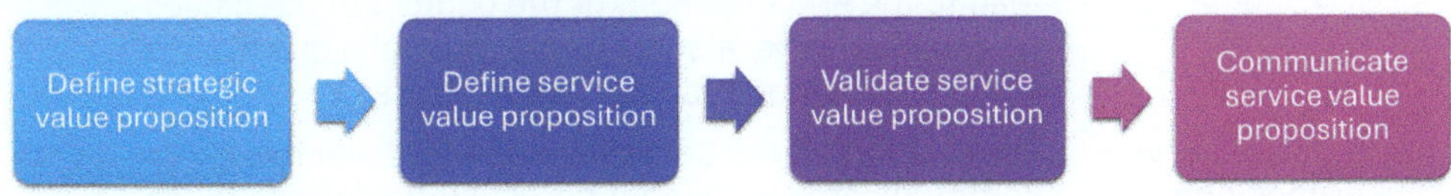

These activities are described in Table 6.1.

The key attributes required to form a value proposition identified by Kaplan and Norton are shown in Figure 6.3.

These elements are described in Table 6.2.

Figure 6.3 Value proposition elements (Adapted from Kaplan and Norton, 1996)

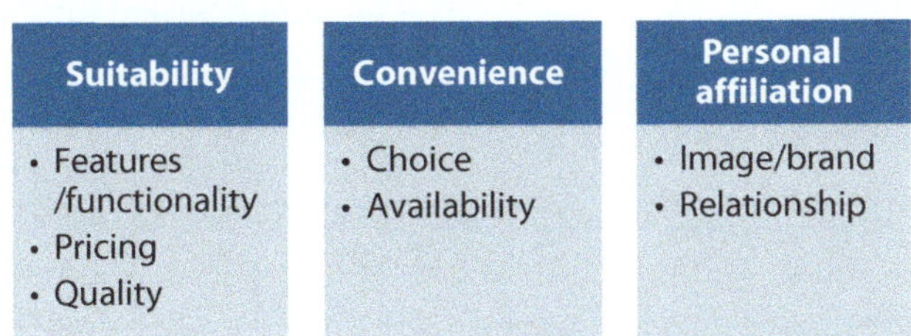

Table 6.1 Value proposition analysis activities

Activity	Description
Define strategic value proposition	The value proposition for the organisation that aims to deliver the defined strategy should be understood and defined prior to defining a value proposition for an individual service. Insights obtained from investigation of the situation and voice of the customer research provide context to this work.
Define service value proposition	Several frameworks can be used as a basis for the definition of the service value proposition including those proposed by Kaplan and Norton (1996) (see Figure 6.3 and Table 6.2) and Osterwalder et al. (2014) (see Table 6.3). Each element of the value proposition is defined. Alignment to the strategic value proposition is also assessed.
Validate service value proposition	The defined service value proposition should be reviewed with identified stakeholders. Feedback provided can lead to the enhancement of the content of the value proposition. Where appropriate, formal sign off of the value proposition may also be necessary.
Communicate service value proposition	Once validated the service value proposition is communicated with identified stakeholders, both inside and outside of the organisation. Internal stakeholders could include those co-creating the service with the service designer.

Table 6.2 Kaplan and Norton value proposition descriptions

Category	Element	Description
Suitability	Features/functionality	The features provided by the product or service.
	Price	The amount charged for the product or service.
	Quality	The level of performance offered by the product or service, including aspects such as robustness, accuracy and speed.

(Continued)

Table 6.2 (Continued)

Category	Element	Description
Convenience	Choice	The ability to customise and personalise the product or service.
	Availability	The level and timing of access to the product or service and responsiveness to customer requests.
Personal affiliation	Image/brand	The image or brand of the organisation and its perception by customers. Where positive, this can increase the desirability of the product or services offered. The image or brand may also lead to a sense of satisfaction and assurance for the customer.
	Relationships	The nature of the engagement between the organisation and its customers. This relates directly to the experience offered by an organisation (and encountered by customers) throughout the entire customer journey.

Osterwalder et al. (2014) defined an alternative framework for defining a value proposition. This framework considers the perspective of both the organisation and customer – see Table 6.3.

Table 6.3 Osterwalder et al. value proposition dimensions (Adapted from Osterwalder et al., 2014)

Customer view	Organisational view
Pains: The gains experienced by the customer that need to be overcome or reduced.	**Pain relievers:** Product or service features that resolve the root causes of customer pain or mitigate the impact.
Gains: The gains required to realise value.	**Gain creators:** Service features that enable the realisation of value.
Customer jobs: The functional, social and emotional jobs that a customer is attempting to complete.	**Products and services:** The list of products and services offered by the organisation.

Benefits of value proposition analysis

A value proposition offers service designers the benefits shown in Figure 6.4:

Figure 6.4 Benefits of a value proposition analysis

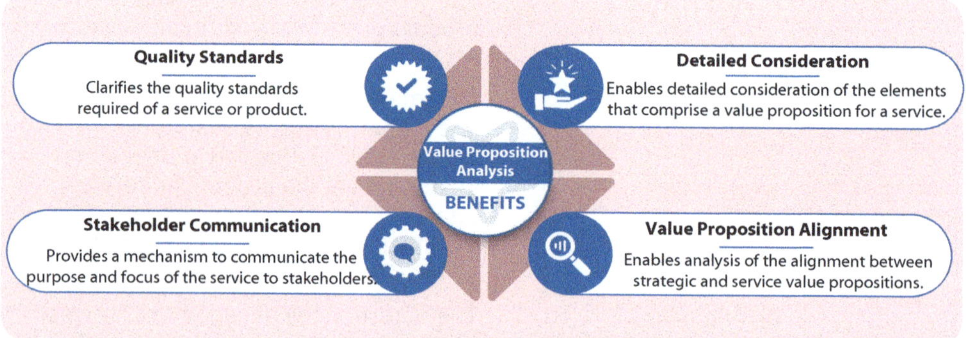

Example value proposition

An example service value proposition for the restaurant scenario using the Kaplan and Norton attributes is shown in Table 6.4.

Table 6.4 Example application of Kaplan and Norton value proposition

Category	Element	Description
Suitability	Features/functionality	• extensive menu of food items; • food items offered describe ingredients clearly; • wide-ranging menu of drink items.
	Price	• reasonably priced meals; • range of prices for drinks offered.
	Quality	• fresh, locally sourced ingredients; • high quality food preparation and presentation; • drinks menu includes premium products.

(Continued)

Table 6.4 (Continued)

Category	Element	Description
Convenience	Choice	• extensive range of food and drink options; • customers can either select individual dishes or order from a set menu.

	Availability	• restaurant open between:
		  • 9.00 a.m. and 2.30 p.m. (breakfast and lunch);
		  • 6.00–11.00 p.m. (dinner);
		• instant response to booking enquiries;
		• staff available to respond to customer requests and queries during restaurant opening hours.

Personal affiliation	Image/brand	The restaurant offers high quality food made with fresh local ingredients, prepared by skilled chefs.
	Relationships	The restaurant engages with customers to obtain information on their requirements, request feedback and build long-term relationships.

Through analysing the value proposition for the restaurant, the service designer is able to start to identify opportunities for service improvement. While the value proposition offered forms a basis for developing the value stream of activities intended to deliver the stated proposition. This does not guarantee that the value proposition is actually delivered – it is a statement of intent. In the course of the restaurant scenario, there have been complaints about food quality and perceptions on drinks prices, and the restaurant is struggling to develop long-term customer relationships. Negative customer experiences have resulted in critical feedback and potential damage to the brand.

Analysing the value proposition enables the service designer to identify where there are issues and offers an opportunity for service enhancement.

Value stream analysis

Purpose

The value stream is a diagram that represents, in overview, the activities needed to deliver a product or service to either an internal or external stakeholder. The model enables a shared understanding of the service activities and how they are linked.

The technique is conceptual in nature and as a result provides a basis for imagining and defining the service without real-world constraints. The activities documented may include those that are conducted within the organisation or are provided by external third party suppliers.

The value stream can be used for further analysis of services using techniques such as Customer Journey Maps (see Glossary of Terms and Techniques) and Service Blueprints (see discussion below).

In addition, the technique can be used to identify and analyse the following aspects:

- The capabilities needed to support execution of value stream activities.
- The events encompassed by each value stream activity and the detailed business processes applied to respond to the events.
- The identification and analysis of interested and impacted stakeholders.

Process

The process for the development and validation of a value stream is shown in Figure 6.5.

Figure 6.5 Value stream development process

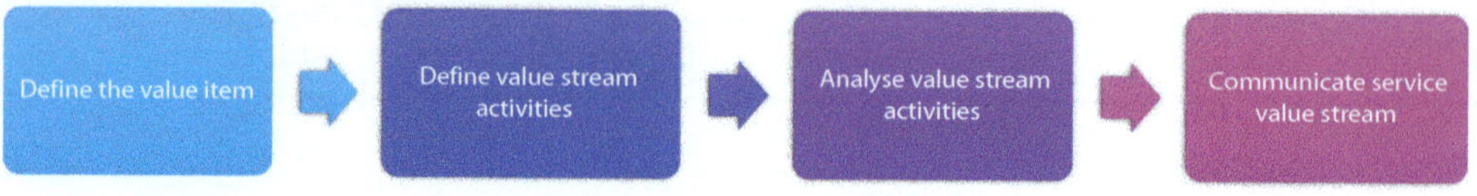

These activities are described in Table 6.5.

Table 6.5 Value stream development process stages

Stage	Description
Define the value item	The 'value item' is defined first. This provides a focus on the product or service being delivered to the customer as a result of the activities within the value stream.
Define value stream activities	Once the value item is defined, the service designer can work backwards to identify and define the activities needed to deliver the value item. Activities should be abstract or conceptual in nature.

(Continued)

Table 6.5 (Continued)

Stage	Description
Analyse value stream activities	The analysis stage is concerned with the assessment and validation of the defined service value stream. Where necessary this activity will lead to the update and enhancement of the value stream as a result of stakeholder feedback. Where appropriate, the value stream is formally approved and baselined.
Communicate service value stream	The stakeholders who should be aware or advised of the value stream are identified. The stakeholders may be internal and external to the organisation, and includes stakeholders responsible for co-creating the service. The service designer identifies the most relevant means of communication with each stakeholder or stakeholder group.

Benefits of a value stream

A value stream offers service designers the benefits shown in Figure 6.6:

Figure 6.6 Benefits of a value stream

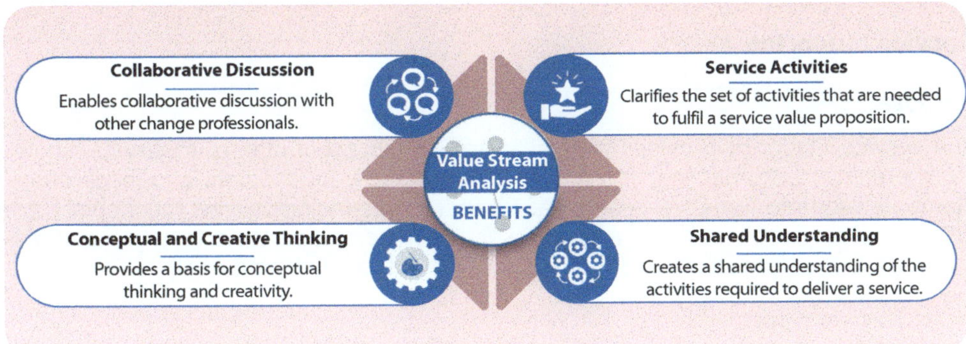

The value stream technique can be used to analyse and document different views, including:

- an existing or current state service;
- a desired or target state service;
- the gap between the current and desired or target state service.

Example value stream

An example service value stream for the restaurant scenario showing the delivery of a value item (in this instance a breakfast) is shown in Figure 6.7.

Figure 6.7 Example value stream for the restaurant scenario

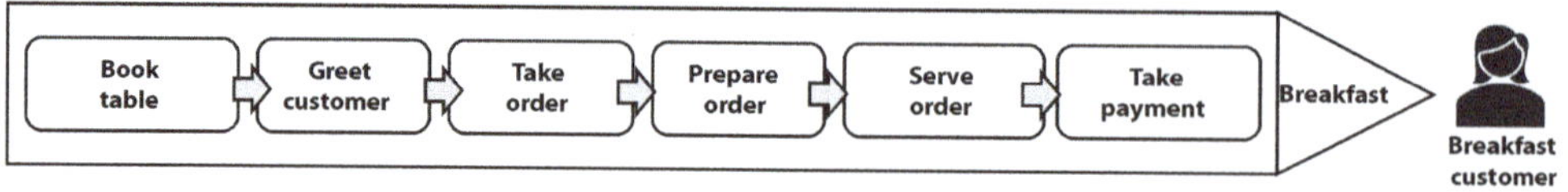

An alternative approach for the development and documentation of a value stream, which highlights the triggering event for the value stream, is shown in Figure 6.8.

Figure 6.8 Example value stream for the restaurant scenario (with event)

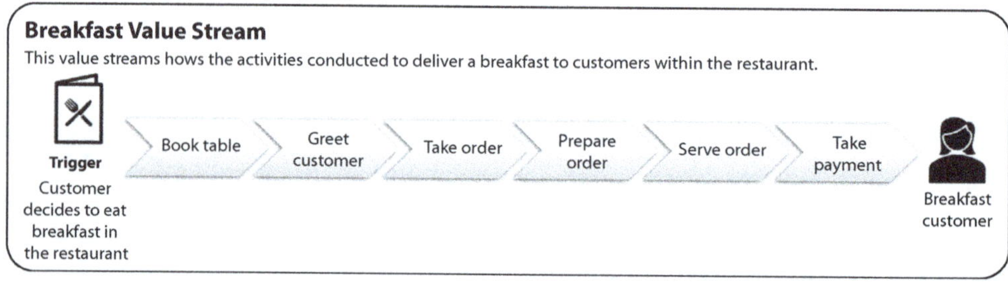

Service blueprint

Purpose

The service blueprint provides a detailed visual representation of a service, showing the entire customer journey, including the stages, touchpoints and 'back office' elements required to deliver a service. The customer-facing service touchpoints are known as the 'front stage' and are represented in the blueprint along with the corresponding 'back stage' elements that support the customer-facing work.

PROCESS

The process for the development of a service blueprint is shown in Figure 6.9.

Figure 6.9 Service blueprint development process stages

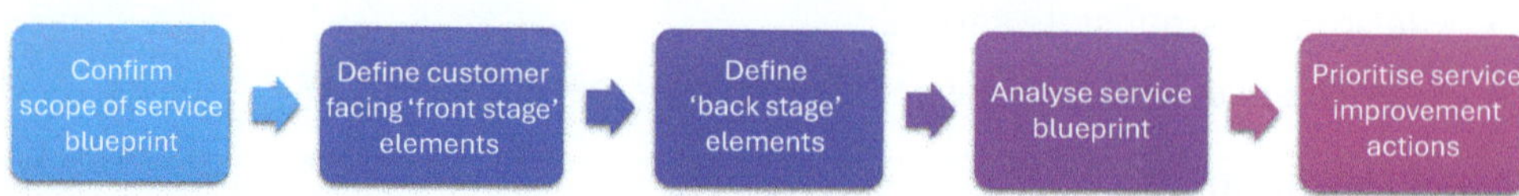

These stages are described in Table 6.6.

Table 6.6 Service blueprint development process stages

Stage	Description
Confirm scope of service blueprint	During this stage, the service designer analyses the customer journey to identify and confirm the scope to be modelled within the service blueprint. Aspects to consider include the customer journey map and persona that the service blueprint relates to. For example, will the service blueprint be focused on the provision of a meal to a customer irrespective of special dietary requirements? Will the blueprint be focused on a general meal offered on the menu or relate to a special celebratory meal offered to customers that have pre-booked this with the restaurant? In addition, the focus of the application of the technique needs to be confirmed. For example, will the service blueprint be used in order to: • Analyse and document a current state/existing service? When applied to this context, will the blueprint also be used to identify opportunities for service improvement? • Analyse and document a target state/new or modified service?
Define customer facing 'front stage' elements	Where a customer journey map exists, this is used as a basis for defining the 'front stage' elements of the service blueprint. Where the customer journey map does not exist, these elements need to be developed (see Glossary of Terms and Techniques). Where the service blueprint is used to define a target state (new or modified) service, the service designer should define the proposed customer journey.
Define 'back stage' elements	Once the 'front stage' elements are defined, the service designer can analyse and describe the 'back stage' elements required to support each touchpoint of the customer journey. These elements include the supporting: • processes; • data/information; • roles/skills; • physical items; • measures; • applications.
Analyse service blueprint	This stage includes the assessment and validation of the service blueprint. Where appropriate this will lead to the update and enhancement of the content of the service blueprint as a result of stakeholder feedback. Where appropriate, the service blueprint is formally approved and baselined.
Prioritise service improvement actions	This stage concerns reviewing the identified service improvement actions and deciding their relative level of priority. The Kano technique may be used to prioritise the improvements (see Glossary of Terms and Techniques).

The back stage elements of the service blueprint are described in more detail in Table 6.7.

Table 6.7 Service blueprint 'back stage' elements

'Back stage' element	Description
Processes	The processes that underpin the work of the customer facing touchpoint.
Data/information	The data and information that is required for the work conducted during the touchpoint.
Role/skills	The supporting roles and skills required to conduct the work of the touchpoint.
Physical items	The physical items that are used to undertake the work of the touchpoint.
Measures	The measures applied by the organisation to the work of the touchpoint.
Applications	The technology used to support the work of the touchpoint.

Benefits of a service blueprint

A service blueprint offers service designers the benefits shown in Figure 6.10:

Figure 6.10 Benefits of a service blueprint

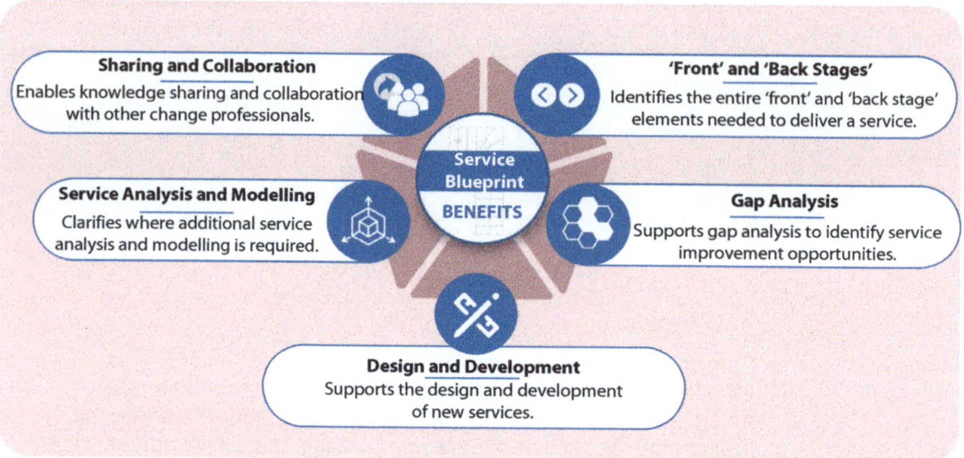

Example service blueprint

Figure 6.11 shows an example service blueprint – based on the customer journey map from Chapter 5.

Figure 6.11 Example of a service blueprint for the restaurant scenario

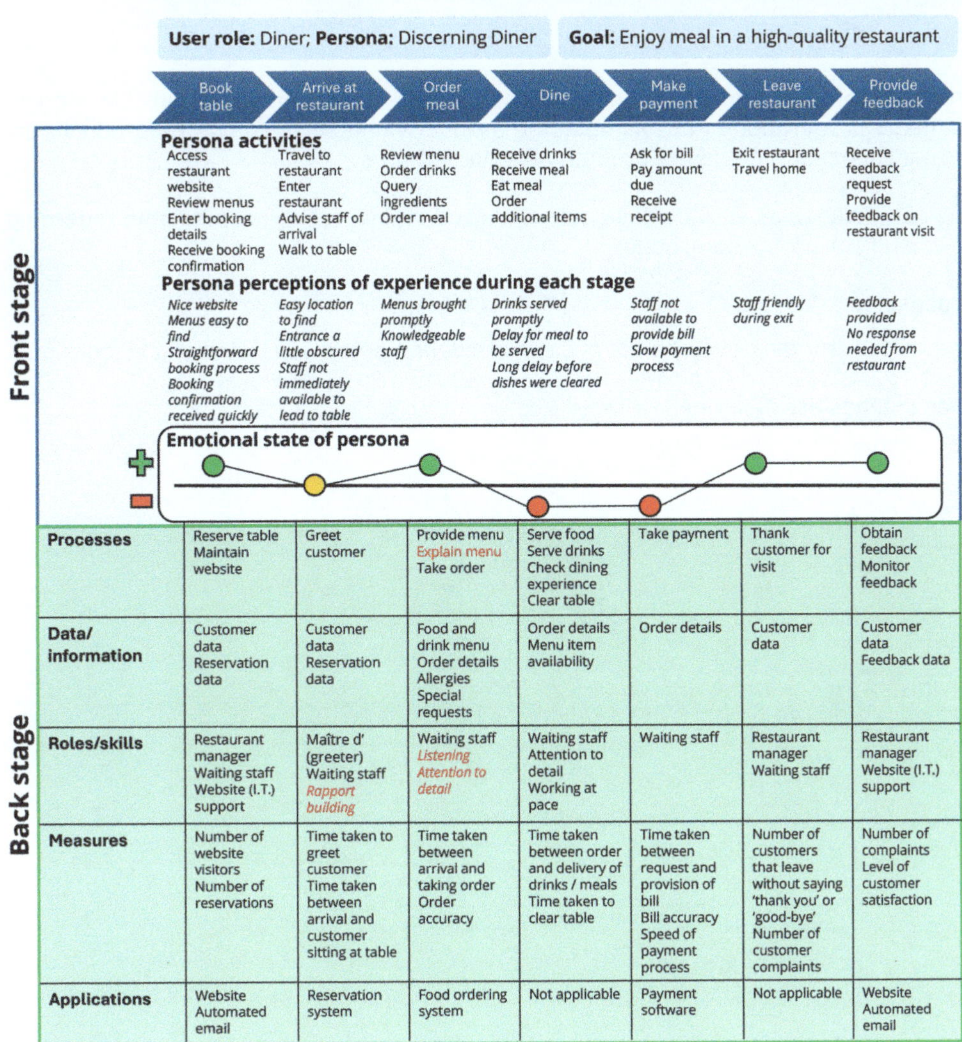

	Book table	Arrive at restaurant	Order meal	Dine	Make payment	Leave restaurant	Provide feedback
Processes	Reserve table Maintain website	Greet customer	Provide menu Explain menu Take order	Serve food Serve drinks Check dining experience Clear table	Take payment	Thank customer for visit	Obtain feedback Monitor feedback
Data/ information	Customer data Reservation data	Customer data Reservation data	Food and drink menu Order details Allergies Special requests	Order details Menu item availability	Order details	Customer data	Customer data Feedback data
Roles/skills	Restaurant manager Waiting staff Website (I.T.) support	Maître d' (greeter) Waiting staff *Rapport building*	Waiting staff *Listening* *Attention to detail*	Waiting staff Attention to detail Working at pace	Waiting staff	Restaurant manager Waiting staff	Restaurant manager Website (I.T.) support
Measures	Number of website visitors Number of reservations	Time taken to greet customer Time taken between arrival and customer sitting at table	Time taken between arrival and taking order Order accuracy	Time taken between order and delivery of drinks / meals Time taken to clear table	Time taken between request and provision of bill Bill accuracy Speed of payment process	Number of customers that leave without saying 'thank you' or 'good-bye' Number of customer complaints	Number of complaints Level of customer satisfaction
Applications	Website Automated email	Reservation system	Food ordering system	Not applicable	Payment software	Not applicable	Website Automated email

Service definition canvas

Purpose

The service definition canvas is an adaptable template used for the discovery, analysis and communication of the key elements related to a service. The canvas elements are concerned with describing the 'why', 'what', 'how' and 'who' for a service plus the 'service revenue streams' and 'service costs'.

Figure 6.12 shows the service definition canvas.

The service definition canvas may also be used to define and communicate the key elements of a product. For example, the product value proposition, the product performance measures and the product revenue streams.

The canvas enables service designers and product owners to gain insights regarding an existing or proposed product.

Process

The process for the development of a service definition canvas is shown in Figure 6.13.

These stages are described in Table 6.8.

Figure 6.12 The service definition canvas (© Assist Knowledge Development)

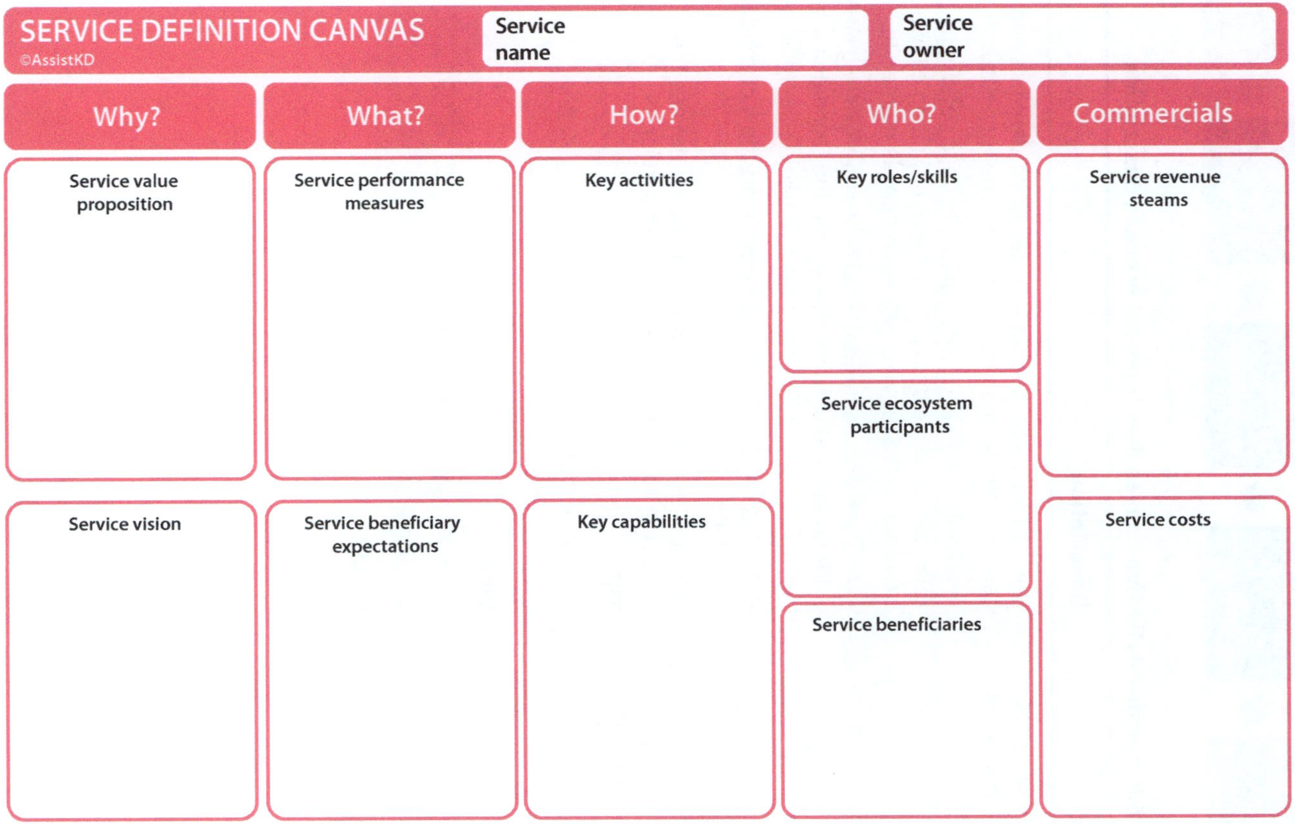

SERVICE DEFINITION CANVAS
©AssistKD
Service name
Service owner
Why?
What?
How?
Who?
Commercials
Service value proposition
Service performance measures
Key activities
Key roles/skills
Service revenue steams
Service ecosystem participants
Service vision
Service beneficiary expectations
Key capabilities
Service costs
Service beneficiaries

Figure 6.13 Service definition canvas development process

Table 6.8 Service definition canvas development process description

Stage	Description
Identify scope of service definition canvas	During this stage, the service designer identifies and confirms the scope of the service to be modelled. In addition, the service designer needs to determine the rationale for developing the service definition canvas. For example, is the service definition canvas needed to: • Analyse and document a current state/existing service? When applied to this context, will the technique also be used to identify service improvement opportunities? • Analyse and document a target state/new or modified service?
Develop core elements of the service definition canvas	During this stage, the service designer defines the following aspects for the identified service: **Title** • service name; • service owner. **Why?** • service value proposition; • service vision. **What?** • service performance measures; • service beneficiary expectations. **How?** • key activities; • key capabilities. **Who?** • key roles/skills; • key service ecosystem participants; • key service beneficiaries.

(Continued)

Table 6.8 (Continued)

Stage	Description
Develop commercial elements of the service definition canvas	The commercial aspects for the identified service are investigated and analysed. These elements concern: • service revenue streams; • service costs.
Analyse service definition canvas	The information documented in the service definition canvas is reviewed and validated. This stage may require amendments to be made to the service definition canvas as a result of the analysis and any stakeholder feedback. Where appropriate, the service definition canvas is formally validated and used to determine actions.
Communicate service definition canvas	The service definition canvas is communicated to relevant stakeholders. This includes stakeholders responsible for co-creating the service.

The elements of the service definition canvas are described in more detail within Table 6.9.

Table 6.9 Service definition canvas elements

Category	Element	Description
Title	Service name	The name by which the service is identified.
	Service owner	The named individual that has overall accountability for the service.
Why?	Service value proposition	The value proposition for the service (see earlier section on value proposition analysis).
	Service vision	The aspirational target state for the service. The 'vision' element of Vision, Mission, Objectives, Strategy and Tactics (VMOST) (see Glossary of Terms and Techniques) can support this element of the canvas.
What?	Service performance measures	The performance measures for the service. These should support the measurement of progress towards the achievement of the service vision.

(Continued)

Table 6.9 (Continued)

Category	Element	Description
		Techniques that support this element of the canvas include the 'objectives' element of VMOST, the balanced scorecard, critical success factors (CSFs), KPIs, objectives and key results (OKRs) (see Glossary of Terms and Techniques).
	Service expectations	The expectations of service beneficiaries and ecosystem participants.
How?	Key activities	The key activities required to deliver the service.
		Value stream analysis (see previous technique) can be used to aid with the identification of activities.
	Key capabilities	The key capabilities required to deliver the service.
		Business Capability Modelling (see Glossary of Terms and Techniques) can be used to aid with the identification of capabilities.
Who?	Key roles/skills	The key roles/skills that are required to carry out the work leading to the delivery of the service.
	Key service ecosystem participants	The key **internal** and **external** ecosystem participants. This comprises the service entities that conduct the work required to deliver the service.
	Key service beneficiaries	The key service beneficiaries. This will include the primary customer or user of the service but can also include other secondary beneficiaries of the service.
Commercials	Service revenue streams	The key sources of revenue for the service. This will include revenue obtained from the sale of products or services.
		For non-commercial organisations, this will include aspects such as: • donations; • allocated budgets or grants.
	Service costs	The key costs associated with delivering the service.

Benefits of a service definition canvas

A service definition canvas offers service designers the benefits shown in Figure 6.14:

Figure 6.14 Benefits of a service definition canvas

Service Definition Canvas
BENEFITS

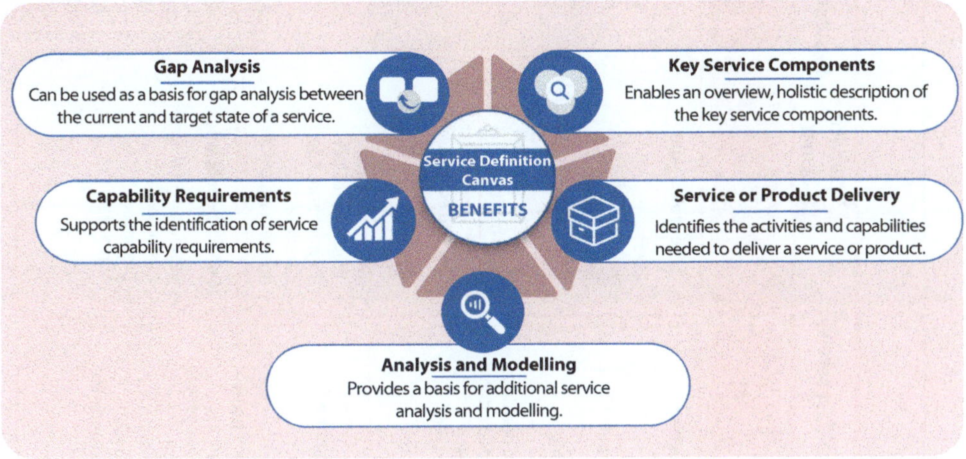

Gap Analysis
Can be used as a basis for gap analysis between the current and target state of a service.

Key Service Components
Enables an overview, holistic description of the key service components.

Capability Requirements
Supports the identification of service capability requirements.

Service or Product Delivery
Identifies the activities and capabilities needed to deliver a service or product.

Analysis and Modelling
Provides a basis for additional service analysis and modelling.

Example service definition canvas

An example service definition canvas for the restaurant scenario is shown in Figure 6.15.

Figure 6.15 Example service definition canvas

SERVICE DEFINITION CANVAS
©AssistKD

Service name: Breakfast service
Service owner: Restaurant manager

Why?

Service value proposition

- High quality breakfast food and drink
- Provide a positive end-to-end customer experience

Service vision

- To be the breakfast restaurant of choice for local residents

What?

Service performance measures

- Customer satisfaction
- Number of repeat customers
- Total breakfast revenue
- Profitability of breakfast service offer

Service beneficiary expectations

- Restaurant manager – profitable service that enhances reputation
- Customers – high quality food and drink at a reasonable price
- Employees – Positive and rewarding work environment
- Suppliers – Ongoing profitable relationship

How?

Key activities

- Creating menus / recipes
- Co-ordinating suppliers
- Taking table bookings
- Preparing food / drink
- Taking orders
- Taking payments
- Cleaning

Key capabilities

- Supplier management
- Menu design
- Customer experience management
- Food preparation
- Drink preparation
- Booking management

Who?

Key roles/skills

- Chef
- Waiting staff
- Relationship management
- Empathy
- Attention to detail
- Food hygiene

Service ecosystem participants

- Food suppliers
- Drink suppliers
- Website provider
- Payment provider
- Landlord
- Insurance provider

Service beneficiaries

- Restaurant manager
- Customers
- Employees
- Suppliers

Commercials

Service revenue streams

- Food sales
- Drinks sales

Service costs

- Employee salaries
- Food / drink purchases
- Cleaning
- Employee training
- Rent
- Insurance
- Banking fees
- Kitchen maintenance
- Utility costs

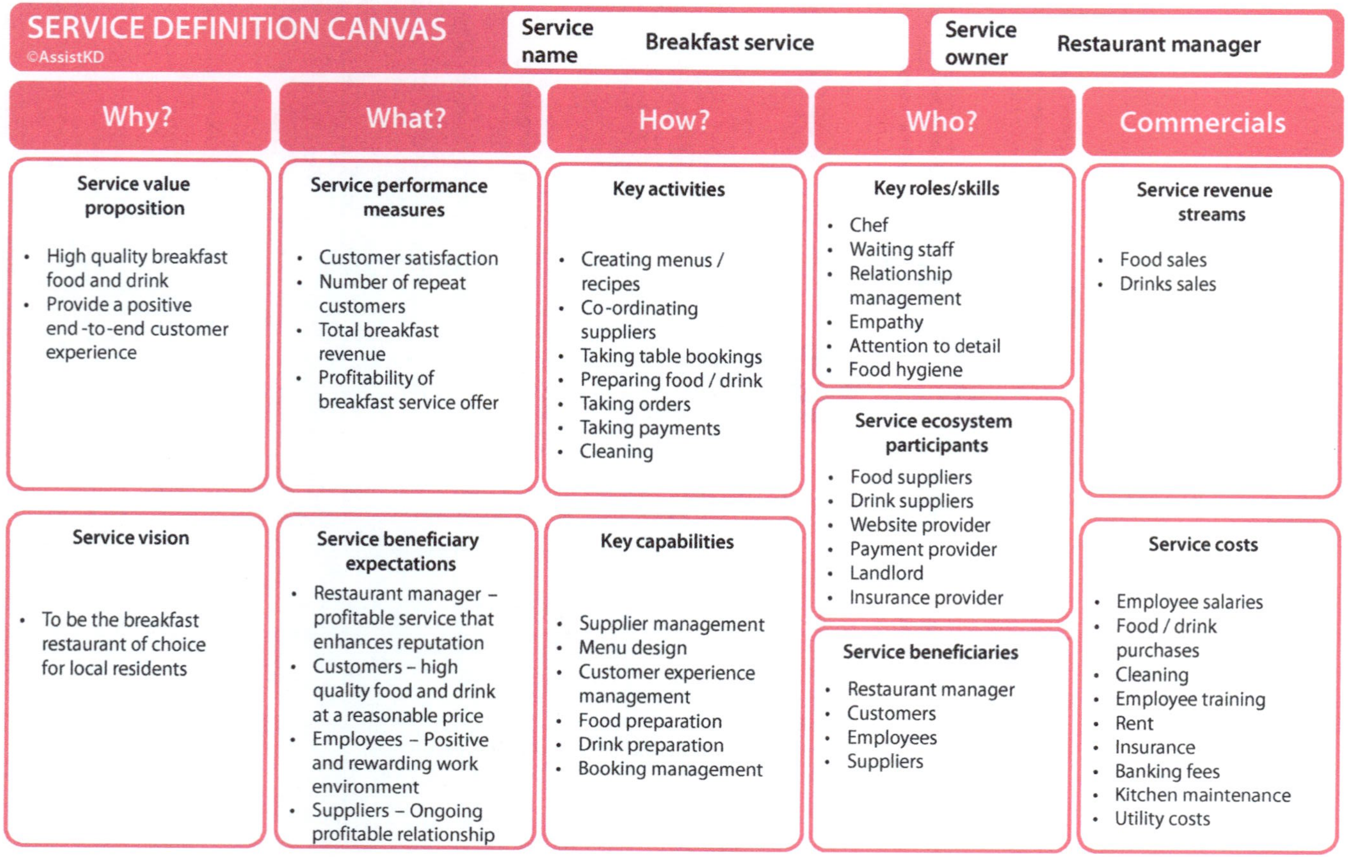

Service capability analysis

Purpose

Service capability analysis aims to provide clarity on both the service requirements for an individual service and the necessary business capabilities that are required to support its effective execution.

This service capability requirements concern the following areas:

- The **business outcome** to be achieved by delivering the service.
- The **business constraints** imposed by the legal/regulatory requirements and organisational policies.
- The **customer experience** to be delivered throughout the customer journey for the service.
- The **technical constraints** imposed by the organisation's technology policies and infrastructure.
- The **utility** to be provided to the customers by the service.
- The **service quality** requirements (see Table 6.10).

Table 6.10 SERVQUAL – service quality requirements

Dimension	Description
Tangibility	The physical facilities, equipment and appearance of personnel.
Reliability	The ability to perform the promised service dependably and accurately.
Responsiveness	The willingness to help customers and provide prompt service.
Assurance	The knowledge and courtesy of employees and their ability to inspire trust and confidence.
Empathy	The caring individualised attention the firm provides to its customers.

The service quality requirements are based on the SERVQUAL dimensions (Parasuraman et al., 1985) outlined within Table 6.10. Once the service requirements are defined, the business capabilities (see Glossary of Terms and Techniques) needed to enable effective execution can be identified. Where appropriate, enhancement of underpinning capabilities can then be prioritised.

Process

The process applied to develop a set of service capability requirements is shown in Figure 6.16.

Figure 6.16 Service capability requirements development process

These stages are described in Table 6.11.

Table 6.11 Service requirements development process description

Stage	Description
Elicit service requirements	During this stage, service designers apply a range of investigation and elicitation techniques (see Glossary of Terms and Techniques) to identify stakeholder 'wants' and 'needs' for the service. This includes exploration of both tacit and explicit knowledge.
Analyse service requirements	This stage involves reviewing and updating the elicited service requirements. The work of this activity includes the following aspects: • removing any identified gaps, overlaps or errors; • negotiating with stakeholders to resolve any conflicts and to determine priorities; • scrutinising the requirements to ensure that they are accurate, complete, feasible and testable.
Validate service requirements	This stage is concerned with requesting the review and feedback of the identified service requirements, and updating the service requirements in collaboration with the stakeholders. Through a process of iteration and continuous improvement, the intent is to enhance shared understanding and the overall quality of the identified requirements. In some contexts, it may be appropriate to use this activity to obtain formal approval of the service requirements.
Analyse required business capabilities	This stage involves using the service requirements to identify and analyse the business capabilities that are required to deliver a service (see Glossary of Terms and Techniques). The work involves: (1) Identifying the business capabilities needed to support the defined service.

(Continued)

Table 6.11 (Continued)

Stage	Description
	(2) Exploring any business capability gaps. This involves analysing a capability to determine if it offers the qualities required by the service. This analysis should also identify where a new business capability is required to deliver the service in line with the value proposition. (3) Prioritising any necessary enhancements to the organisation's business capabilities. These enhancements may require changes to the capability components, in particular the people skills, technology, information, equipment and processes. Where a new capability is required, these components will need to be established.

Benefits of service capability analysis

The service capability analysis technique offers the benefits shown in Figure 6.17:

Figure 6.17 Benefits of a service capability analysis

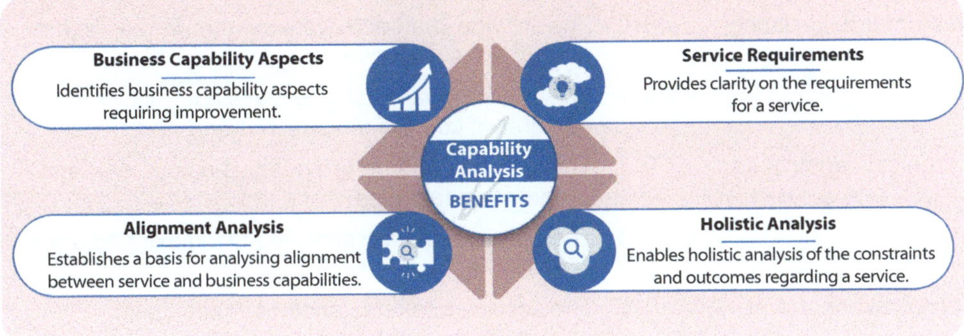

Example service capability requirements

An example set of service requirements for the breakfast service within a restaurant is shown in Table 6.12.

Table 6.12 Example draft service requirements for a breakfast service

Category	Ref	Description
Business outcome	001	The service shall be profitable in first year of operation.
	002	The service shall enhance the overall reputation of the restaurant.
	003	The service shall leverage existing business capabilities.
Business constraints	004	The service shall be offered between 8.30 a.m. and 11.00 a.m. – seven days per week.
	005	The service shall be delivered in compliance with food safety standards.
	006	The service shall be delivered in compliance with employment regulations.
	007	The service shall be delivered in compliance with taxation regulations.
	008	The service shall be advertised in compliance with advertising laws.
	009	The delivered service shall align with the strategic value proposition.
Customer experience	010	The service shall achieve a customer satisfaction of four stars or above.
	011	The service shall result in fewer than 1% of customers complaining each month.
Technical constraints	012	The service shall be provided using current food preparation facilities.
	013	The service shall be provided using existing drink preparation facilities.
Technical constraints	014	The service bookings shall be made using existing restaurant booking facilities.
	015	The service payments shall be made using existing payment facilities.
	016	The service customers shall use the existing Wi-Fi network.

(Continued)

Table 6.12 (Continued)

Category		Ref	Description
Utility		017	The service shall provide a range of food options that align with non-meat food preferences.
		018	The service shall provide a variety of alcoholic/non-alcoholic drink options.
		019	The service shall be adjusted to ensure food allergies/intolerances are accommodated.
Service quality	Tangibility	020	The service shall be provided in a restaurant where all areas are visibly clean.
		021	The service staff shall meet the restaurants high presentation standards (including alignment to dress code, hygiene standards).
		022	The service tableware (cutlery, plates, cups, glasses) shall be visibly clean.
	Reliability	023	The service standards shall be reliable and adhered to at all times.
	Responsiveness	024	The service staff shall provide prompt responses to customer requests and queries.
	Assurance	025	The service staff shall demonstrate knowledge of the service offer.
		026	The service staff shall be courteous to customers at all times.
	Empathy	027	The service staff shall provide individualised care and attention to customers.

For the restaurant breakfast service, the following capabilities are deemed necessary:

- supplier management;
- menu design;
- customer experience management;
- food preparation;
- drink preparation.

An example output from the analysis of 'drink preparation' capability in relation to the breakfast service is shown in Table 6.13.

Table 6.13 Example analysis of business capabilities for a breakfast service

<table>
<tr><td>Service</td><td>Breakfast service</td></tr>
<tr><td>Capability</td><td>Drink preparation</td></tr>
<tr><td>Capability existence</td><td>Capability exists.

All expected elements of a capability available and in use. This includes:

<table>
<tr><th>Element</th><th>Existence</th></tr>
<tr><td>Skilled personnel</td><td>✓</td></tr>
<tr><td>Facilities and equipment</td><td>✓</td></tr>
<tr><td>Process, routines and standards</td><td>✓</td></tr>
<tr><td>Authority</td><td>✓</td></tr>
<tr><td>Information</td><td>✓</td></tr>
</table>

The 'drink preparation' capability is utilised during the afternoon and evening opening hours.</td></tr>
<tr><td>Capability maturity</td><td>Skilled personnel
• In general, the majority of restaurant employees have the necessary skills and competence to execute capability effectively.
• Additional barista training required for some employees.
Facilities and equipment
• Restaurant has necessary equipment to execute capability.
• Current coffee machine may need to be upgraded.</td></tr>
</table>

(Continued)

Table 6.13 (Continued)

Service	**Breakfast service**
Capability	**Drink preparation**
	• **Processes, routines and standards** • Restaurant has in place necessary processes, routines and standards to execute capability effectively. **Authority** • Established authority in place; there is clear ownership and accountability. **Information** • Appropriate information available and in use.
Capability capacity	• Cold drink preparation capacity adequate for expected volumes. • Tea and hot chocolate capacity adequate for expected volumes. • Coffee preparation capacity is limited. An upgrade to a larger coffee machine is required to support expected volumes.
Capability performance	• The capability requires some improvement to meet expectations for the new breakfast service.

When assessing the capability in relation to the breakfast service, a decision would need to be made on whether to implement enhancements to the capability. In the example, this includes additional barista training for employees and also the consideration of an upgrade of the existing coffee machine.

CASE STUDY: SERVICE DESIGN AT HMRC

Bruce Prendergast explains the approach taken to embed a service mindset within the UK government department, HMRC.

The context: empathy, define and ideation

The Chief Digital and Information Office (CDIO) at HMRC was on a transformation journey and I had responsibility for developing a new Operational Strategy. That strategy set out clear outcomes – we would create better value for our service consumers, which we would achieve sooner, safer and with happier colleagues. Essentially, we would transform HMRC CDIO into a modern service organisation. HMRC CDIO do an incredible job and this new strategy, befitting the importance of our purpose

– collecting the money that powers UK public services – was rightly ambitious. I was looking for methods that could help develop a service mindset across the organisation both rapidly and in a truly collaborative way. I needed to be able to connect people right across the organisation with 'service thinking' and was developing the concept of 'strategy as a service' or StraaS, aiming to test ideas that might then provide a prototype for others to adopt or build from. I mentioned this in conversation with the founder members of the Service Design Forum, who suggested looking at the new 'service definition canvas' technique. At the inaugural meeting of the Service Design Forum, we took our first look at the prototype canvas and tested it as a group. I instantly saw the potential for the service definition canvas and offered to help further develop and test it back at HMRC.

Prototype and test

I started socialising the canvas with a couple of colleagues, who shared my thinking regarding the potential it might have. We discussed and iterated the canvas, tailoring it for use in HMRC and sharing these changes and ideas back to members of the Service Design Forum. I used this HMRC branded version to set out how my concept of Strategy as a Service (StraaS) might work, along with a coffee shop example and blank canvas to share with peers. I also shared the strategy canvas at the IRM Service Design Conference Europe and WRK Leaders in Tech conferences inviting feedback from their expert audiences. Interest was high. At HMRC, colleagues in both governance and supplier management instantly recognised the potential for the canvas, helping them to both develop their service offer for internal users whilst also helping think about services being supplied to HMRC by commercial partners, providing further testing for the canvas and confirming the positive benefits for service thinking within their teams. Whilst this was ongoing, I was also leading on the adoption of (OKRs) across CDIO as part of the approach to strategy realisation. With growing exposure, mounting evidence of the clear benefits being realised from the service definition canvas and support amongst senior colleagues, it was agreed that the strategic operations functions would adopt an objective to 'Drive CDIO to become a service organisation'. The service definition canvas has a central role to play in this drive.

Early adoption, continuous improvement, and going mainstream?

During this time, other members of the Service Design Forum had also been testing and further developing the canvas and shared an updated version. I took this opportunity to update our early efforts on the StraaS service definition canvas, making further changes to arrive at a final version of the canvas for our use, which was even more focused on service value and service beneficiaries. Strategy is one of over forty practices adopted by HMRC CDIO to create our digital services, and I proposed that each of these practices might benefit from utilising the service definition canvas to enhance their thinking in terms of service and value that they are offering. Practice managers who had tested the canvas immediately spoke up in support of the idea, with both architecture and service design practices offering to lead on and support future use of the canvas, bringing it – and a service mindset – into the mainstream across CDIO.

Figure 6.18 Example (HMRC) service definition canvas

Service name: Strategy Practice [Strategy as a Service – StraaS]

Service Definition Canvas

Why?

Service value proposition

To translate HMRC's purpose into clear direction for CDIO—formulating mission, outcomes and courses of action; aligning strategic choices and decisions, turning strategy into coherent, prioritised and sustainable delivery through nested strategies and OKRs

Service vision

Strategies are the driving force for purposeful action across CDIO.

What?

Service beneficiary expectations

- Strategies that create better value for HMRC Consumers
- Clear alignment between CDIO and HMRC strategic direction
- Co-creation and maintenance of the CDIO Operational Strategy
- Co-Creation of CDIO Strategic Annual OKRs
- Support and guidance for strategy and OKR creation across CDIO

Service performance measures

- People survey results for colleagues who report that their work is aligned to service user requirements
- Qualitative Peer review of HMRC alignment
- CDIO Operational Strategy published and up to date
- CDIO Strategic Annual OKRs published and progress evidenced through performance reviews
- Customer satisfaction with support and guidance offering

How?

Service Offerings

1. Strategy Formulation [CDIO Operational] and alignment
2. Strategic Narrative development
3. Strategic Annual OKR development
4. Support for nested strategy creation and alignment
5. Support for OKR development
6. Analysis for Strategy and OKR creation, alignment and continuous improvement opportunities.

Key capabilities

- Strategic Analysis
- Strategy Co-creation
- OKR formulation
- Practice Management

Key skills

- Strategic thinking
- Business Acumen
- Design Thinking
- Stakeholder Management
- Leadership
- Influencing
- Coaching and facilitation
- Communication
- Narrative and Storytelling
- Environmental Scanning & Analysis
- Problem Solving
- Systems thinking
- Continuous Improvement

Who?

Service beneficiaries

Tax-payers & UK Public services
HMRC ExCom
CDIO Leadership
Practice Owners
Tax regime leadership and Service Owners
Product Teams
Functional Teams

Service ecosystem participants

- CDIO Strategic Leadership
- Practices: Portfolio; Risk; Architecture; Service Financial Management; Demand; Comms; Measurement and Reporting
- Nominated strategy and OKR development leads
- Strategy and OKR Champions

Commercials?

Service revenue streams

- Operational Transformation Team cost allocation
- Joint Value Initiatives

Service costs

- G6 Practice Owner (F/T)
- G7 Practice Manager (F/T)
- + on-costs

Unfunded

- Strategy Practice Officer (F/T)
- Coaches? Strategy + OKR

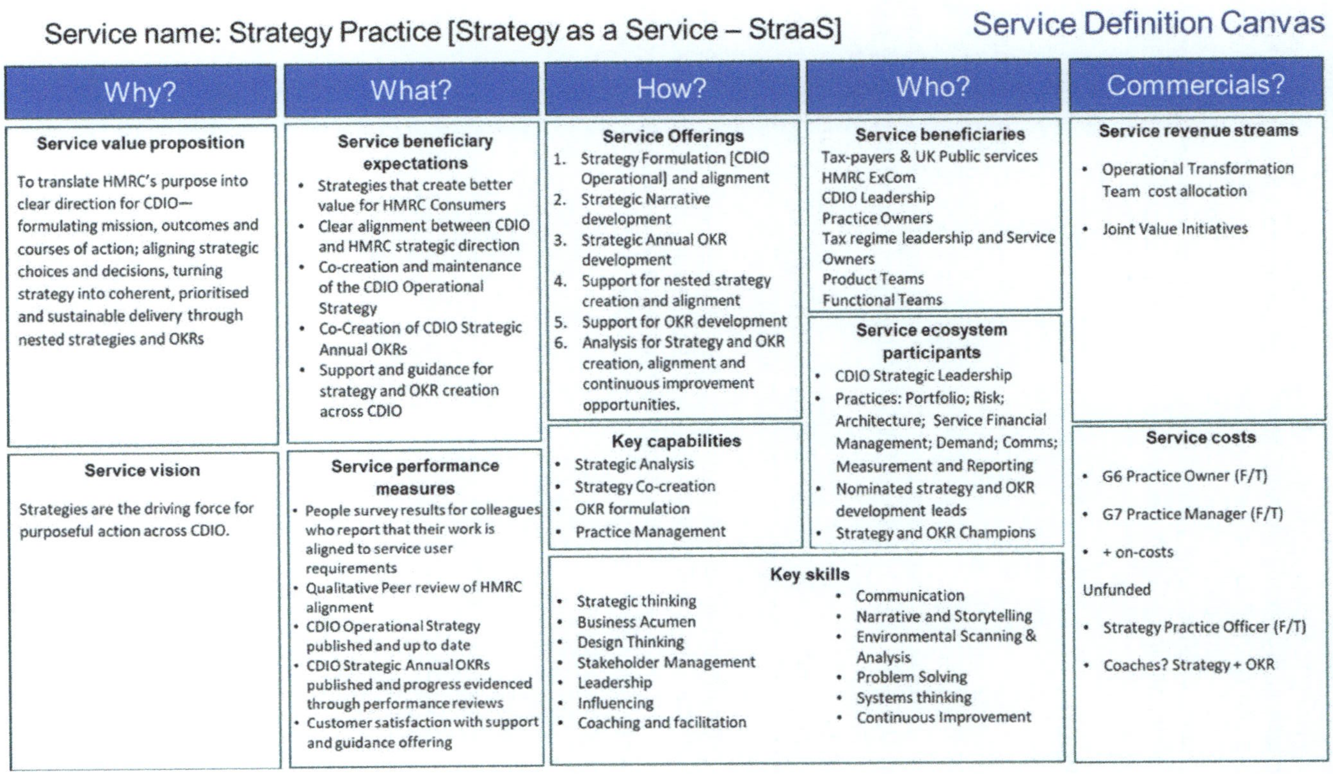

Case study conclusions

Using aspects of service design, in both the design of strategy and then taking strategy into delivery has been pivotal to early successes in HMRC CDIO transformation into a modern service organisation. These design approaches and techniques have themselves contributed to the development of the service definition canvas, which in turn is playing an impactful role in creating a culture typified by a service mindset. Whilst early days, there's no doubt in my mind that service design approaches and the service definition canvas have helped give us a great start (Figure 6.18).

CONCLUSION

Service Definition provides a foundation for the design and development of either an enhanced or entirely new service. Where service designers omit the Service Definition, the basis for Service Experimentation is likely to be flawed. Through a process of iteration and feedback from Service Experimentation, understanding of Service Definition can evolve further. The development of the value proposition, value stream, service blueprint, service definition canvas and service requirements provides a basis for understanding service capability requirements. This enables shared understanding with other change professionals including business architects, enterprise architects and business analysts.

The value stream activities enacted to conduct this service ensure there is a clear definition of the service. The techniques described in this chapter enable service designers to define a service holistically. They may also be applied when conducting other service design services.

7 SERVICE EXPERIMENTATION

This chapter covers the work conducted by service designers during the Service Experimentation service. The key activities of this service and techniques that may be applied to carry out these activities are described in this chapter. These techniques may be supplemented by other techniques, in particular those described in Chapters 10 and 11. However, the techniques described in Chapters 3–6 and 8–9 may also offer additional insights.

INTRODUCTION

This service is focused on identifying, prototyping and testing a range of potential solutions. Through iterative feedback and continuous improvement, information is obtained on whether design ideas and solutions will work in practice. Knowledge is also obtained on the feasibility, benefits, disbenefits, risks and impacts of potential solutions. This service provides further insight regarding the voice of the customer and the service requirements. The execution of this service provides a foundation for the deployment of a target state service.

The Service Experimentation service

This service includes the following service activities:

- Support the design and development of service prototypes.
- Elicit and analyse feedback against prototypes to enable iteration and continuous improvement.

The service value items offered by this service are defined as:

- service prototypes designed and developed;
- qualitative and quantitative feedback elicited and analysed.

Figure 7.1 shows a value stream diagram for this service, including the service deliverables.

Figure 7.1 Value stream: Service Experimentation

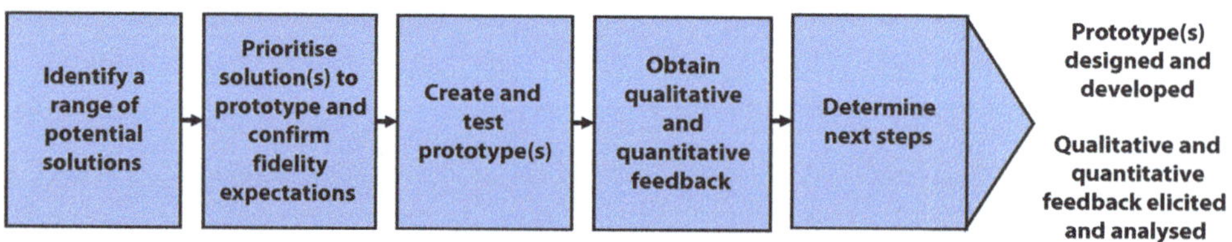

Table 7.1 describes the benefits offered by the Service Experimentation.

Table 7.1 Service Experimentation benefits

Potential Benefit	Description
Risk reduction	Service Experimentation can lead to an enhanced understanding of the risks associated with Service Deployment. This includes obtaining enhanced understanding of the: • feasibility and desirability of the product or service; • impact of the introduction of the product or service.
Early value co-creation	Service Experimentation provides an opportunity for early access to a product or service for selected customers (or other stakeholders). Consequently, any benefits offered by the product or service are made available sooner. In addition, any insights obtained through feedback can lead to product or service enhancement.
Increased stakeholder awareness and engagement	Service Experimentation can lead to an increased volume of stakeholders being aware of the product or service and its associated value proposition. This can also lead to increased credibility and engagement with stakeholders.
Increased innovation	Service Experimentation can help identify opportunities to enhance a product or service. In addition, opportunities to enhance the value proposition of the organisation through other products and services may be identified.

THE TECHNIQUES

Many techniques are used to carry out the work of this service. The generic techniques used in support of Service Experimentation work are described in Chapters 10 and 11. The specific techniques relevant to this service are:

- storyboarding;
- hypothesis trees;

- scenario analysis;
- decision trees;
- prototyping;
- A/B testing.

Storyboarding

Purpose

A storyboard provides a graphical representation of the steps within a customer journey. The technique can be used in conjunction with a customer journey map or service blueprint (see Glossary of Terms and Techniques).

A storyboard is a form of low-fidelity prototype (see prototyping) when used to explore potential target state business services or information technology solutions. Storyboarding can also be applied to analyse and assess current state services and technology solutions.

Process

The process for the development and validation of a storyboard is shown in Figure 7.2.

Figure 7.2 Storyboard development process

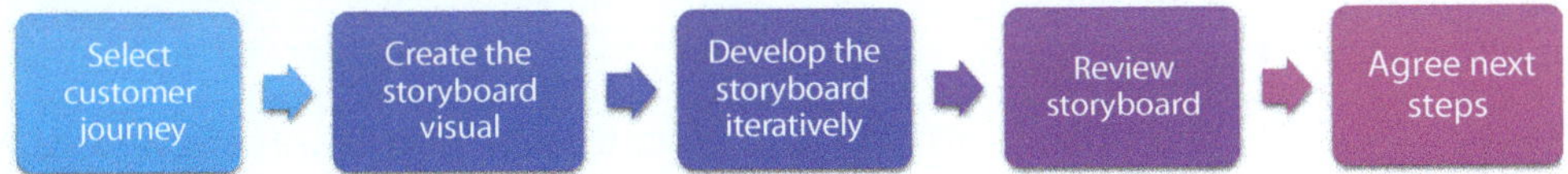

These stages are described in Table 7.2.

Table 7.2 Storyboard development process stages

Stage	Description
Select customer journey	The customer journey to be represented by the storyboard must be selected before developing the storyboard. Whether the storyboard will represent a current or target state customer journey must also be decided at the outset.
Create the storyboard visual	The draft storyboard can be developed once the scope of the storyboard has been confirmed. This involves identifying the main stages of the storyboard and developing the visual content for each stage.

(Continued)

Table 7.2 (Continued)

Stage	Description
Develop the storyboard iteratively	This stage focuses on the exploration of the touchpoints of the customer journey that will be represented within the storyboard. Various aspects can be represented regarding touchpoints, including: • The order of the touchpoints. • The underpinning backstage elements supporting the touchpoint (see service blueprints, Glossary of Terms and Techniques). • The reaction to the touchpoint by the actors within the storyboard (for example, whether the touchpoint is perceived to be positive or negative). Shared understanding of the customer journey is developed through iterative storyboard exploration. Where appropriate multiple storyboards can be developed that show different: • front and back stage elements; • personas and actors; • touchpoints; • scenarios.
Review storyboard	The output(s) from the storyboard development are reviewed. This includes sharing the outputs with stakeholders to obtain feedback.
Agree next steps	This stage is focused on agreeing next steps. For example, will a particular storyboard be selected for further analysis and refinement? Will a particular storyboard scenario be prioritised for development?

Benefits of storyboarding

Storyboarding offers the benefits shown in Figure 7.3.

Figure 7.3 Benefits of storyboarding

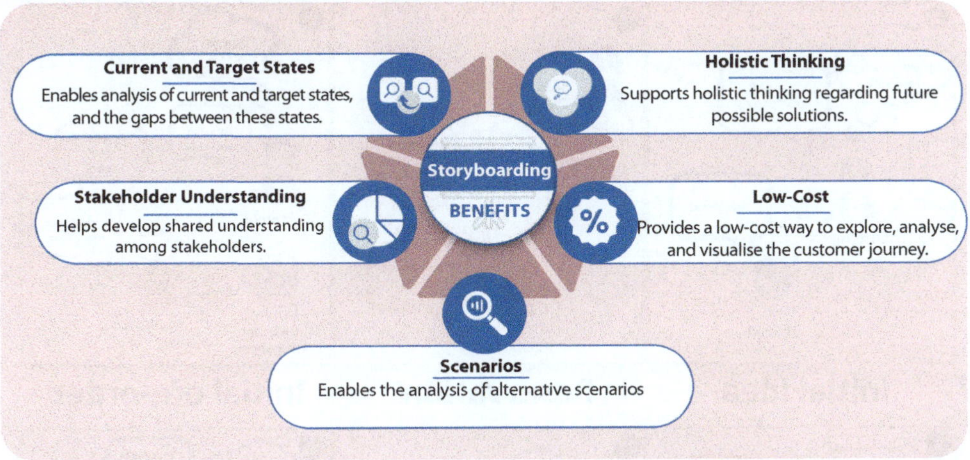

Current and Target States
Enables analysis of current and target states, and the gaps between these states.

Holistic Thinking
Supports holistic thinking regarding future possible solutions.

Storyboarding
BENEFITS

Stakeholder Understanding
Helps develop shared understanding among stakeholders.

Low-Cost
Provides a low-cost way to explore, analyse, and visualise the customer journey.

Scenarios
Enables the analysis of alternative scenarios

Example storyboard

An example target state storyboard for the restaurant scenario is shown in Figure 7.4. This storyboard represents a possible target state journey following the restaurant introducing a new artificial intelligence (AI) chatbot.

An explanation of the steps taken within the storyboard is provided in Table 7.3.

Table 7.3 Example storyboard steps

Step	Description
(1) Initial idea	The customer decides to ask a friend to go for breakfast.
(2) Reservation	The customer reserves the restaurant table using the restaurant website. During this process, an AI chatbot lets the customer know that they will receive a complimentary drink if they pre-order their food.
(3) Initial pre-order	The customer agrees to pre-order their food. The AI chatbot sends a confirmation of the order and asks if they can contact the other guest(s).
(4) Final pre-order	The AI chatbot contacts the other guest(s) and offers the complimentary drink. The guest confirms their order and is also sent an order confirmation.
(5) Meal	The restaurant serves the food order to the guests and provides the complimentary drink.
(6) After the meal	The customer is pleased with the food and overall service of the restaurant and decides to leave a positive review.

Figure 7.4 Example target state storyboard for the restaurant scenario

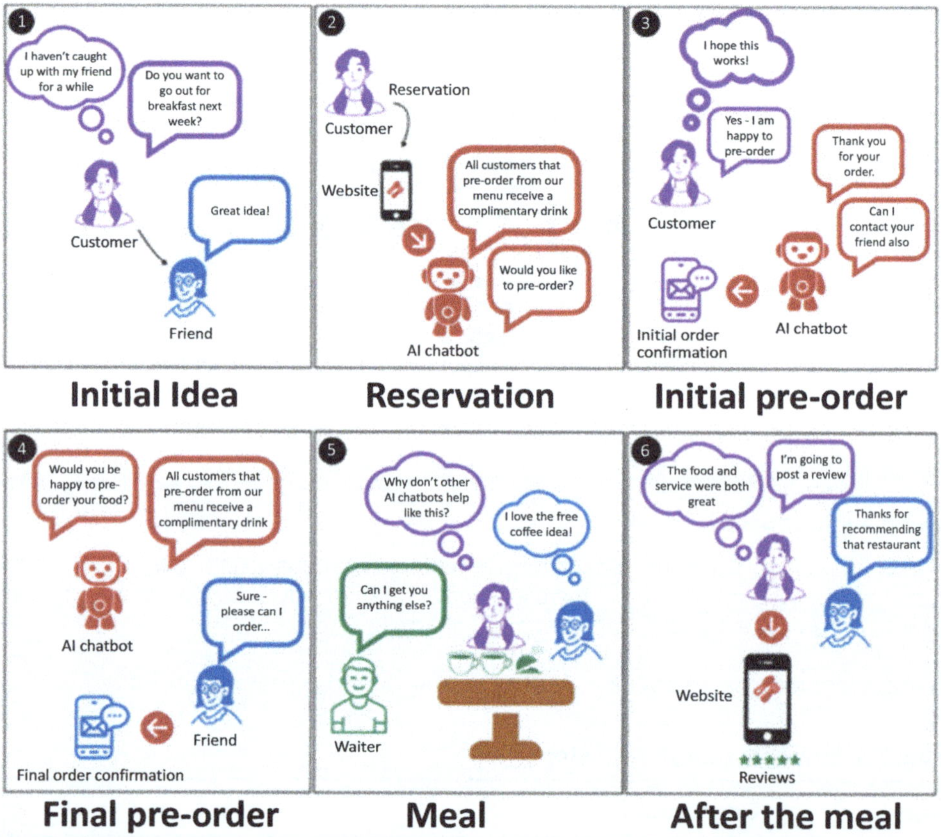

Storyboards can also be used as a technique to visualise a technology-based solution. The storyboard shown in Figure 7.5 represents a partial target state technology-based journey once the restaurant has introduced a new AI chatbot.

Figure 7.5 Example target state technology-based storyboard for the restaurant scenario

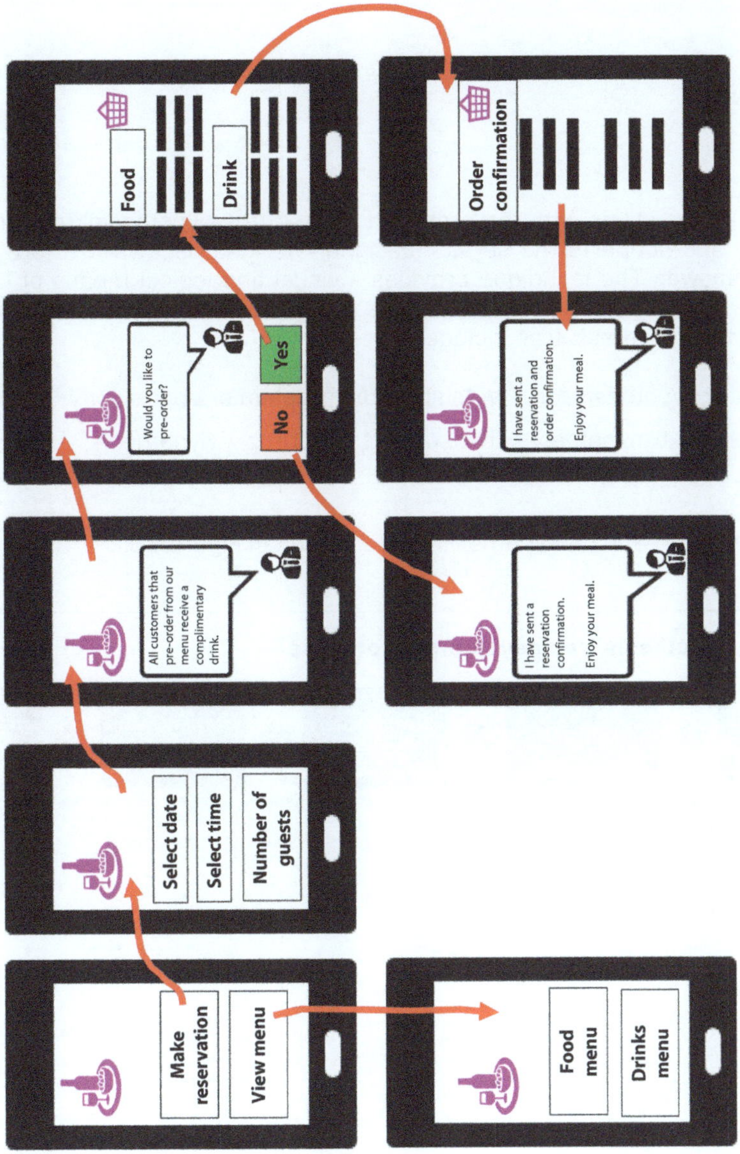

Hypothesis trees

Purpose

A hypothesis is:

> 'An idea or explanation for something that is based on known facts but has not yet been proved'.
>
> (www.dictionary.cambridge.org)

A hypothesis tree starts with the proposed answer (the hypothesis) to a problem or opportunity and supports the service designer working backward to prove or disprove that answer. The technique provides a visual and logical means of identifying and exploring a range of different solutions to a given problem or opportunity. When completed, the hypothesis tree includes:

- A primary hypothesis for how to solve the problem or opportunity in focus.
- A range of sub-hypotheses that support the primary hypothesis.

Process

The process for creating a hypothesis tree is shown in Figure 7.6.

Figure 7.6 Hypothesis tree development process

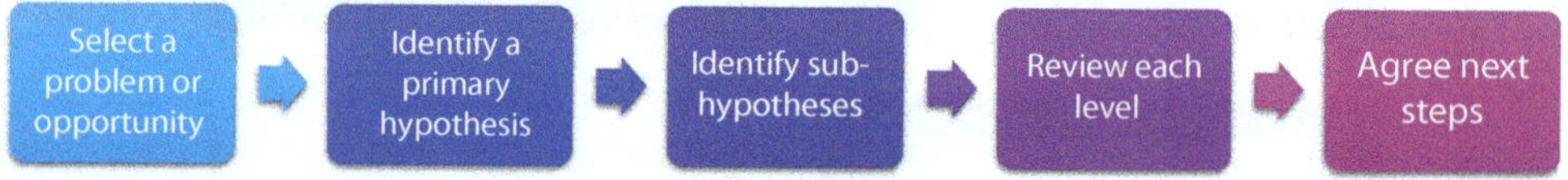

These stages are described in Table 7.4.

Table 7.4 Hypothesis tree development process stages

Stage	Description
Select a problem or opportunity	This stage involves selecting and defining the problem or opportunity that will be focused on within the hypothesis tree.
Identify a primary hypothesis	This stage involves defining the highest-level hypothesis (or answer) for how the problem or opportunity might be solved. This is known as a 'level 1' hypothesis.
Identify sub-hypotheses	This stage involves defining the various lower-level hypotheses (or answers) for how the problem or opportunity might be solved. These are known as 'level 2' and 'level 3' hypotheses.
Review each level	This stage involves reviewing and validating the hypothesis tree. Each level of the hypothesis tree should be examined using the Mutually Exclusive, Comprehensively Exhaustive (MECE) framework. This aids in ensuring that there are no gaps in the logic of the hypothesis tree and also helps to ensure that there are no overlaps in the identified hypotheses (or answers) for the defined problem or opportunity. In some situations, it may also be beneficial to determine the probability of each hypothesis.
Agree next steps	This stage is focused on agreeing next steps. For example, will individual hypotheses be prioritised for further analysis and exploration? How will each hypothesis be objectively tested?

Benefits of using hypothesis trees

A hypothesis tree offers service designers the benefits shown in Figure 7.7.

Figure 7.7 Benefits of hypothesis trees

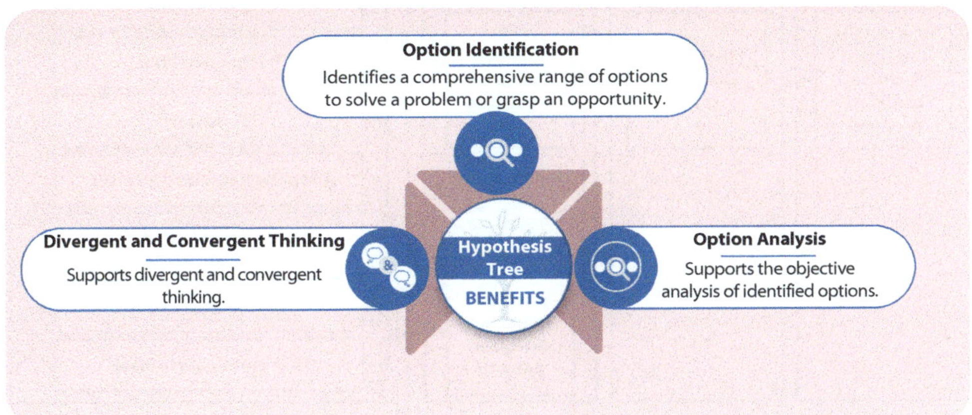

On occasion, a solution to a problem or opportunity is presented that may not have been subjected to thorough analysis. For example, to increase productivity within a team, a senior stakeholder may want to invest in a new technology solution or create a new role within their department. The hypothesis tree can be used to explore the solution option with the stakeholder and to encourage objective consideration of alternative options. This includes the assessment of the business case for each option (see Glossary of Terms and Techniques).

Stakeholders may perceive the hypothesis tree or its application to be a direct challenge to their logic and authority within the organisation. The risk of this reaction can increase if the stakeholder has invested significant effort into a selected 'hypothesis' or solution. Accordingly, service designers should carefully consider the context for applying the hypothesis tree technique.

Example hypothesis tree

An example hypothesis tree for the restaurant scenario is shown in Figure 7.8. This example represents one level 1 hypothesis but an extended hypothesis tree would include other level 1 hypotheses such as 'reduce breakfast costs'.

Figure 7.8 Example hypothesis tree for the restaurant scenario

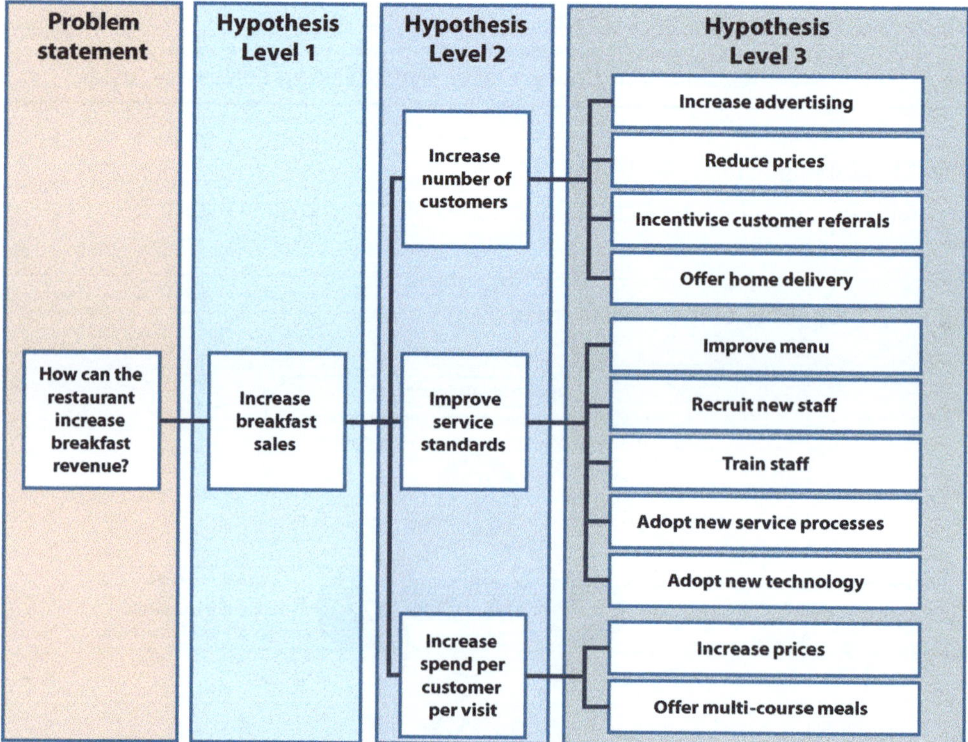

Scenario analysis

Purpose

Scenarios explore the way in which actors interact with one of the organisation's internal or external services. Each scenario is triggered by a business event that initiates a sequence of actions including a response.

The scenario analysis technique encourages exploration of different circumstances, triggering events, actions and responses. Application of the technique can aid with ensuring that deployed services are robust and help to achieve desired outcomes for both the organisation and its customers. For example, a situation where an organisation offers a service that is supported by a key ecosystem partner. This could be a retailer distributing packages with the support of an external logistics provider. If there is an issue with the logistics provider during service delivery, this could lead to the retailer failing to deliver packages. If the retailer has not identified how it will respond in advance to this scenario, this could lead to an unplanned or emergency response. If the response is not co-ordinated or is ill thought through, this could result in additional customer complaints, additional costs for the retailer and increased reputational damage.

Scenario analysis is often used to encourage stakeholders to share tacit knowledge within the context of interviews or workshops (see Glossary of Terms and Techniques). While it is almost impossible to identify every scenario, the technique helps to ensure that both Service Definition and Experimentation activities are as comprehensive as possible. For example, the service designer could ask a stakeholder about the standard sequence of events and actions during the delivery of a service. If 'what if' style questions are asked, further insight can be obtained. Examples include:

- What happens if the customer has accessibility needs?
- What happens if the customer is new to the organisation?
- What happens if we have run out of product or reached capacity for service delivery?
- What happens if an ecosystem partner fails to deliver their product/service?
- Would the service offer change if the customer was also an employee?

Process

The process for applying scenario analysis is shown in Figure 7.9.

Figure 7.9 Scenario analysis process

These stages are described in Table 7.5.

Table 7.5 Scenario analysis process stages

Stage	Description
Select interaction to be analysed	This stage involves selecting the specific interaction to be analysed. The trigger, or event that causes the interaction to take place, should be identified. A start point for the identification of interactions to be analysed could be touchpoints within a customer journey map or service blueprint. Consideration of the user role or persona in focus for the analysis may also be beneficial.
Define standard sequence of steps/ actions	This stage is focused on identifying and defining the standard sequence of steps/actions that take place following the triggering event.
Review movement between steps/ actions	This stage is focused on identification of the conditions that need to be met to move forward to the next step/action.
Identify and define alternative paths	This stage is focused on the identification, definition and analysis of alternative paths. Analysis of conditions to move forward to the next step/action can aid with the identification of alternative paths. Each alternative path should be explored to determine the desired sequence.

Benefits of scenario analysis

Scenario analysis offers the benefits shown in Figure 7.10.

Figure 7.10 Benefits of scenario analysis

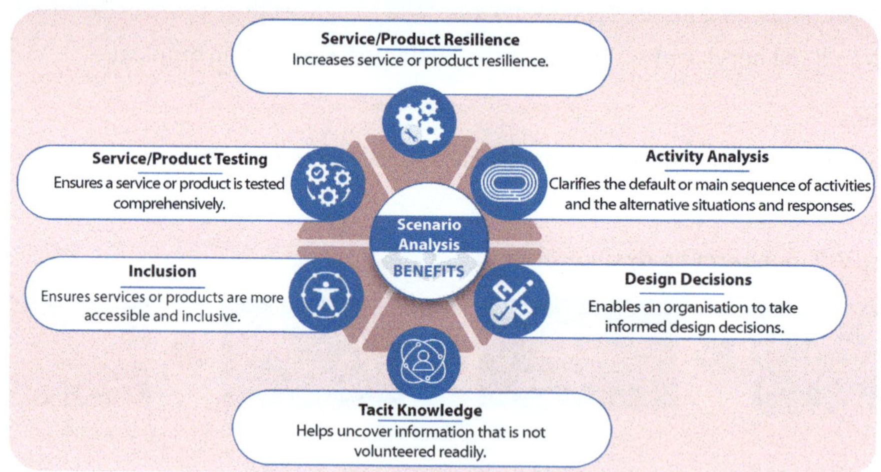

Example scenario analysis

The application of the scenario analysis technique involves interactive discussion between the service designer and a stakeholder or group of stakeholders. Outputs from this discussion could include a description of the business use case. An example of this is shown in Table 7.6.

Table 7.6 Business use case description

Business use case	Pay bill (or check).
User role or persona	Standard customer.
Brief description	This use case will allow a customer to pay for their meal and drinks consumed during the visit to the restaurant.
Trigger/event	Customer requests to pay the bill.
Main flow of events	(1) Customer requests to pay. (2) Waiting staff bring the bill to the table. (3) Customer requests to pay by card. (4) Waiting staff return with card payment machine. (5) Customer pays by card.
Alternative flows	(1a) Customer requests a discount on their bill due to a complaint. (1b) Customer requests a discount on their bill due to being a member of discount/loyalty scheme. (1c) Employee decides to offer the customer a discount. (3a) Customer requests to pay by cash. (3b) Customer requests for service charge to be removed from the bill. (3c) Customer requests to split bill with a member of their dining party. (3d) Customer requests to pay part of the bill with cash and part with a card. (4a) Card payment machine faulty. (5a) Customer card is declined.

Diagrammatic techniques such as the unified modeling language (UML) activity diagram or UML sequence diagram may also be used to represent scenarios.

When compiling the business use case, the service designer could explore questions surrounding each aspect of the scenario and the service. While not exhaustive, example questions for the main flow of the business use case 'pay bill (or check)' are shown in Table 7.7.

Table 7.7 Example scenario analysis questions for business use case 'pay bill (or check)'

Business use case aspect	Example questions

User role or persona	• How is a standard customer defined?
	• Does the process differ if the customer:
	  • Is also a restaurant employee, manager owner, partner or supplier?
	  • Is a new or repeat customer?
	  • Has accessibility needs?
	  • Is vulnerable or a child?
	  • Is a business or corporate customer?
	  • Is rude, aggressive or intoxicated?
	  • Is attempting to avoid payment?

Brief description	• Would it be possible for the customer to pay in advance or after their visit to the restaurant?
Trigger/event	• Are there any other events that could trigger this process? For example, the customer doesn't request to pay – is there a timescale where the waiting staff will proactively bring the bill to the table? Does the timescale differ depending on: • How busy the restaurant is? • Who the customer is? • The size of the bill?

(Continued)

Table 7.7 (Continued)

Business use case aspect	Example questions
Main flow of events	1. Customer requests to pay: • See trigger/event questions above. 2. Waiting staff bring the bill/check to the table: • What happens if the waiting staff are not available to bring the bill to the table? • What happens if the point-of-sale system/cash register is not functioning? 3. Customer requests to pay by card: • What happens if the card payment machine is not available? • What happens if the card payment machine is not functioning? 4. Waiting staff return with card payment machine. • What happens if the waiting staff are not available to bring the card payment machine to the table? 5. Customer pays by card: • What happens if the customer is not able to pay by either card or cash? • What happens if the customer requests to pay in a different currency? • What happens if the customer attempts to leave without paying?

In addition to the above questions, the service designer could also ask broader questions about the context for the provision of the service. While not exhaustive, example questions could include:

- What happens if there is an issue with:
  - broadband connectivity?
  - electricity supply?
  - card payment services?
  - banking services?

In addition to the above, the service designer may also start to enquire about other aspects of the service. For example, it may be necessary to consider aspects such as the distribution of service charges to employees or to review the calculation of taxation charges.

The analysis and investigation of the scenario can lead to the identification of opportunities to enhance the service. For example, in the context of the bill payment service, options such as allowing the customer to pay when they order could be considered. In addition, efficiencies could be obtained by allowing the customer to pay online or at the point when they receive the bill from the waiting staff (as opposed to having to wait for the card payment machine to be brought to them).

Decision trees

Purpose

The decision tree technique is used to identify, model and analyse business rules and the actions that apply to a combination of those rules. It offers a clear view of the different scenarios that result from answering 'yes' or 'no' to a series of questions that have been derived from a set of business rules.

This technique also clearly identifies the action to be taken as a result of a combination of circumstances or characteristics.

Process

The process for developing a decision tree is shown in Figure 7.11.

Figure 7.11 Decision tree development process

Identify decision criteria → Identify actions → Plot decision criteria → Develop tree structure → Allocate actions

These stages are described in Table 7.8.

Table 7.8 The stages of the decision tree technique

Stage	Description
Identify decision criteria	The service designer identifies the business rules that form the basis for the decision criteria.
Identify actions	The service designer identifies the actions that may be taken based upon a combination of decision criteria.
Plot decision criteria	The service designer place an initial decision criterion in a box at the top of the tree. Two lines are drawn emerging from the box: one represents a 'yes' answer while the other represents a 'no' answer.

(Continued)

Table 7.8 (Continued)

Stage	Description
Develop tree structure	The service designer places further decision criteria beneath the 'yes' and 'no' answers to build a tree structure.
Allocate actions	An action is shown once a point is reached where an action applies. The decision tree is complete when a clear decision pathway is shown to each action and all the actions identified are represented.

It is sometimes necessary to rework a decision tree to optimise the clarity of the pathways represented. For example, where a decision criteria is shown several times, the decision may be improved by moving the particular decision so that it is placed at an earlier point.

A decision table is an alternative approach used to represent combinations of decisions and the resultant actions. A decision table uses a grid structure rather than a tree structure. Examples of both approaches are shown below.

Benefits of using decision trees

A decision tree enables detailed analysis of the rules leading to a particular action. The technique results in a clear structure that is easily understood and applied. Figure 7.12 shows the benefits of a decision tree.

Figure 7.12 Benefits of decision trees

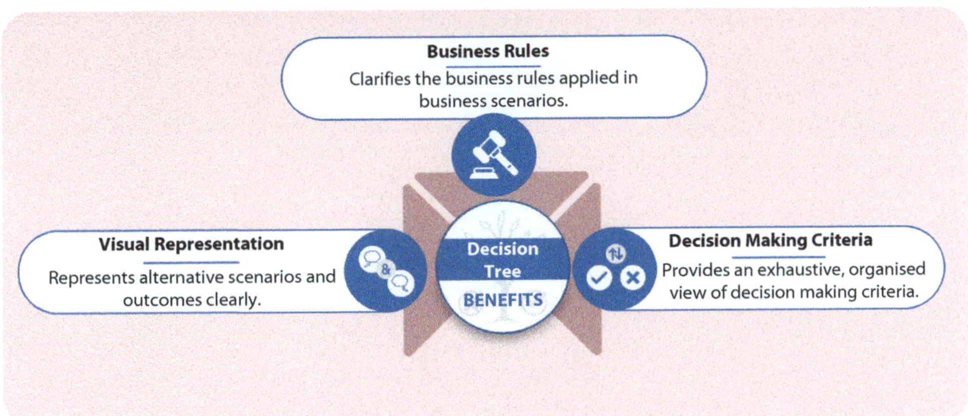

Example decision tree

An example decision tree has been completed to help with the management of decisions concerning the level of service provision in the restaurant. In this example, customers either receive a 'priority' or 'normal' service from the restaurant waiting staff. The priority service could include aspects such as the offer of a complimentary drink. Figure 7.13 shows this decision tree.

Example decision table

A decision table is an alternative way of representing combinations of conditions that result in defined actions. The steps to develop a decision table are:

1. Identify relevant conditions and list them on the left-hand side of the table.
2. Calculate the combination of conditions using the formula 2^n. The exponential value is the number of conditions. In the example shown in Table 7.9, there are three conditions so the number of possible combinations is 2^3, which equals eight.
3. Insert a column for each combination of conditions. Begin by inserting a row alongside the first condition that shows a series of Y and N entries. Where there are eight possible combinations of conditions, show four 'Y' entries and four 'N' entries. The next row for eight combinations halves the 'Y' and 'N' values further (two 'Y', two 'N', two 'Y', two 'N') and the final row alternates between the values. If there were more combinations, the total should be halved to begin. For example, 16 combinations would result in an initial row with 8 'y' and eight 'N' entries.
4. Identify the actions and list them below the conditions on the left-hand side of the table.
5. Indicate the required action for each combination of conditions.

An example decision table for the restaurant scenario is shown in Table 7.9.

Figure 7.13 Example decision tree for the restaurant scenario

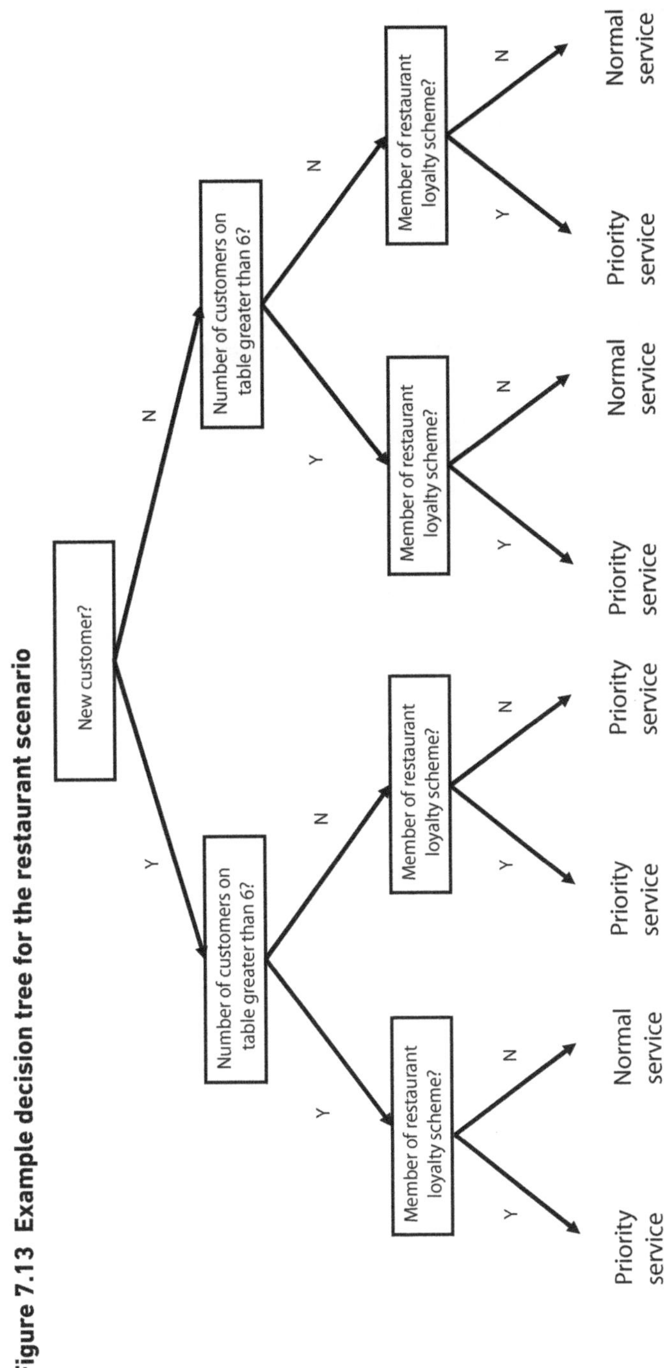

Table 7.9 Example decision table for the restaurant scenario

	1	2	3	4	5	6	7	8
Conditions								
New customer?	Y	Y	Y	Y	N	N	N	N
Number of customers on table greater than six?	Y	Y	N	N	Y	Y	N	N
Member of restaurant loyalty scheme?	Y	N	Y	N	Y	N	Y	N
Actions								
Priority service	X		X	X	X		X	
Normal service		X				X		X

Prototyping

Purpose

A prototype involves building a model or representation of a product or service to test assumptions, obtain feedback and evolve understanding.

Insights obtained through prototyping include learning about costs, benefits, risks and impacts of proposed solutions. Prototyping also aids with the testing and validation of assumptions. Where applied within a culture of continuous improvement, prototyping can be used as a basis for ongoing product or service enhancement. The technique can be applied in combination with other techniques. Examples include:

- holding a focus group or workshop focused on obtaining feedback on a prototype (see Glossary of Terms and Techniques);
- using prototyping as a mechanism to test the hypotheses that are outlined within a hypothesis tree;
- creating prototypes to test out different scenarios identified within scenario analysis;
- conducting A/B tests against different prototypes.

The concept of a minimal viable product (MVP) has become synonymous with agile software development. The MVP concept can be used to aid with determining the scope of a product prototype. Within the context of service design, the concept of a minimal viable service (MVS) can be applied as an alternative to an MVP. An MVS should be holistic and take into consideration all aspects of the service. The AssistKD POPIT™ model can be used as a basis to support consideration of the MVS and, as a consequence, the prototype for a service.

Process

The process for the development and validation of a prototype is shown in Figure 7.14.

Figure 7.14 Prototype development process

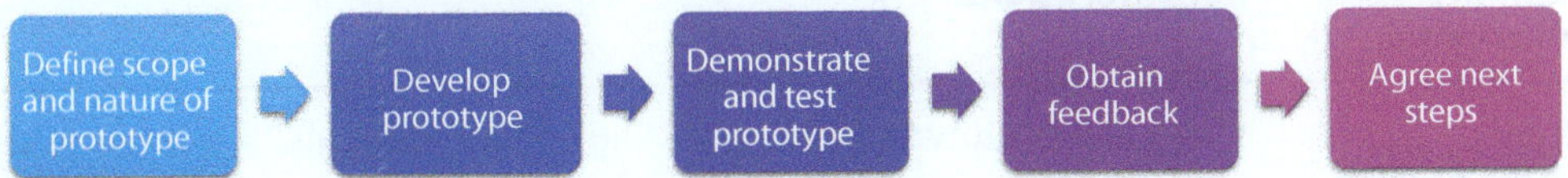

These stages are described in Table 7.10.

Table 7.10 Prototype development process stages

Stage	Description
Define scope and nature of prototype	This stage involves defining the nature and scope of the prototype. Aspects to consider include: • **Objective:** What goal(s) will be achieved as a result of prototype development? • **Scope:** Which aspects of an MVP or MVS are in scope? • **Evolution:** Will it be possible to evolve the prototype into a deployed product or service? • **Testing:** Will the prototype be tested with real customers? Will the prototype be tested in a real-world context/environment? • **Fidelity:** How closely will the prototype represent the final product or service? (See prototype fidelity dimensions within Table 7.11.) Service designers should also confirm aspects such as the available resources to support prototype development. Constraints (including budget, timescales and expected quality standards) should also be confirmed.
Develop prototype	This stage involves the development of the prototype in alignment with the defined scope.
Demonstrate and test prototype	This stage is focused on demonstrating and testing the prototype.
Obtain feedback	This stage is focused on capturing both qualitative and quantitative feedback on the prototype.
Agree next steps	This stage is focused on analysing the results of insights obtained and determining next steps. This could involve repeating the prototype development process in its entirety or going back to one of the previous stages. If prototyping has been a success, a decision could also be made to move forward with the deployment of the product or service (see Glossary of Terms and Techniques).

To aid with confirming the scope of the proposed prototype, service designers should also consider aspects such as the fidelity dimensions shown in Table 7.11.

Table 7.11 Prototype fidelity dimensions (Adapted from McCurdy et al., 2006)

Fidelity dimension	Considerations
Visual	• Will the prototype have low or high-fidelity visuals? • Will the visuals of the prototype be realistic in comparison to the final product or service?
Interaction	• To what extent will end users or customers be able to interact with the prototype?
Data	• Will the prototype contain a low or high amount of data/ information? • Will the prototype contain real world data/information?
Functional width	• How broad will the functionality be that is contained within the prototype? • Will the breadth of the functionality be representative of the end product or service?
Functional depth	• How deep will the functionality be that is contained within the prototype? • Will the depth of functionality be representative of the end product or service?

Benefits of prototyping

The benefits of prototyping are shown in Figure 7.15.

Figure 7.15 Benefits of prototyping

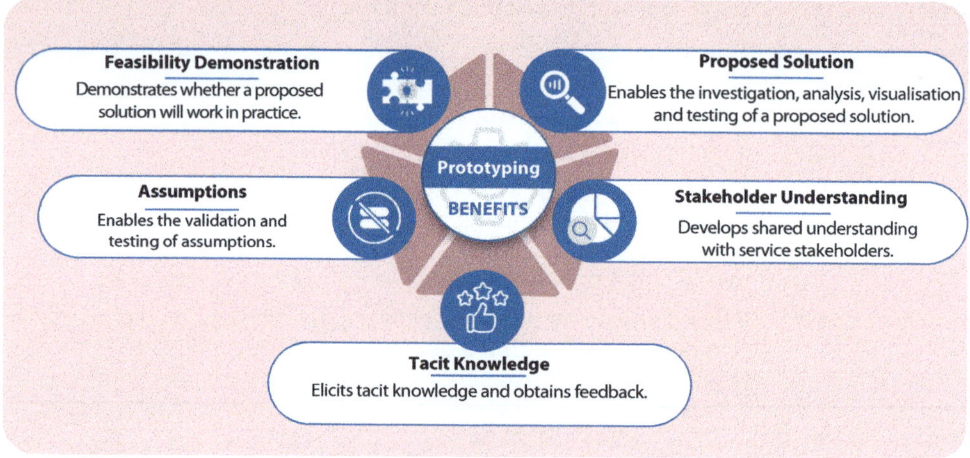

Example prototype

A prototype could be used for many different challenges or contexts within a restaurant scenario. For example, a prototype could be created for a new or changed:

- restaurant logo;
- staff induction process;
- layout of the restaurant or kitchen;
- menu;
- individual drink or meal;
- staff uniform;
- website or app (including an individual feature);
- payment solution;
- organisation chart;
- internal policy.

The precise nature of a prototype is dependent on the context in which the technique is applied. For example, a prototype of a new restaurant logo would be very different from a prototype of a new meal or staff induction process.

Within the context of service design, the development of a prototype should align with the concept of an MVS. Figure 7.4 shows an example target state storyboard for the restaurant scenario. In particular this storyboard is focused on the introduction of a new AI chatbot in support of the breakfast service. The storyboard in itself can be considered to be an early service prototype. If this service were to be developed into an MVS, example aspects to be considered would include those shown in Table 7.12.

Table 7.12 MVS considerations for new restaurant service

POPIT™ dimension	Considerations
People	• How will customers react to an AI chatbot requesting order details when making a reservation? • Will customers choose not to reserve a table because of the use of the use of AI? • Will restaurant staff be trained to answer any customer queries or complaints about the AI chatbot service? • How will staff be trained to ensure that the customer receives the complimentary drink? • Does the organisation have the skills and expertise to update and maintain the AI chatbot service?

(Continued)

Table 7.12 (Continued)

POPIT™ dimension	Considerations
Organisation	• Will the introduction of the AI chatbot feature impact the culture of the organisation? • How will the AI chatbot comply and associated processes align with regulatory, compliance and policy expectations? • Who will be responsible for owning and maintaining the AI chatbot? • How will changes to the chatbot be communicated to stakeholders? • How does the use of AI in this context impact the wider organisational strategy?
Process	• What processes are impacted by the introduction of the new service? • Will customers that reserve a table in person or over the phone also be offered the opportunity to pre-order their meal? • Will customers be able to change their pre-ordered meal? • How will reservation cancellations be impacted?
Information	• Will the AI chatbot have access to the latest menu and prices? • How will information be kept secure? • Will the customer need to register or provide their name and email address in order to use the new service? • Will the chatbot need to know the age of the customer? For example, what happens if a minor attempts to order a complimentary alcoholic drink? • How will staff know that a customer has pre-ordered their meal and drink? • What metrics will be used to measure the success or failure of the new service? • How will information on pre-ordered meals be used? Will this help drive efficiencies? • What happens if the information captured by the chatbot is incorrect? For example, the wrong meal or drink is ordered. • Does the processing of information captured align with data protection and compliance regulations and policies?
Technology	• What technology (or technologies) will be used to support the provision of the AI chatbot? • Will the chatbot work with assistive technologies?

A/B testing

Purpose

A/B testing is used to objectively compare the outcomes from the result of using two or more variations of a product or service. The technique can be combined with CX Analysis techniques (see Chapter 5) to obtain both quantitative and qualitative data.

The results of A/B testing are used as a basis from which to make informed design decisions. This could include the decision to:

- Conduct additional experimentation activities (including further A/B testing).
- Deploy the new or modified product or service.
- Stop a planned change to a product or service.
- Conduct additional investigation into the situation.
- Update business case assumptions and feasibility assessments.
- Revise proposed service definitions.

The process for A/B testing is shown in Figure 7.16.

Figure 7.16 A/B testing process

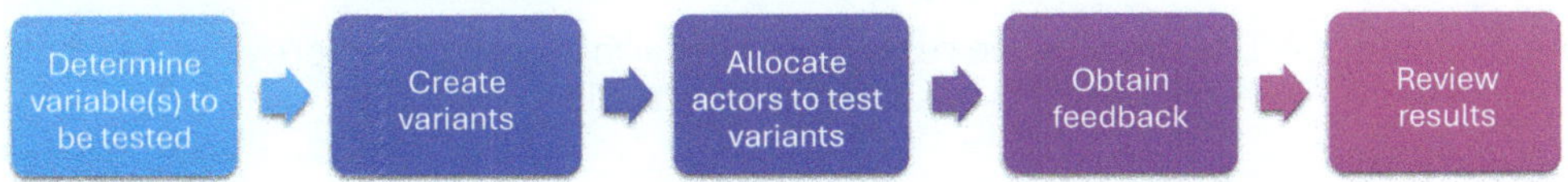

These stages are described in Table 7.13.

Table 7.13 A/B testing process stages

Stage	Description
Determine variable(s) to be tested	This stage involves specifying the precise variable or variables that will be tested. The context of the environment and scope of the A/B testing activities should also be determined.
Create variants	This stage involves creating the A/B variants.
Allocate actors to test variants	This stage involves allocating actors to test the different variants.
Obtain feedback	This stage involves obtaining both quantitative and qualitative feedback on the A/B variants.
Review results	This stage involves assessing the feedback obtained and determining next steps.

Benefits of A/B testing

A/B testing offers the benefits shown in Figure 7.17.

Figure 7.17 Benefits of A/B testing

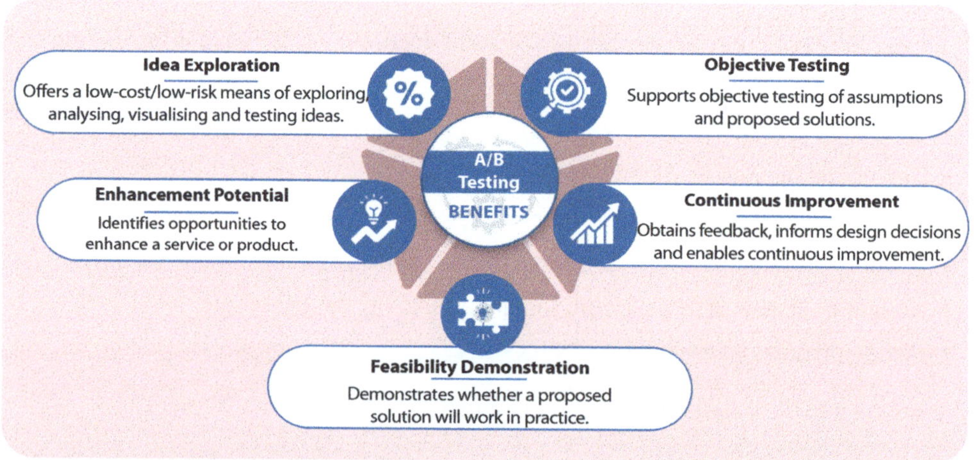

Example application of A/B testing

An example of A/B testing for the restaurant scenario (based on the previous example storyboard shown in Figure 7.5) is shown in Figure 7.18.

Figure 7.18 Example of A/B testing for the restaurant scenario

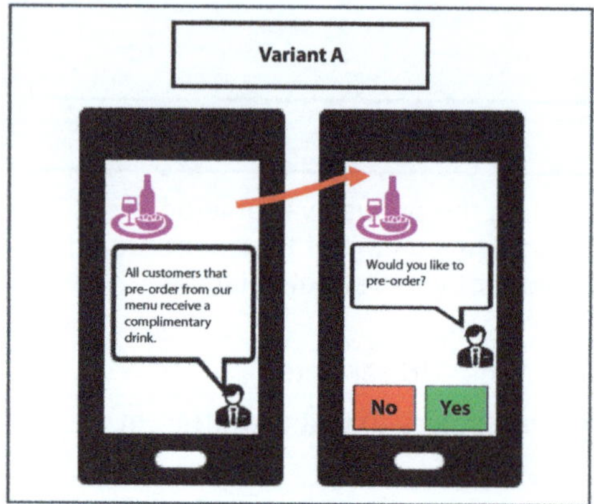

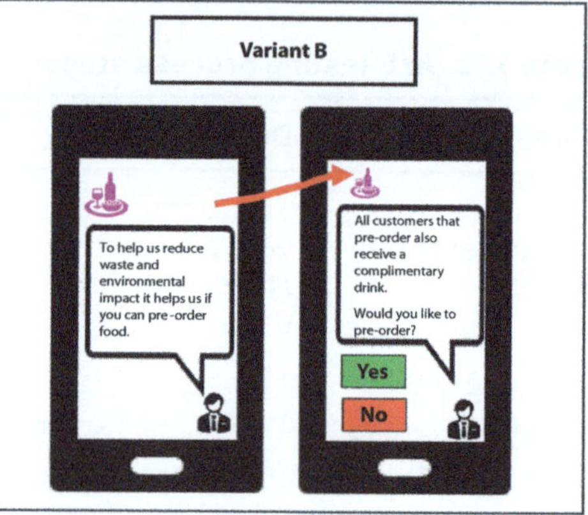

In this instance, a variation to both the wording and layout of the text shown on screen during the optional pre-order element of the service is being tested. Once created, the two paper-based designs (or low-fidelity prototypes) could then be shown to a selected group of actors. This could include customers or employees. Feedback could then be obtained in order to determine next steps.

As an alternative, the variations could be tested using a technology (or high-fidelity) prototype. This would involve making a change to the live website for a selected number of website users for a selected period of time. The results of this test could then be analysed in order to determine next steps.

CONCLUSION

Service Experimentation provides a foundation for the effective design and development of products and services. It enables an early assessment of the viability and desirability of proposed products and services.

Service Experimentation provides a basis to deploy service or product changes based on objective and holistic insight. Understanding of Service Definition and the voice of the customer is likely to evolve and deepen when applying the Service Experimentation approach using iteration and feedback.

Where this service is not conducted thoroughly, or even omitted completely, organisations face significant dangers including the risks of:

- reputational damage;
- damaged customer (and broader stakeholder) relationships;
- unintended consequences being encountered as a result of deployed changes;
- failure to realise expected benefits from change investments.

In contrast, organisations that effectively apply Service Experimentation are able to benefit from:

- enhanced long-term customer (and stakeholder) relationships;
- reduced unexpected consequences as a result of deployed changes;
- increased confidence in the realisation of expected benefits from change investments;
- improved decision making.

The effective application of Service Experimentation supports the development of a culture of continuous improvement and customer centricity.

8 SERVICE DEPLOYMENT

This chapter covers the work conducted by service designers during the Service Deployment service. The key activities of this service and techniques that may be applied to carry out these activities are described in this chapter. These techniques may be supplemented by other techniques, in particular those described in Chapters 10 and 11. However, the techniques described in Chapters 3–7 and 9 may also offer additional insights.

INTRODUCTION

This service is focused on the deployment of a product or service into operation. The service is often conducted in collaboration with other change professionals such as change managers, project managers and business analysts.

Initially, this service involves assessing business readiness to adopt the new product or service. Business readiness assessment provides a basis for understanding the transition requirements (including where stakeholders need to be supported or trained). Once identified, the service designer supports the development of necessary outputs and the adoption of the service change itself. Once the service is deployed, the service designer should seek objective, constructive feedback from service users and take action to enhance the service, where necessary.

Service Deployment needs to be executed effectively if the beneficial outcomes from the service design are to be realised. If Service Deployment is not executed effectively, the following risks may result:

- Reduced trust in the organisation and its products and services. This may result from the organisation not delivering against its stated value proposition(s).
- Brand reputation is damaged. There may be an impact on an organisation's reputation where a service fails to meet customer expectations.
- Limited (or zero) co-creation of value or benefit.
- Missed learning opportunities. This includes knowledge that could have led to the enhancement of the design and delivery of the organisation's products and services.
- Unintended consequences not being identified. This includes both positive and negative consequences to ecosystem participants – including the organisation itself and its customers.

Unintended consequences can result in increases in 'failure demand' or 'value demand' (Seddon, 2008). Failure demand refers to demand that is caused by a failing to do something, or by doing something that does not meet the customer's needs. Examples of failure demand include a customer requesting updates regarding the delivery of a product or service, or having to contact the organisation repeatedly to resolve an issue or complaint. Failure demand causes additional work for the organisation and frustration for its customers. In contrast, 'value demand' concerns doing something that customers want. For example, a product or service meeting or exceeding the customer's value expectations.

While other root causes, such as effective or ineffective processes, exist in some instances, increased 'failure demand' or 'value demand' can be linked to the failure or success of the Service Deployment service.

THE SERVICE DEPLOYMENT SERVICE

The service value proposition offered by this service is defined as:

- Service Deployment supported;
- business value co-created and realised;
- service stakeholder feedback elicited, analysed and actioned.

Figure 8.1 shows a value stream diagram for this service that represents the service activities and deliverables.

Figure 8.1 Value stream: Service Deployment

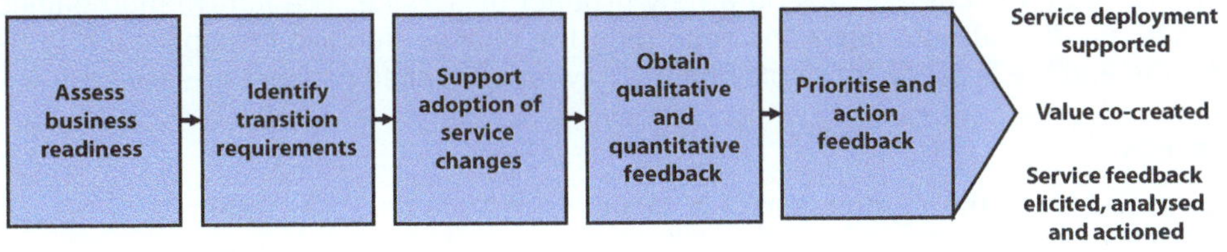

THE TECHNIQUES

A range of techniques may be used to carry out the work of this service. The generic techniques used in support of Service Deployment work are described in Chapters 10 and 11.

Several techniques described in earlier chapters may be of use when conducting the work of this service. For example, empathy maps, rich pictures and Kano analysis. In addition, the techniques described within Chapter 9 are particularly relevant to help service designers navigate stakeholder concerns and expectations.

The specific techniques relevant to this service and described in this chapter are:

- business readiness assessment;
- feedback capture grid;
- objectives and key results (OKRs);
- net promoter score (NPS);
- customer effort score (CES).

These techniques may be used to gain insights into different situations and contexts, some of which may emerge during the deployment process. Given this, the use made of the techniques should be adapted and repeated as necessary.

Business readiness assessment

Purpose

The completion of a business readiness assessment provides insight into:

- how prepared the organisation and other ecosystem participants are for the deployment of a new or enhanced product or service;
- the actions required to ensure that the organisation and ecosystem participants are prepared for product or Service Deployment;
- the risks and impacts related to a Service Deployment.

The completion of a business readiness assessment is intended to provide evidence of the extent to which an organisation is ready for change. Readiness assessment considers whether an organisation or business unit is positioned to embrace the changes that are required when deploying a new product or service. The information gained is used as an input into decisions regarding the change deployment approach to be adopted and the timeline for deploying the new or enhanced product or service.

Process

The process for the completion of a business readiness assessment is shown in Figure 8.2.

Figure 8.2 Business readiness assessment process

These stages are described in Table 8.1.

Table 8.1 Business readiness assessment process stages

<table>
<tr><th>Stage</th><th>Description</th></tr>
<tr><td>Agree scope of assessment</td><td>This stage concerns agreeing the elements to be included within the scope of the business readiness assessment and associated timescales for completion.

Elements for scope consideration include those within the CPPOLDAT framework:
• Customer
• Product
• Process
• Organisation
• Location
• Data
• Application
• Technology</td></tr>
<tr><td>Conduct assessment</td><td>This stage concerns reviewing each of the in-scope elements and identifying recommended actions to support business readiness.</td></tr>
<tr><td>Communicate assessment result</td><td>This stage concerns communicating the results of the business readiness assessment to relevant stakeholders.</td></tr>
<tr><td>Agree next steps</td><td>This stage concerns agreeing the next steps. For example,
• Prioritising any recommended actions.
• Agreeing ownership and timescales for completion of recommended actions.
• Scheduling further business readiness assessment(s). Further assessments are usually planned once recommended actions have been completed.
• Deciding to deploy the new product or service. This is usually due to the organisation being deemed ready for product or Service Deployment.
• Deciding to defer the deployment of the product or service in order to address any readiness issues.
• Deciding to abandon Service Deployment entirely. This could be due to several factors including the business readiness assessment reporting significant gaps to achieve business readiness and/or substantial risks and impacts of product or Service Deployment.</td></tr>
</table>

An explanation of the elements of the CPPOLDAT technique is provided in Table 8.2.

Table 8.2 CPPOLDAT elements

Element	Description
Customer	The beneficiary (or beneficiaries) of the product or service. Beneficiaries include internal or external customers or users.
Product	The product(s) or service(s) to be provided to the customer.
Process	The processes that support the product or service offer to the customer.
Organisation	The organisational elements required to support the product or service offer to the customer. Includes: • organisational policies and culture; • external ecosystem participants (for example, partners, suppliers, regulators); • internal ecosystem participants (for example sales and marketing, finance and operations).

Location	The environment for the delivery of the product(s) or service(s) to the customer.
	Includes:
	• locations that are both physical and virtual in nature;
	• locations where the product(s) or service(s) will be available to the customer. This includes:
	  • locations that the customer can access (for example the dining area or bar area within a restaurant);
	  • locations that are non-customer facing (for example the kitchen or storage area within a restaurant).

Data	The data and information required to deliver the products or services to customers. Includes aspects such as: • processing data and information securely; • processing data and information in alignment with regulatory and compliance expectations.
Application	The software needed to deliver the products or services to the customer.
Technology	The technology infrastructure required to deliver the products or services to the customer.

Example questions that can be considered when applying the CPPOLDAT technique are provided in Table 8.3.

Table 8.3 CPPOLDAT example questions

<table>
<tr><th>Element</th><th>Example questions</th></tr>
<tr><td>Customer</td><td><ul>
<li>Have all impacted/interested customer segments been identified and considered?</li>
<li>Are customers aware of planned changes?<ul>
<li>Is there a need for further communication with customers to explain planned changes?</li>
<li>Will customers be likely to resist changes? Are any actions needed to address this?</li>
<li>Have the 'optics' of the change been considered from the customer perspective?</li></ul></li>
<li>Has a comprehensive risk and impact assessment of the proposed change been conducted?<ul>
<li>Are any actions necessary to reduce risks and impacts?</li></ul></li>
<li>Will customers require any support or guidance to use the enhanced or new product or service?<ul>
<li>Have support processes and guidance been thoroughly tested?</li>
<li>Has sufficient consideration been given to different scenarios?</li></ul></li>
</ul></td></tr>
<tr><td>Product</td><td><ul>
<li>Has the product or service been fully tested?<ul>
<li>Is the product or service ready for deployment?</li></ul></li>
<li>What is the implementation strategy and are there any arrangements that need to be made to enable this strategy?</li>
<li>Are there any risks or issues associated with the product or service?<ul>
<li>Are any actions necessary to reduce risks and impacts?</li></ul></li>
</ul></td></tr>
<tr><td>Process</td><td><ul>
<li>How does the deployment of the new product or service impact the organisation's processes?<ul>
<li>Does the change align with existing processes?</li>
<li>Does the change introduce new processes?</li>
<li>Have the new (or changed) processes been designed, tested and communicated?</li></ul></li>
<li>Will any process change introduce waste or inefficiency into the organisation?<ul>
<li>Can processes be streamlined?</li>
<li>How can waste or inefficiency be minimised?</li></ul></li>
</ul></td></tr>
</table>

(Continued)

Table 8.3 (Continued)

Element	Example questions

Organisation	• How does the deployment of the new product or service impact the organisation?
	  • What is the impact on the policies and culture of the organisation?
	  • What is the impact on the external ecosystem participants (for example, partners, suppliers, regulators)?
	  • What is the impact on internal ecosystem participants (for example sales and marketing, finance and operations)?
	• Are any actions necessary to reduce organisational risks and impacts?
	• Are any actions necessary to enhance the potential for benefit realisation?

Location	• How does the deployment of the new product or service impact the organisation's locations? • Is each location ready for the deployment of the product or service?
Data	• How does the deployment of the new product or service impact the organisation's collection and use of data? • Will data be processed in alignment with organisational policies and compliance expectations? • Will the capture and processing of data positively or negatively impact the overall customer journey? • How will the performance of the new product or service be monitored and reported on?
Application	• How does the deployment of the new product or service impact the organisation's software applications? • Have any changes to applications been comprehensively defined, designed and tested?
Technology	• How does the deployment of the new product or service impact the organisation's use of technology? • Have any changes to technology been comprehensively defined, designed and tested?

CPPOLDAT provides a comprehensive view of the elements to be considered during a business readiness assessment. Other frameworks, such as POPIT™, may also be used.

Benefits of business readiness assessment

Business readiness assessment offers the benefits shown in Figure 8.3.

Figure 8.3 Benefits of business readiness assessment

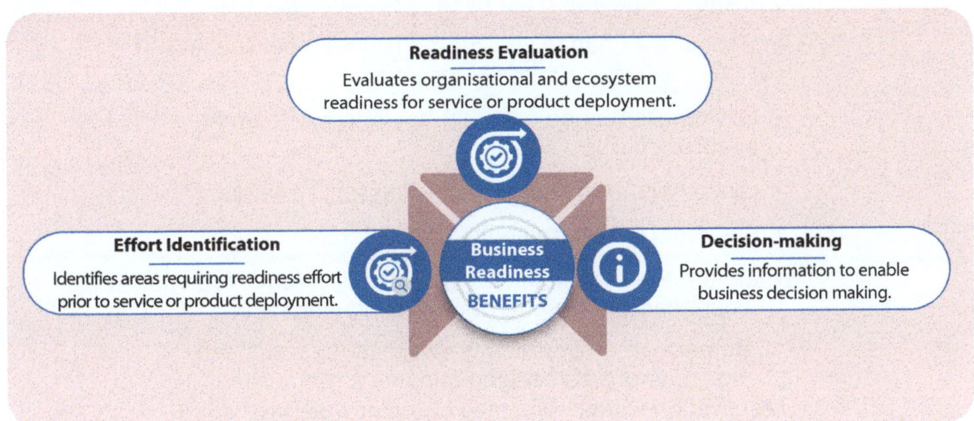

Example business readiness assessment

An example business readiness assessment for the restaurant scenario is shown in Table 8.4. This assessment is aligned to the restaurant introducing a new AI chatbot to support online reservations. Each aspect of the assessment has been assessed using the red, amber, green (RAG) rating as follows:

- **Red:** Significant business readiness issue identified.

  Substantial action required to ensure successful deployment of the product or service.
- **Amber:** Moderate business readiness issue identified.

  Actions required to address can be completed within planned timescales and with existing resources.
- **Green:** Insignificant business readiness issue identified.

  Limited action required to address this issue.

Table 8.4 Example business readiness assessment

Element	Comments	RAG rating

Customer	• Only customers booking directly on the restaurant website will be impacted by the new AI chatbot service.
	• Impact of the change considered from the perspective of various customer personas including:
	  • Customers that do not want to engage with an AI enabled chatbot.
	  • Customers with a variety of accessibility needs.
	  • Customers that are adults and children.
	  • Customers that speak English as a first language and those that have English as a second language.
	• Customers are not currently aware of the proposed change. Customers seeking to make a restaurant reservation will be informed of the new service at the point service is deployed.
	• Some customers may resist the change due to an aversion to AI chatbots. This could lead to a subset of customers failing to complete table reservations.
	• Some customers may be frustrated if the AI chatbot is not able to deal with questions on other topics such as:
	  • Requesting a change to an existing reservation.
	  • Providing information on group bookings or private events.
	  • Providing accurate information on
	    • Restaurant opening hours.
	    • Restaurant location.
	    • Restaurant parking.
	    • Menu and dietary information.
	• A comprehensive risk and impact assessment of the proposed change has not been conducted.
	• The AI chatbot has not been comprehensively tested with a range of customers.
		Red

Product	• The AI chatbot has not been fully tested. • There is a significant risk of negative impact to the overall customer experience.	Red

(Continued)

Table 8.4 (Continued)

Element	Comments	RAG rating

Process	• The new AI chatbot impacts processes for
	  • Reserving tables.
	  • Placing orders.
	  • Ordering supplies.
	  • Preparing food.
	  • Verifying age (due to the potential for children to place orders for alcohol).
	• There is a risk that the AI chatbot will cause additional work for restaurant staff due to an increased volume of questions and queries about pre-ordered food and complimentary drinks.
		Red

Organisation	• The new AI chatbot would need to capture information in alignment with organisational policies. • Limited change is anticipated to the organisational culture. • Limited change is anticipated to external ecosystem participants. A new contract will be required with a third party to update and maintain the chatbot. • Significant potential change to internal ecosystem participants due to potential process changes. • Significant detrimental impact to the reputation of the restaurant if concerns surrounding Service Deployment not resolved.	**Red**
Location	• The restaurant operates from a single physical location and uses a single website. If the new service were to be deployed minimal change is anticipated.	**Green**
Data	• The AI chatbot significantly impacts the collection and use of customer data. A thorough impact assessment is required.	**Red**
Application	• The AI chatbot would in the short term only impact the restaurant website.	**Green**
Technology	• The AI chatbot would be updated and maintained by a third party. Minimal impact anticipated.	**Green**

Following completion of the business readiness assessment, it is highly unlikely that the proposed AI chatbot service would be deployed without considerable change. Given the volume of issues identified within the assessment, a review of the effectiveness of the execution of other service design services would also be likely.

FEEDBACK CAPTURE GRID

Purpose

The feedback capture grid is a four-box grid that can be used to capture and organise insights obtained from customers regarding a specific product or service. This technique focuses on eliciting feedback from customers regarding the experience they have encountered when accessing a new or enhanced service or product.

The technique supports the capture of the following areas of customer feedback:

- positive feedback;
- constructive criticism;
- questions customers wish to ask as a result of their experience;
- new ideas that customers wish to suggest.

The feedback capture grid can be used to obtain feedback during the development of a service or product, or once deployment has taken place. For example, service designers may use the feedback capture grid when undertaking Service Definition or Experimentation to gain insights into customer views at an early stage of service development. Alternatively, the feedback capture grid offers a helpful structure to elicit customer views about products or services once they have been launched.

Essentially, the feedback capture grid is used when evaluating a product or service. While this is essential post-deployment, this technique can also help to identify ideas for improvement at many points in the service design process.

The structure of the feedback capture grid is shown in Figure 8.4.

Figure 8.4 Feedback capture grid

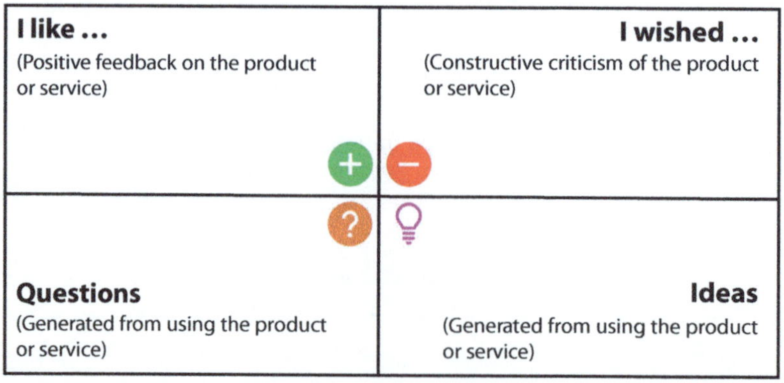

I like ... (Positive feedback on the product or service) +	− **I wished ...** (Constructive criticism of the product or service)
? **Questions** (Generated from using the product or service)	**Ideas** (Generated from using the product or service)

Process

The process for using the feedback capture grid is shown in Figure 8.5.

Figure 8.5 Feedback capture grid process

These stages are described in Table 8.5.

Table 8.5 Feedback capture grid process stages

Stage	Description
Identify product or service	This stage involves identifying the product or service where feedback is required. This can include either a prototype for a product or service or an existing deployed product or service.
Determine approach to capture feedback	This stage involves planning the approach to capturing feedback on the product or service in alignment with the quadrants of the feedback capture grid.
Capture feedback	This stage involves capturing feedback in alignment with the planned approach. Feedback captured is allocated into each of the quadrants of the feedback capture grid.
Determine next steps	This stage is concerned with agreeing the next steps. For example, does any aspect of feedback provided require further investigation? Does the feedback suggest any issues with the product or service (or prototype) that need to be addressed? Does the feedback provide any useful insights into customer behaviour or strengths of the product or service?

Benefits of the feedback capture grid

The feedback capture grid offers the benefits shown in Figure 8.6.

When used in conjunction with a prototype, the feedback capture grid can be a useful input into the decision on whether to deploy the new product or service. For example, if the feedback provided is positive this could contribute to a decision to move forward with deployment of the product or service.

If, in contrast, the feedback captured is negative, this could lead to a decision to delay or cancel deployment. The organisation may decide to conduct further Service

Figure 8.6 Benefits of the feedback capture grid

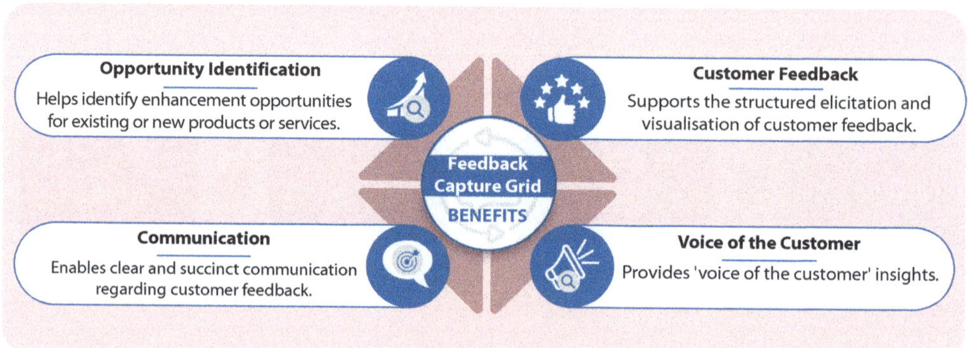

Experimentation work or to revisit understanding of the 'voice of the customer' and Service Definition. Subsequent completion of corrective actions (such as modification or enhancement work) may help the organisation avoid a situation where a deficient product or service is deployed, helping the organisation evade significant reputational damage and deployment costs.

Example feedback capture grid

An example completed feedback capture grid for the restaurant scenario is shown in Figure 8.7. The feedback represents feedback obtained from business customers that hired the restaurant for a private event.

Figure 8.7 Example feedback capture grid

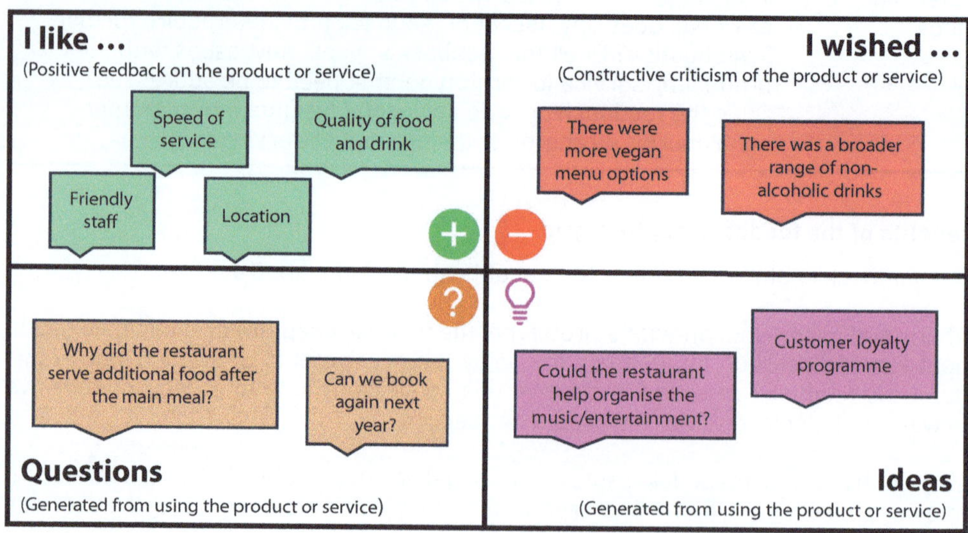

Following completion of the feedback capture grid, the restaurant could seek to investigate the current range of vegan menu options and non-alcoholic drinks. It may also be possible to reduce service costs by choosing not to provide additional food late in the evening for guests after completion of a main meal. Finally, the restaurant could also seek to investigate the ideas of assisting customers in sourcing entertainment and the concept of a customer loyalty programme.

Objectives and key results (OKRs)

Purpose

OKRs consist of a goal (or objective) coupled with a limited range of performance measures that can be used to track progress towards completion of the goal. The approach provides objective and clear feedback on progress towards achieving desired outcomes. OKRs can be used in a range of different contexts, including monitoring organisational, departmental, product or service performance. Where used to measure product or service performance, OKRs can result in feedback that supports the identification of continuous improvement opportunities.

Process

The process for the creation and application of OKRs is shown in Figure 8.8.

Figure 8.8 OKR creation and application process

Identify objective → Determine key results → Monitor key results → Determine next steps

These stages are described in Table 8.6.

Table 8.6 OKR creation and use process stages

Stage	Description
Identify objective	This stage involves the identification, analysis and validation of the key strategic objective.
Determine key results	This stage involves determining the key results that will be utilised to monitor progress towards the achievement of the identified objective. Consideration should be given to aspects such as the: • alignment of the OKRs to strategic goals and objectives; • alignment of the OKRs to the value proposition for the product or service;

(Continued)

Table 8.6 (Continued)

Stage	Description
	• specific measurements that will be used to measure progress towards achieving each key result; • expected targets for each key result; • timescale for achieving each key result.
Monitor key results	This stage involves monitoring the key results against expected targets, to determine progress towards achieving the overall key strategic objective.
Determine next steps	This stage is focused on agreeing and prioritising next steps. For example, what action is required to ensure that the objective or key results are achieved? What lessons can be learned from a successful outcome or a failure to achieve the objective or key results?

Where appropriate, the OKR creation and use process can be repeated for multiple strategic objectives. For example, OKRs could be defined for a specific focus such as financial performance or customer satisfaction.

Benefits of OKRs

Figure 8.9 shows the benefits that may be realised when applied to product or service performance.

Figure 8.9 Benefits of OKRs

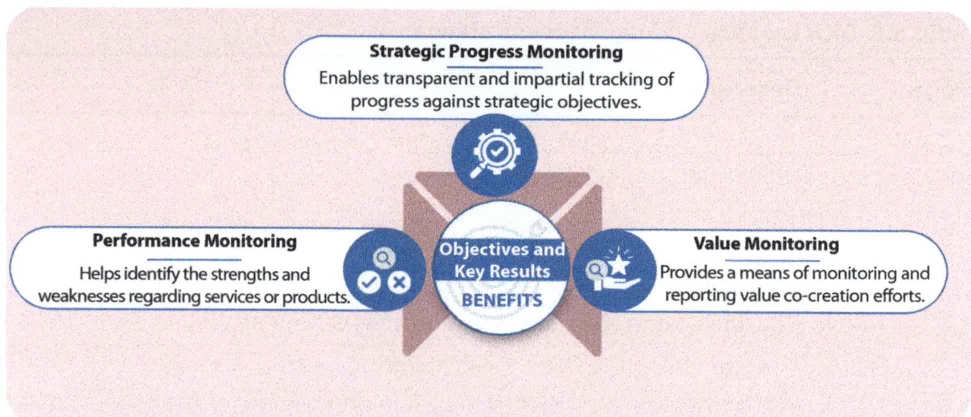

Example OKRs

An example application of the OKR technique for a new 'breakfast service' offer within the restaurant scenario is shown in Figure 8.10.

Figure 8.10 Example OKRs for restaurant scenario

Objective:

Become the breakfast restaurant of choice for local residents by the end of the calendar year.

Key Results	Q3 Score	Performance Status
Increase 'breakfast service' revenue by 15% every calendar month.	8% monthly increase in revenue.	Partial progress towards target. AMBER
Obtain 1,200 new members of the 'breakfast club' loyalty scheme by the end of the year.	1,400 new members.	Target exceeded. GREEN
Publish 2 social media posts per month focussed on the 'breakfast service' offer.	2 social media posts published in the past 6 months.	Limited progress towards target. RED
Less than 0.5% of 'breakfast service' customers complain.	Less than 0.1% of customers complain.	On track. GREEN

The achievement of key results for obtaining new members of the 'breakfast club' loyalty scheme and receiving just a small number of customer complaints should be considered successes and celebrated. While breakfast revenue has increased, there may be a need to investigate why revenue growth expectations have not been met. Perhaps the original 15 per cent monthly revenue increase target was unrealistic and therefore not achievable. The restaurant could also consider making improvements to the breakfast service and extending the marketing strategy. For example, the failure to post consistently on social media about the new service could be having a detrimental effect. An investigation into why social media posts are not being published could be conducted. In addition, the restaurant may need to look at its wider social media and marketing activities and how this specific key result fits within this context.

Net promoter score (NPS)

Purpose

NPS calculates the percentage of customers that are promoters of an organisation minus the percentage of detractors. The technique was developed by Frederick F. Reichheld (2003) as a means of enabling organisations to monitor customer loyalty and satisfaction. NPS focuses on asking customers the question:

- 'How likely is it that you would recommend this company to a friend or colleague?'

Responses to the NPS question are captured against a scale of 0–10. Zero indicates the lowest level of the satisfaction and likelihood of the customer recommending the company to others. Ten indicates the highest level of the satisfaction and that the customer is likely to recommend the organisation to others and to remain loyal. The NPS scale is described in Table 8.7.

Table 8.7 NPS categories

NPS response	Category	Description
9–10	Promoters	Customers that are likely to recommend the organisation to others. These customers are likely to remain loyal to the organisation.
7–8	Neutrals (or passively satisfied)	Customers that are not likely to actively recommend the organisation to others. These customers could be tempted to move to other organisations.
0–6	Detractors	Customers that are extremely unlikely to recommend the organisation to others. These customers are highly likely to spread negative views of the organisation to others and would also be highly likely to move to other organisations.

The NPS responses are categorised and calculated into a ratio. The steps needed to calculate the NPS ratio are:

- Calculate the percentage of customers that are promoters.
- Calculate the percentage of customers that are detractors.
- Subtract the percentage of detractors from the percentage of promotors.

The NPS concept is that an organisation is more likely to be successful over the longer term if a greater percentage of its customers are promoters than detractors. This success can be achieved if the organisation is able to learn from NPS feedback to enhance its offering. Where NPS is applied to a specific product or service the technique provides feedback that can be invaluable for the continuous improvement efforts.

Process

The process for NPS capture is shown in Figure 8.11.

Figure 8.11 NPS capture process

These stages are described in Table 8.8.

Table 8.8 NPS capture process stages

Stage	Description
Define NPS strategy	This stage involves reviewing and assessing the broader strategy for customer engagement, monitoring and reporting and considering the alignment of NPS to this context. Where appropriate the NPS strategy can then be defined. Consideration should be given to questions such as: • How is NPS currently used within the organisation? • What is the desired target state for the use of NPS? • How will the organisation move from its current to desired target state?

Define NPS question(s)	This stage involves identifying touchpoint(s) for the capture of NPS and also determining the specific question(s) to be posed.
	When determining the touchpoint(s) consideration should be given to the:
	• Specific channel for the NPS question and response (for example, email, text message, online or face to face survey, telephone call).
	• Timing of the NPS question in relation to the overall customer journey (for example, will the NPS question be at the start, middle or end of the customer journey?).
	• Focus of the NPS question. This could be focused on the customers view of:
	  • The overall organisation (for example, 'How likely is it that you would recommend our organisation to a friend or colleague?').
	  • The specific product or service that they have engaged with (for example, 'How likely is it that you would recommend our delivery service to a friend or colleague?').
	• Wording of any follow up questions (such as 'What is the rationale for the score provided?').

Deploy NPS question(s)	This stage involves deploying the NPS question and associated reporting mechanisms into the organisation as part of its business-as-usual activities.
Monitor NPS results	This stage involves monitoring NPS results and feedback.
Determine next steps	This stage is focused on agreeing and prioritising next steps. For example, what insights have been obtained from NPS feedback? What can the organisation do to increase the number of promoters/reduce the number of detractors?

Benefits of NPS

NPS offers the benefits shown in Figure 8.12.

Figure 8.12 Benefits of NPS

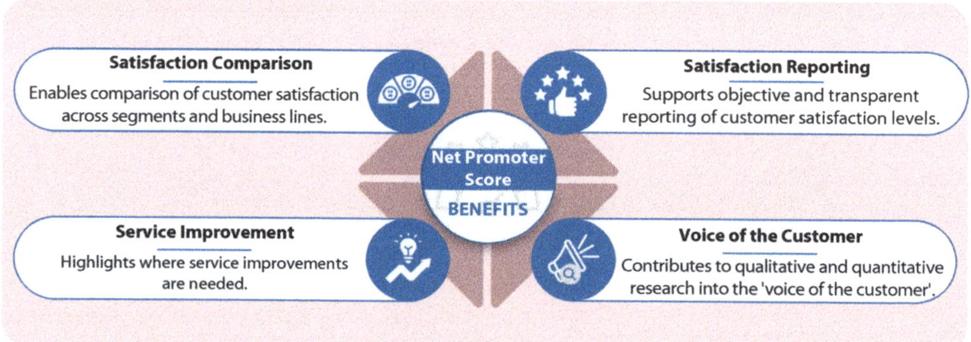

Example of NPS

An example application of the NPS capture process for the restaurant scenario is described in Table 8.9.

Table 8.9 NPS capture process example

Stage	Description
Define NPS strategy	The restaurant has not used NPS previously. A decision has been made to use NPS to develop insight into the 'voice of the customer' and to aid with the identification of improvement opportunities.

Define NPS question(s)	The restaurant has decided to ask for NPS feedback using an online survey that is completed when customers request to log in to the Wi-Fi.
	The specific questions to be asked will be:
	• How likely is it that you would recommend our restaurant to a friend or colleague?
	  • Answers to be captured using a scale of 0–10.
	• Do you have any specific comments about the service you received?
	  • Answers to be captured using a free format text box.

Deploy NPS question(s)	The restaurant will deploy NPS within the next month. Reports will be provided to the leadership team of the restaurant on a weekly basis.
Monitor NPS results	NPS feedback will be monitored on an ongoing basis by the leadership team and discussed within the monthly team meeting.
Determine next steps	NPS feedback will be considered as part of continuous service improvement opportunities.

Example NPS feedback from customers of the restaurant is shown in Table 8.10

Table 8.10 NPS data capture example

	July	August	September
% Promoters	42	38	43
% Detractors	8	13	9
NPS Score	**34**	**25**	**34**

An example visualisation of NPS feedback is also shown in Figure 8.13.

Figure 8.13 NPS feedback example

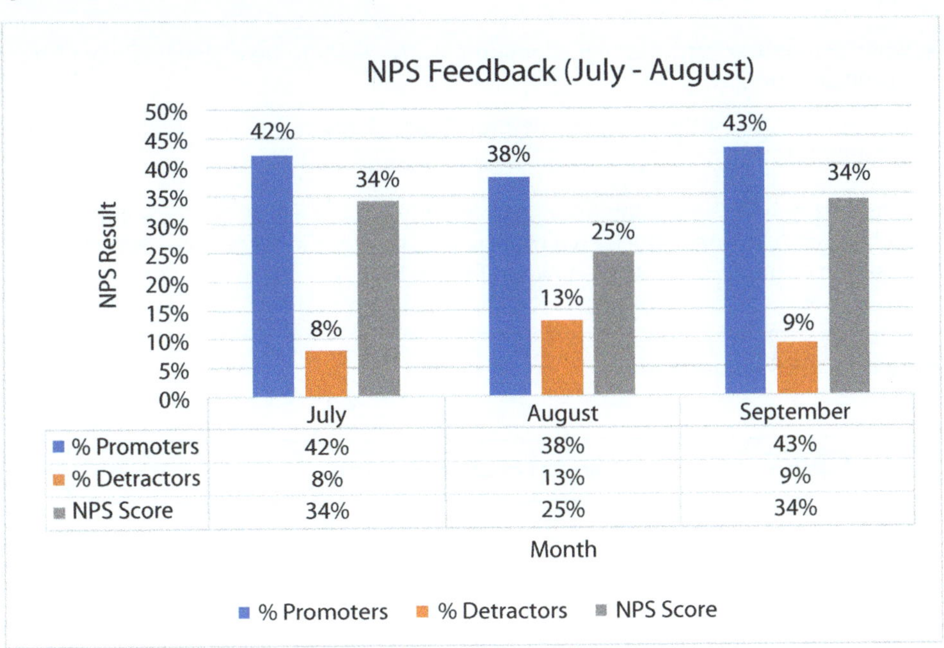

The restaurant leadership may select to review the NPS feedback in more detail in order to:

- Identify any voice of the customer insights provided through responses to the question 'Why did you provide this score?'
- Identify if there were any root causes behind the decrease in promoters and increase in detractors during the month of August.

Following the review, opportunities to enhance the service offer provided by the restaurant could be reviewed and prioritised.

Customer effort score (CES)

Purpose

CES provides a means of measuring customer satisfaction. The technique was developed by Matthew Dixon, Karen Freeman and Nicholas Toman (2010) as a means of enabling organisations to monitor customer loyalty and satisfaction. CES is focused on asking customers to rate how much effort they were required to spend when attempting to solve a problem with an organisation's product or service. The premise here is that customers want quick and effective solutions to problems that they raise. For example, a customer seeking assistance with a query, making a change or resolving a complaint would not want to spend several hours making calls to rectify the situation.

Advocates of CES argue that:

- where customer effort is high, consumers are likely to be disloyal (likely to move to competitors);
- where customer effort is low, customers are likely to be loyal (unlikely to move to competitors).

Responses to the CES question are captured against a scale of 1–5. One indicates the lowest level of customer effort. Five represents the highest level of customer effort. A visualisation of the CES scale is shown in Figure 8.14.

Figure 8.14 CES visualisation

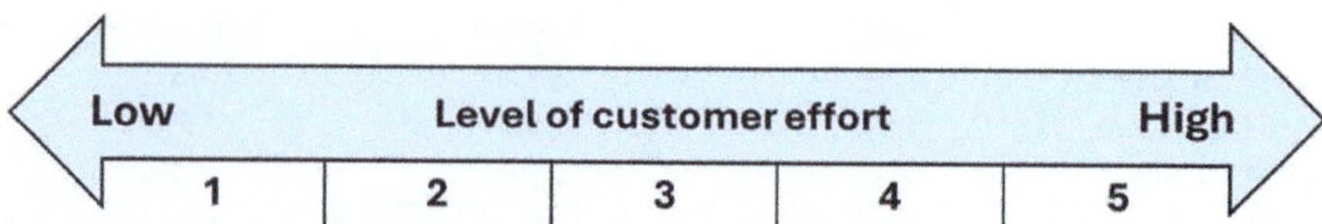

Once completed, CES survey responses can be categorised and the percentage of customers calculated.

Process

The process for CES capture is shown in Figure 8.15.

Figure 8.15 CES capture process

These stages are described in Table 8.11.

Table 8.11 CES capture process stages

Stage	Description
Define CES strategy	This stage involves reviewing and assessing the broader strategy for customer engagement, monitoring and reporting, and considering the alignment of CES to the context. The CES strategy can then be defined. Consideration should be given to questions such as: • How is customer feedback currently captured in the organisation? Does the proposed use of CES align or misalign with this approach? • What is the desired target state for the use of CES? • Which products or services will the CES question be focused on? • How will the organisation move from its current state to its desired target state?
Define CES question(s)	This stage involves identifying touchpoint(s) for the capture of CES and also determining the specific question(s) that will be asked. When determining the touchpoint(s) consideration should be placed on the: • Specific channel for the CES question and response (for example, will email, text message, online or face to face survey or telephone call be used?). • Timing of the CES question in relation to the overall customer touchpoint and journey (for example, will the CES question be asked immediately after the end of a transaction with a customer or some time afterwards?). • Wording of the CES question and explanation of the response scale. Example variations of the question include: • How much personal effort did you put into handling your recent request? An example explanation of the response scale is: • Answers are scored on a scale from one (very low effort) to five (very high effort). • Wording of any follow up questions (such as 'What is the rationale for the score provided?').
Deploy CES question(s)	This stage involves deploying the CES question and associated reporting mechanisms into the organisation as part of its business-as-usual activities.
Monitor CES results	This stage involves monitoring CES results and feedback.
Determine next steps	This stage is focused on agreeing and prioritising next steps. For example, what insights have been obtained from CES feedback? What can the organisation do to reduce customer effort levels? How can CES data be used to promote a culture of continuous improvement?

Benefits of CES

CES offers the benefits shown in Figure 8.16.

Figure 8.16 Benefits of CES

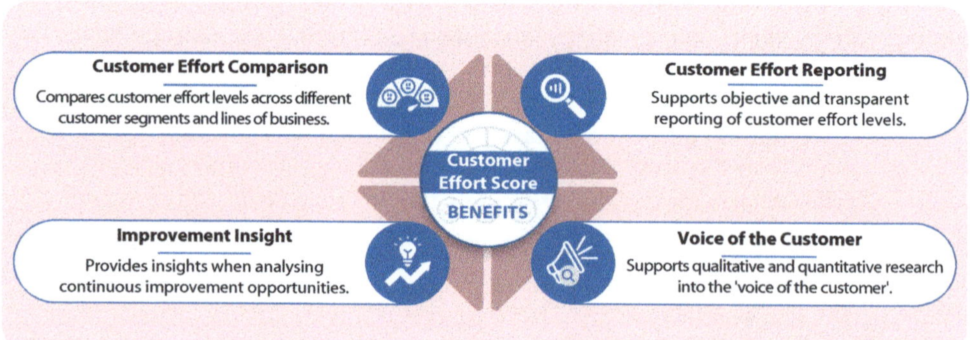

Example CES

An example application of the CES capture process for the restaurant scenario is described in Table 8.12.

Table 8.12 CES capture process example

Stage	Description
Define CES strategy	The restaurant has not used CES previously. A decision has been made to use CES to develop insight into the 'voice of the customer' and to aid with the identification of improvement opportunities.
Define CES question(s)	The restaurant has decided to ask for CES feedback using an online survey that is completed when customers make specific requests such as: • changing a table or private dining reservation; • requesting specialist dietary, location or other restaurant information (that is not available on the restaurant website); • other ad-hoc requests or queries that the restaurant manager deems that a CES survey should be deployed against.

(Continued)

Table 8.12 (Continued)

Stage	Description
	The specific questions to be asked are: • How much personal effort did you have to spend gaining a satisfactory outcome to your request? Answers to be captured using a scale of 0–10. • Why did you provide this score? • Answers to be captured using a free format text box.
Deploy CES question(s)	The restaurant will deploy CES within the next month. Reports will be provided to the leadership team of the restaurant on a monthly basis.
Monitor CES results	CES feedback will be monitored on an ongoing basis by the leadership team and discussed within the monthly team meeting.
Determine next steps	CES feedback will be considered as part of continuous service improvement opportunities.

Example CES feedback from customers of the restaurant is shown in Table 8.13.

Table 8.13 CES data capture example

	Customer Effort Level				
	1 – very low	**2 – low**	**3 – medium**	**4 – high**	**5 – very high**
Changing reservations (%)	46.73	37.38	9.35	4.67	1.87
Request for specialist advice (%)	6.90	10.34	3.45	27.59	51.72
Ad-hoc requests (%)	50.00	50.00	0.00	0.00	0.00

An example visualisation of CES feedback is shown in Figure 8.17.

Figure 8.17 Example CES feedback for the restaurant scenario

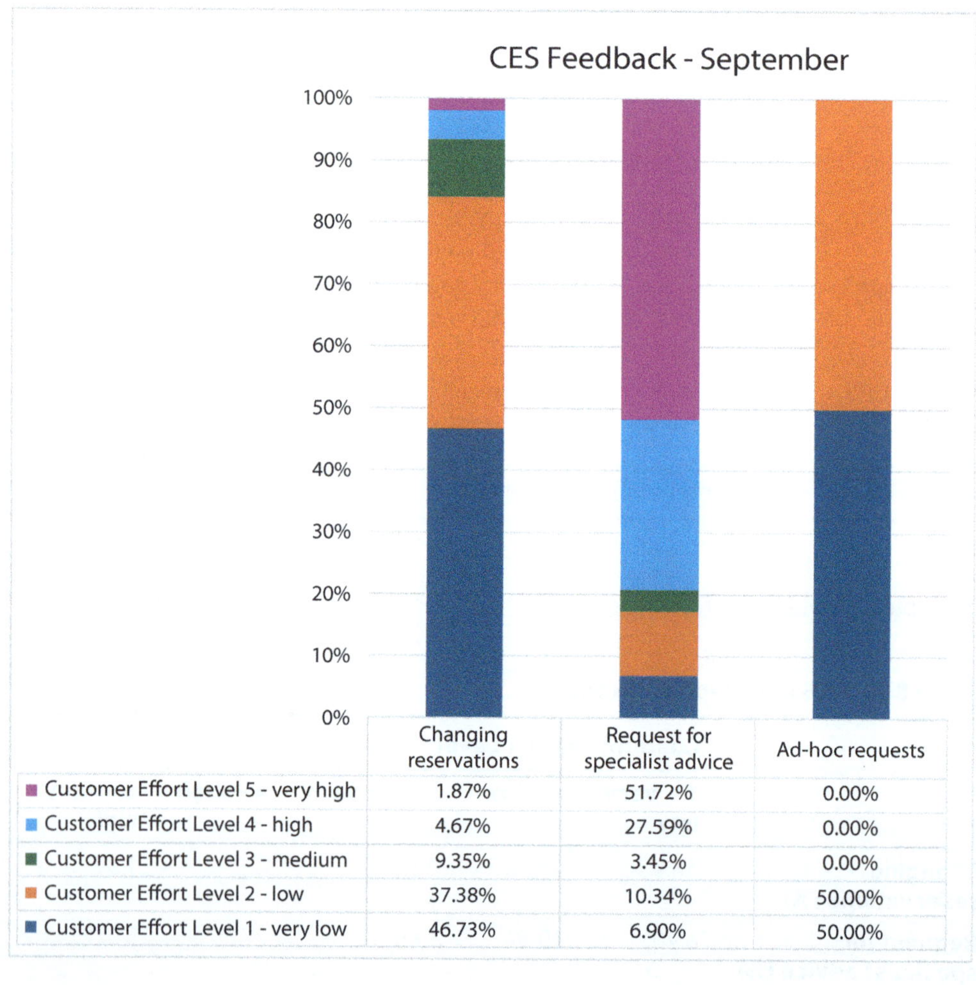

	Changing reservations	Request for specialist advice	Ad-hoc requests
Customer Effort Level 5 - very high	1.87%	51.72%	0.00%
Customer Effort Level 4 - high	4.67%	27.59%	0.00%
Customer Effort Level 3 - medium	9.35%	3.45%	0.00%
Customer Effort Level 2 - low	37.38%	10.34%	50.00%
Customer Effort Level 1 - very low	46.73%	6.90%	50.00%

The restaurant leadership may elect to review the CES feedback in more detail in order to:

- Identify any voice of the customer insights provided through responses to the question 'Why did you provide this score?'
- Identify if there are any root causes behind the challenges in providing responses to specialist advice.
- Identify if there are any root causes behind the customers that are required to extend effort to make changes to reservations.

Following the review, opportunities to enhance the service offer provided by the restaurant should be reviewed and prioritised.

CONCLUSION

Service Deployment provides a foundation for establishing effective and customer-centric products and services. Where applied effectively, deployed services:

- support value co-creation with stakeholders;
- enable the organisation to work towards the achievement of strategic goals and objectives;
- enhance the reputation of the organisation.

Any issues identified with the deployment of a product or service should be investigated and, where possible, resolved. Positive product or service feedback should be celebrated and reflected upon; it may also offer lessons that can help improve future service design initiatives.

9 STAKEHOLDER ENGAGEMENT

This chapter covers the Stakeholder Engagement service, which is an auxiliary service within the Service Design Service Framework (SDSF). The Stakeholder Engagement service is applied when conducting each of the SDSF services as they all require service designers to collaborate with their customers and other stakeholders.

Hunsley et al. (2025) provide the following value proposition for the Stakeholder Engagement service:

> To support the achievement of business change success through effective stakeholder relationship management and communication.

Business change success encompasses many areas of concern, including service design.

Given that value co-creation is one of the key elements of 'service thinking', service designers need to understand their stakeholders and collaborate with them effectively. They must apply a range of frameworks and techniques for identifying, researching, analysing and engaging with stakeholders. They also require the ability to work effectively with people. This requires the following skills: collaborative working, emotional intelligence, cultural awareness and sense-making.

Many activities are conducted within the Stakeholder Engagement service. Some activities are conducted proactively and others are initiated by events. Hunsley et al. (2025) defined the various activities performed when conducting the Stakeholder Engagement service. These activities are shown in Figure 9.1.

Figure 9.1 Stakeholder engagement activities (Hunsley et al., 2025)

A summarised, linear view of the stakeholder engagement activities, and the techniques used when conducting the activities, are described in this chapter.

INTRODUCTION

Every service offered by an organisation is designed to meet the needs of the relevant stakeholders. The key stakeholder group is the intended audience for the service. For example, if the service value proposition is aimed at a particular market for that service, the customers (or consumers) are from the key stakeholder group. However, there may be other stakeholders – such as regulators or government departments – who also have requirements to be met by the delivered service. The internal stakeholders are also a key group to consider as they may communicate directly with the customers during service delivery.

Techniques to understand the variety of views, perspectives and needs are used to enable service designers to engage with their stakeholders effectively and enable value co-creation. Chapter 5 (CX Analysis) explained the techniques used to research and model the different aspects of the customer journey as they access a service. This chapter provides additional insights, explaining the techniques that support service designers as they engage with stakeholders and manage difficult situations.

THE STAKEHOLDER ENGAGEMENT SERVICE

Service description

This service encompasses the following activities:

- Identify the stakeholders (both individuals and groups) for the service design initiative.
- Research the areas of concern for each stakeholder, including any particular requirements to be met.
- Analyse the stakeholders' views and allocate priorities to determine the extent of the engagement activities.
- Decide the stakeholder engagement strategy to be adopted.

Service value proposition

The service value items offered by the service are as follows:

- All stakeholders are identified and their views are clarified.
- The stakeholders are prioritised and the means of engagement are determined for each stakeholder.
- The stakeholder engagement strategy is defined.

Figure 9.2 shows a value stream diagram for this service.

Figure 9.2 Value stream: stakeholder engagement service

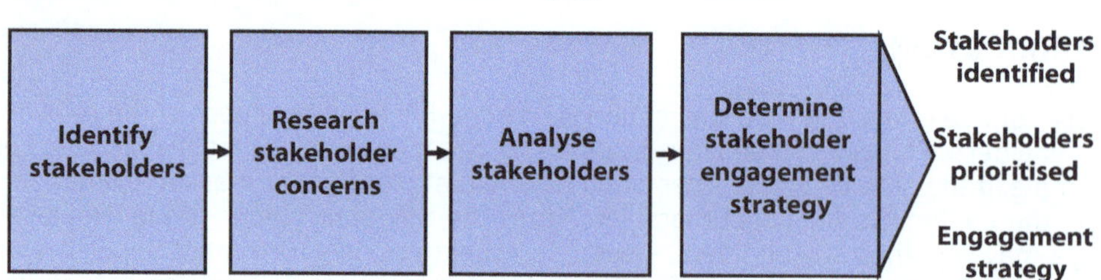

THE TECHNIQUES

A range of techniques is needed to enable successful stakeholder engagement. Stakeholders are likely to have beliefs and opinions that impact their behaviours, communications and expectations. Further, the situations that arise can be highly variable and often unpredictable, requiring significant analysis to ensure they are resolved effectively. Applying various techniques helps to develop an effective stakeholder engagement strategy and ensures this is reviewed and adapted when necessary.

Generic techniques used to identify and research stakeholders are described in Chapters 10 and 11. The following techniques are particularly relevant to this service and are described in this chapter:

- stakeholder wheel;
- customer, actor, transformation, world view, owner, environment (CATWOE);
- RACI matrix;
- power/interest grid;
- principled negotiation.

These techniques are used to identify, analyse and manage stakeholders. They underpin the other service design services as they ensure a holistic understanding of the relevant stakeholders and their different viewpoints. The techniques described in this chapter are also relevant to other business improvement roles, in particular, business analysts, business architects and user researchers.

Identify stakeholders: stakeholder wheel

Purpose

The stakeholder wheel sets out the different actor categories that should be explored to identify relevant stakeholders.

Service designers need to work closely with the various stakeholders involved in delivering or receiving a service. These stakeholders may represent particular organisations, such as regulators or internal business functions. They may be individuals working within the organisation, such as those delivering a service, or may be existing or potential consumers of a service. Therefore, there are various stakeholder groups, each of which is likely to have different priorities, beliefs and value concerns.

The priorities and concerns of a particular stakeholder or stakeholder group reflect their expectations of a service. For example, regulatory stakeholders require a service to comply with the legal framework they represent; customer stakeholders require a service to meet their value needs and expectations.

Paul and Cadle (2020) define a stakeholder as follows:

Stakeholder

An individual, group of individuals or organisation with an interest in the change. Categories of stakeholder include customers, employees, managers, partners, regulators, owners, suppliers and contractors.

Figure 9.3 shows the stakeholder wheel (Paul and Cadle, 2020).

Figure 9.3 The stakeholder wheel (Paul and Cadle, 2020)

The stakeholder groups represented in the stakeholder wheel are described in Table 9.1.

Table 9.1 The stakeholder wheel's stakeholder groups

Stakeholder group	Description
Customers	The individuals or organisations who are the targeted audience for the service. The service may be aimed at individual customers – a business to customer (B2C) service – or may be aimed at an organisational customer – a business to business (B2B) service.
Partners	The organisations that work closely with the organisation and collaborate in the delivery of a particular service. Examples include resellers such as sales organisations or companies that offer technology support.
Suppliers	The organisations that provide goods and services required to enable the service delivery. Examples are companies that supply materials, components or products.
Regulators	Organisations that determine and enforce compliance with the legal framework relevant to a service. For example, the laws and regulations that govern data protection or educational standards.
Employees	The people carry out the work of the organisation in general and the service in particular. The perspectives and concerns of individual stakeholders may be explored or, particularly for larger organisations, the view of employee groups.
Managers	The people who have managerial responsibilities in an organisation. There may be several management layers such as at executive board or middle manager level.
Owners	The shareholders of a commercial organisation or those with trustee status for a non-profit organisation.
Competitors	The organisations that compete in the delivery of a service. These organisations are interested in service improvement or redesign and they may decide to respond in some way. This may affect the viability of the service.

A further stakeholder group should also be considered: the population that has concerns, conducts lobbying or makes comments regarding issues relevant to the service. For example, the increasing public interest in corporate social responsibility and the natural environment.

Process

Service designers should consider the following questions when applying the stakeholder wheel:

- Which customer groups will be the intended recipients or beneficiaries of the service? Will they be internal or external customers or both?

- Which actors will deliver the service? Will employed staff and external partners be involved in delivering the service?
- Which suppliers will provide items that form part of or facilitate the delivered service?
- Which executives or senior managers have ownership and governance responsibility for the service?
- Which external organisations impose legal and regulatory obligations on the service?
- Which competitor organisations will be alert to any new or redesigned service offering?

These questions provide a basis for exploring the service landscape and identifying the full range of relevant stakeholders.

Benefits of applying the stakeholder wheel

Stakeholder identification begins during the investigation of a situation or service. The activities and techniques used to investigate situations often uncover different stakeholder groups, particularly those engaged in delivering a service or receiving its outputs. However, the stakeholder wheel augments the stakeholder identification activity, providing an aide-mémoire that helps achieve the benefits shown in Figure 9.4.

Figure 9.4 Benefits of the stakeholder wheel

Holistic View
Offers a holistic view of the possible stakeholders.
Stakeholder Perspective
Considers the range of different stakeholder perspectives.
Stakeholder Wheel
BENEFITS
Exhaustive Analysis
Ensures relevant stakeholders are not overlooked.

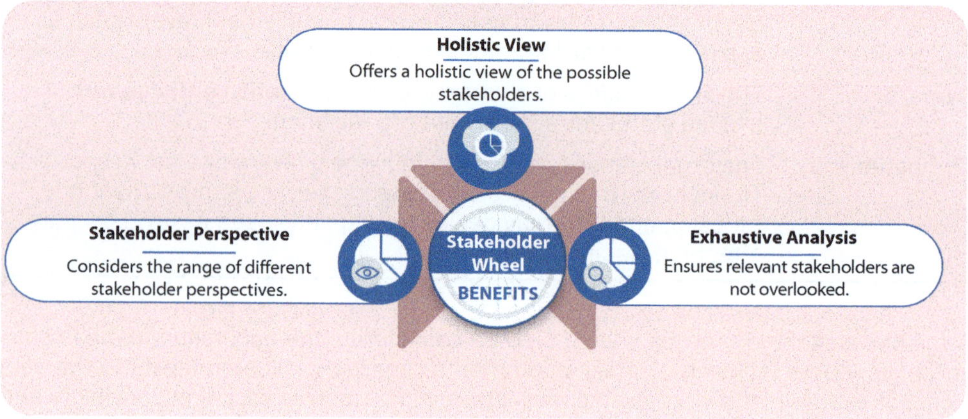

Example application of the stakeholder wheel

The risk that some stakeholders are omitted during stakeholder identification is mitigated by the Stakeholder Wheel. In the restaurant scenario, the following stakeholders are likely to be evident during the initial investigation of the situation:

- Diners; this category may be further decomposed to identify diners with different characteristics.
- Waiting staff.
- Food preparation staff.
- Restaurant manager.

The stakeholder wheel would also raise the possible stakeholders identified in Table 9.2

Table 9.2 The stakeholders for the restaurant scenario

Stakeholder category	Stakeholder explanation/description
Partners	The restaurant has partnered with courier companies to allow customers to order meals online and request home delivery.
Suppliers	The restaurant works with a small number of local suppliers. A redesign of the restaurant service may require changes to the working practices applied to engage with suppliers.
Regulators	The regulatory framework for the restaurant encompasses food hygiene standards, health and safety, data protection and financial conduct. Each regulator should be identified as a potential stakeholder and any changes reviewed in the light of a regulator's compliance criteria.
Owners	The restaurant is jointly owned by two shareholders. They both have perspectives on the services offered by the restaurant.
Competitors	Several local restaurants compete with the restaurant by offering similar dining experiences and dishes.

Research stakeholders: CATWOE analysis

Purpose

The CATWOE technique (Paul and Cadle, 2020, adapted from Checkland, 1981) is used to explore the beliefs, values and priorities held by different stakeholders. Understanding these aspects helps to clarify a stakeholder's world view and vision for the service under examination. CATWOE is a key stakeholder engagement technique as it offers greater understanding of stakeholders, helping to explain their behaviours, requirements and priorities.

Table 9.3 explains the six elements within CATWOE.

Table 9.3 The CATWOE elements

CATWOE element	Description
Customer	The intended recipient of the service.
Actor	The actors conducting the service.
Transformation	The core process or activity undertaken when conducting the service.
World view	The set of values, beliefs and priorities that collectively determine the underlying rationale for the service.
Owner	The individual or group with the authority to govern the service.
Environment	The external factors that constrain or enable the operation of the service.

Exploring the CATWOE elements for a stakeholder helps service designers to gain insights that may have otherwise been missed. These insights may explain why certain features are desired by stakeholders and where constraints lie that may limit a potential design. For example, one diner may prioritise the ability to request changes to dishes offered by the restaurant while other diners may prioritise standard menus at reasonable prices.

Process

The process for conducting CATWOE analysis is shown in Figure 9.5.

Figure 9.5 The process for conducting a CATWOE analysis of a service

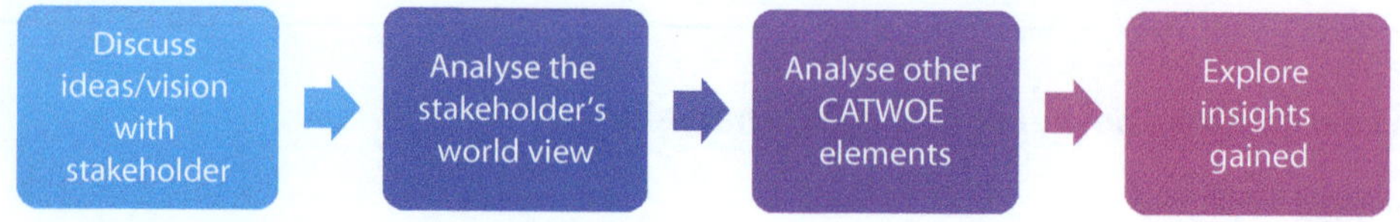

These stages are described in Table 9.4.

Table 9.4 The stages to perform a CATWOE analysis of a service

Stage	Description
Discuss ideas/ vision with stakeholder	The stakeholder's concerns, issues, values, beliefs and priorities regarding the service are explored.
Analyse the stakeholder's world view	The points raised by the stakeholder are analysed to formulate their world view regarding the service.
Analyse other CATWOE elements	The world view is used to determine the core transformation process of the service, the customer who is the primary audience for the service, the key actors conducting the work of the service, the owner governing the service and the environmental factors that impact the service.
Explore insights gained	The complete CATWOE is used to define the service activities that form the customer journey and are required to fulfil the world view.

Benefits of CATWOE analysis

Analysing a stakeholder's CATWOE for a service provides the service designer with insights into aspects such as the nature of value from the stakeholder's perspective and where value may be co-created. Conducting this analysis for several stakeholders helps service designers to understand where different stakeholders' priorities lie and to take a holistic view of the service requirements. CATWOE analysis offers the benefits shown in Figure 9.6.

Figure 9.6 Benefits of CATWOE analysis

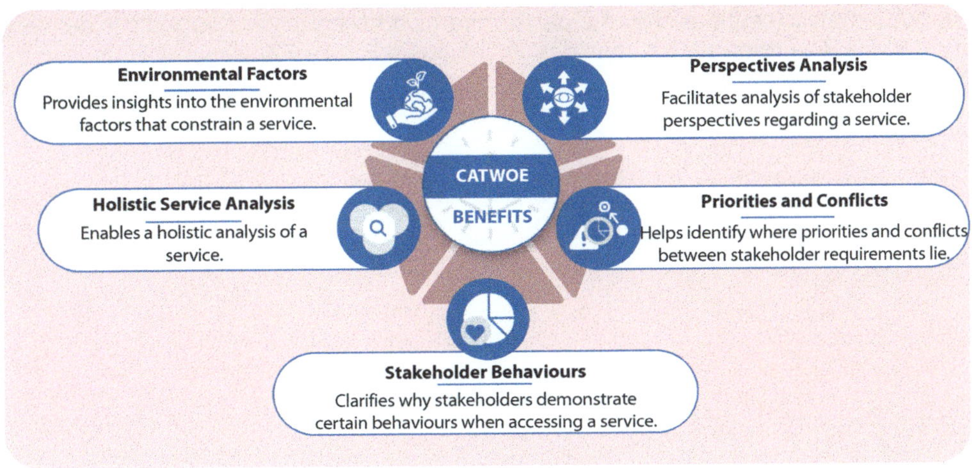

Example CATWOE analysis

An example CATWOE analysis for the restaurant scenario is shown in Table 9.5.

Table 9.5 An example CATWOE analysis for the restaurant scenario

Stakeholder	Restaurant manager
Customer	Diners, many of whom will have particular food requirements and intolerances.
Actor	Menu design, food preparation and waiting staff.
Transformation	Design and deliver menu of quality meals.
World view	The restaurant offers excellent food at competitive prices as part of a flexible, diner-oriented service.
Owner	The two shareholders.
Environment	Regulations regarding food safety; business regulations; food trends; economic factors.

Analyse stakeholders: RACI matrix

Purpose

A RACI matrix is used to analyse areas and levels of responsibility for defined service elements. These elements are either tasks carried out or individual deliverables created that facilitate the design and delivery of a service.

The completed RACI matrix enables the service designer to gain insights into the actors concerned with the delivery of the tasks or deliverables and the role each actor plays. This includes aspects such as ownership and accountability.

The RACI matrix identifies the role performed by different actors during the delivery of a service. The roles are categorised as defined in Figure 9.7.

Figure 9.7 The RACI categories

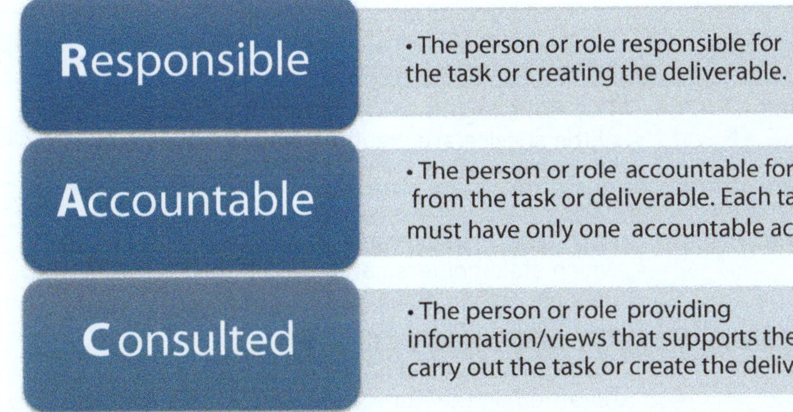

Process

The process for developing a RACI is shown in Figure 9.8.

Figure 9.8 The process to develop a RACI

These stages are described in further detail in Table 9.6.

Table 9.6 The stages to create a RACI matrix

Stage	Description
Record each service element	Each task or deliverable within the service is identified and recorded on a row within the matrix.
List the stakeholders	The stakeholders involved in conducting the work of the service are identified and listed along the top of the matrix. Each stakeholder is allocated to a column.
Analyse each service element	Each task or deliverable is reviewed to identify which stakeholders carry out the work and the role they play when doing this.
Record the RACI categories	The RACI category indicating the role of the stakeholder regarding the service element is recorded on the matrix.
Review the completed matrix	Once all of the elements have been analysed and the role of the stakeholders recorded, the completed RACI is analysed for completeness and consistency. The following is considered: • Is there a single accountable stakeholder for each task/deliverable? • Is there at least one stakeholder responsible for each task/deliverable? • Do some stakeholders have too much responsibility?

Benefits of RACI matrix analysis

Analysing the stakeholder roles and responsibilities required to conduct a service enables the service designer to understand how the actors collaborate in delivering the service. The benefits of creating a RACI are shown in Figure 9.9.

Example RACI matrix

Figure 9.10 is an example of a RACI matrix for the restaurant scenario.

A RACI may be enhanced using colours to highlight different elements. Figure 9.11 shows a RACI where the accountable and responsible actors have been highlighted.

Figure 9.9 Benefits of a RACI

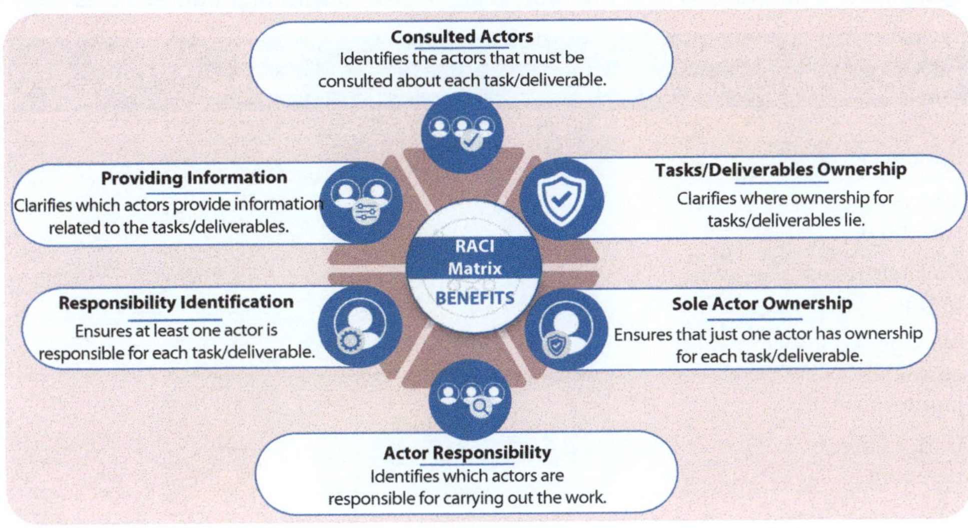

Figure 9.10 Example RACI for the restaurant scenario

Stakeholder/ Task	Restaurant manager	Restaurant actor	Service owner	Service designer	Diner
Produce business case	A	C	R	R	
Interview stakeholders	I	C	A	R	C
Facilitate focus group	I	C	A	R	C
Manage customer journey map	I	C	A	R	C
Design service blueprint	C	C	R	A/R	C

Figure 9.11 Example RACI for the restaurant scenario with highlighted roles

Stakeholder/ Task	Restaurant manager	Restaurant actor	Service owner	Service designer	Diner
Produce business case	A	C	R	R	
Interview stakeholders	I	C	A	R	C
Facilitate focus group	I	C	A	R	C
Manage customer journey map	I	C	A	R	C
Design service blueprint	C	C	R	A/R	C

Determine stakeholder engagement strategy: power/interest grid

Purpose

The power/interest grid technique is used to analyse each stakeholder or stakeholder group and to determine the most effective strategy to engage with them. Each stakeholder is analysed with regard to the following:

- their level of power to govern or change the service;
- the level of interest they have regarding the service.

The power/interest grid is shown in Figure 9.12.

The level of power and interest for each stakeholder or stakeholder group is analysed regarding the service. The stakeholders are placed in the relevant section on the power/interest grid, which helps to identify the required engagement strategy to be adopted.

Figure 9.13 shows the engagement strategies for the sections of the power/interest grid.

Figure 9.12 The power/interest grid (Adapted from Johnson et al., 2005, in Paul and Cadle, 2020)

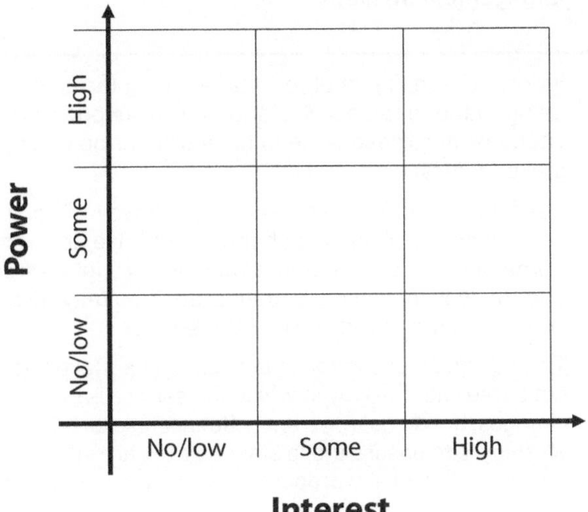

Figure 9.13 The power/interest grid engagement strategies

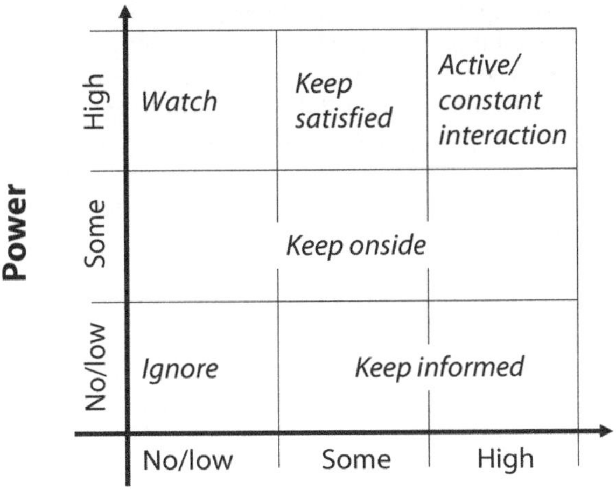

Table 9.7 The power/interest grid engagement strategies

Power/interest grid section	Engagement strategy
Low power/low interest	Ignore: These stakeholders have little interest in the changes being made to the service and have little power to influence those changes. It is reasonable to have little or no engagement with these stakeholders.
Low power/some or high interest	Keep informed: These stakeholders have little power to influence the service or any proposed changes but have at least some interest. Some of these stakeholders may be very interested in the service and the way in which it is delivered. This may be because they conduct some of the work of the service. This can be an uncomfortable situation for stakeholders as they may not agree with the way in which the service is delivered or any proposed changes, but do not have any influence to exert. The recommended strategy is to ensure these stakeholders are informed of the service design work and any proposed changes to the service. Due consideration should be given to the situation faced by these stakeholders as they may resent their lack of influence and may resort to other ways to make their views known. This could include working with staff associations or trade unions, or resorting to social media. Should they do this, the level of power held by these stakeholders may increase, which may create difficulties for the service designers.
Some power/ low, some or high interest	Keep onside: These stakeholders have some power to influence the service or any proposed changes and have at least some interest. Some of these stakeholders may be very interested in the service, and the way in which it is delivered, because they manage those tasked with conducting the work of the service. Given the level of power, these stakeholders should be managed carefully to ensure they remain supportive of the service design work. Their concerns should be researched, understood and addressed as much as possible.
High power/low interest	Watch: These stakeholders have a significant level of power but low interest. They may be senior executives that lead functions with a limited connection to the delivered service, such as human resources or finance. However, their level of interest can increase should any proposed changes or issues arise regarding the service. Where this occurs, the combination of increased interest and the level of power could impede the progress of the service design changes. Given this, it is wise to ensure any particular views or concerns held by these stakeholders are known and considered when change proposals are put forward. Ignoring these stakeholders runs the risk of them engaging at a critical point in the service design and derailing the improvement project.

(Continued)

Table 9.7 (Continued)

Power/interest grid section	Engagement strategy
High power/some interest	Keep satisfied: These stakeholders have a significant level of power and some interest. They may be senior executives that lead functions that contribute to the delivered service, such as production or infrastructure architecture. The level of interest of these stakeholders is likely to increase should any proposed changes to the service design impact their areas of responsibility. This should be anticipated as the service design work progresses and the concerns and view of these stakeholders should be reviewed to ensure they are taken into account.
High power/high interest	Active, constant interaction: These are the key stakeholders who have the power to decide on any proposals or recommendations and are highly interested in any outcomes from the service design. This may be because they are accountable for certain aspects including the service design and delivery. If working within the context of a project, the project sponsor will be one of the stakeholders within this group. It is essential that service designers identify these stakeholders and work with them closely. Their perspectives, possibly analysed using CATWOE, should be clearly understood. They should be given regular progress updates, including the results from any experiments or trials regarding a proposed service design. These stakeholders should not be presented with any unexpected proposals or recommendations. They should be made aware of any issues, successes or innovations as they occur. This approach helps to ensure they remain supportive, which can be fundamental to the success of the service design.

Process

The process for power/interest grid analysis is shown in Figure 9.14.

Figure 9.14 Process for power/interest grid analysis

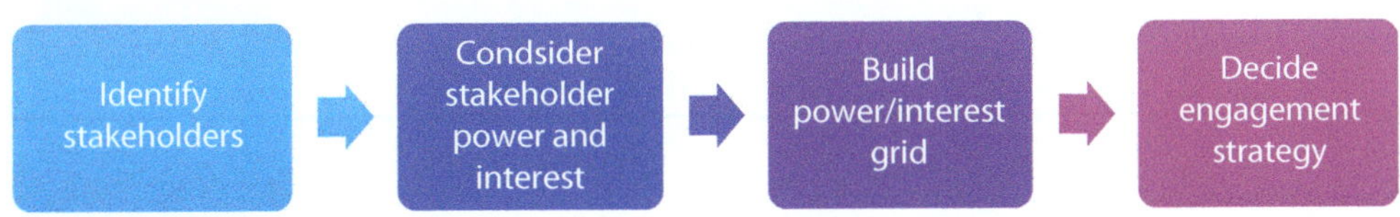

These stages are described in Table 9.8.

Table 9.8 The stages applied to develop a power/interest grid

Stage	Description
Identify stakeholders	The stakeholders involved with the service design are identified using the stakeholder wheel.
Consider stakeholder power and interest	Each stakeholder is analysed to determine the level of power they possess and the extent to which they are interested in the service design. The stakeholders may also be analysed using techniques such as CATWOE and RACI.
Build power/interest grid	Each of the stakeholders are mapped to the power/interest grid. This enables the service designer to view the stakeholder landscape and identify the volume of stakeholders within each of the power/interest grid categories.

Decide engagement strategy	The various engagement strategies suggested by the power/interest grid are reviewed and the approaches to enact the strategies are decided. This typically requires a communication strategy that includes a stakeholder management plan. This plan should include the following for each stakeholder or stakeholder group:
	• Stakeholder role name.
	• Levels of power and interest.
	• Views, concerns, interests and priorities.
	• Attitude demonstrated. This may be categorised as follows:
	  • **Champion or advocate:** A stakeholder who is active in promoting the service design.
	  • **Supporter or follower:** A stakeholder who supports the service design but does not promote it actively.
	  • **Neutral or indifferent:** A stakeholder who does not demonstrate support or opposition to the service design.
	  • **Critic:** A stakeholder who expresses any positive or negative observations regarding the service design.
	  • **Blocker:** A stakeholder who opposes the service design and takes action to impede progress or prevent the delivery of the service.
	• Actions to be taken to engage with the stakeholder and, if required, to manage their opposition.

Benefits of power/interest grid analysis

The benefits of developing and applying a power/interest grid are shown in Figure 9.15.

Figure 9.15 Benefits of power/interest grid analysis

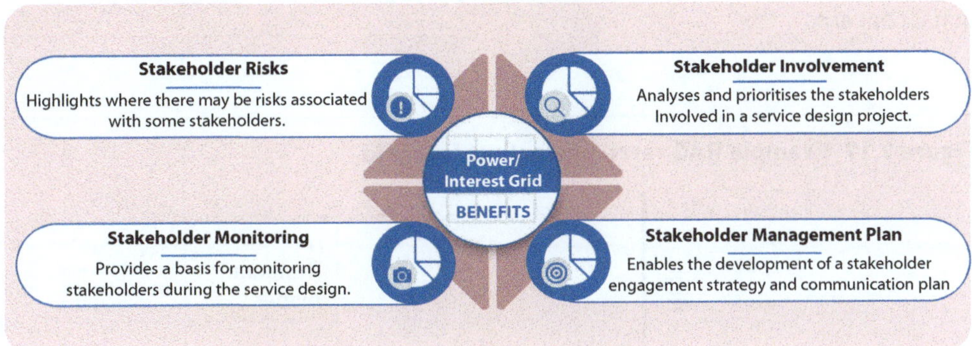

Example power/interest grid

Figure 9.16 shows a power/interest grid for the restaurant scenario.

Figure 9.16 Example power/interest grid

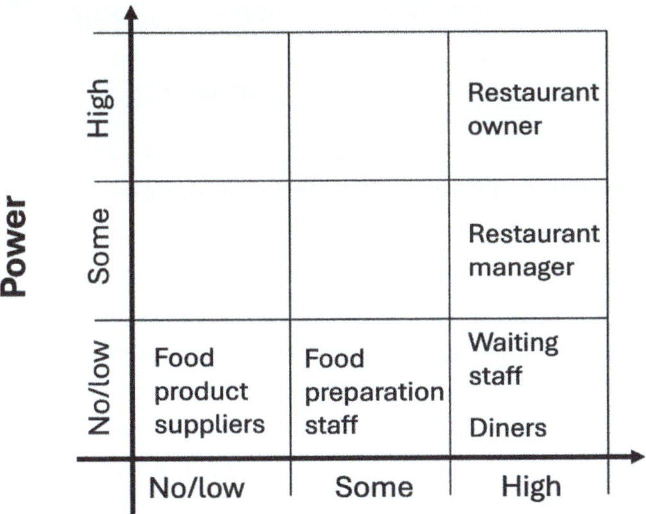

It may be helpful to combine certain techniques as this can increase the visibility of issues or provide additional insights. For example, a completed power/interest grid may use the RAG categories to highlight where there are particular concerns regarding stakeholders. An example based on Figure 9.16 is shown in Figure 9.17. In this figure, red indicates that there are significant concerns regarding a stakeholder that could risk the success of a service design assignment, amber indicates that there are some concerns, so extra care is needed, and green indicates that there are no additional concerns.

Figure 9.17 Example RAG rated power/interest grid

Power
High
Some
No/low
Restaurant owner
Restaurant manager
Food product suppliers
Food preparation staff
Waiting staff
Diners
No/low
Some
High
Interest

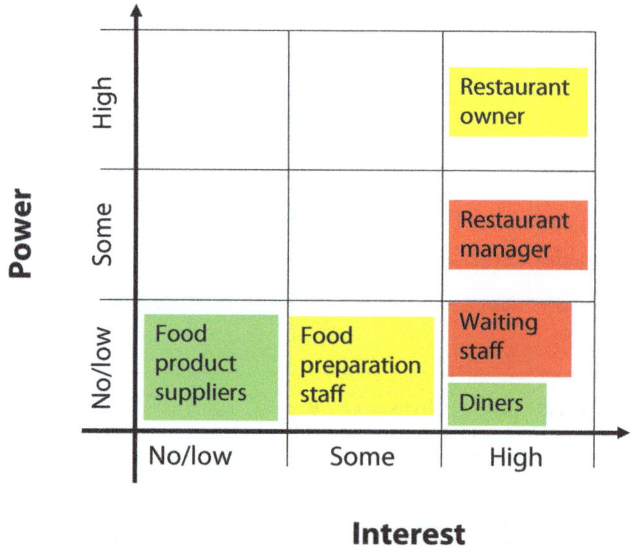

Resolve stakeholder conflicts: principled negotiation

Purpose

Stakeholders often have different views, beliefs, priorities and requirements. Given this, disagreements can arise regarding the service delivered. Service designers may need to apply negotiation approaches to navigate these disagreements in order to help ensure conflict does not result. Where there is conflict, service designers may need to adopt a conflict management strategy.

Negotiation skills help service designers to deal with different disagreement situations and prevent them developing into conflicts. These different situations may require service designers to adapt their approach and outcome focus. When engaging with stakeholders, it is usually preferable to apply an integrative negotiation approach where all stakeholders are encouraged to work together to achieve a mutually agreed outcome. However, there are situations where a distributive negotiation approach may be needed. When applying this approach, stakeholders use data to support their position and focus on meeting their needs.

Thomas and Kilmann (2007) developed a framework of conflict outcome positions that extends beyond integrative and distributive negotiation. This framework identifies different positions depending upon the extent of cooperation on the part of the negotiating parties and the extent to which they assert their need to achieve their desired outcomes. Figure 9.18 shows this framework.

Figure 9.18 Thomas and Kilmann's conflict positions (Thomas and Kilmann, 2007)

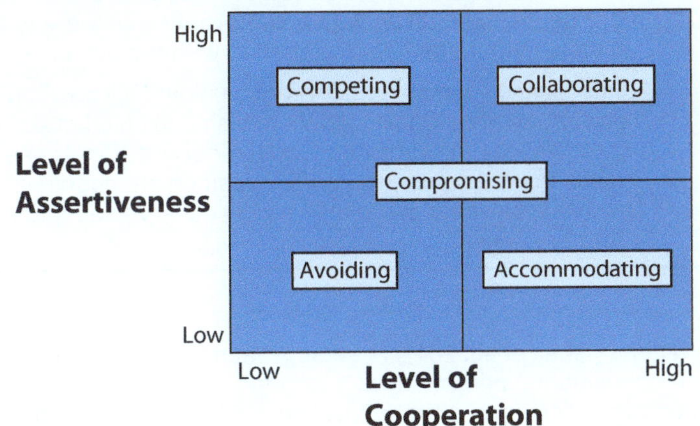

Each of these positions can be relevant depending upon the situation. Table 9.9 describes the five positions and explains when they may be relevant.

Table 9.9 Thomas and Kilmann's conflict positions

Conflict position	Description
Avoiding	Low assertiveness and low cooperation: This position is relevant if a situation arises where action is not needed and could serve to extend the difficulty.
Accommodating	Low assertiveness and high cooperation: This position is relevant if a situation arises where one stakeholder is happy to concede as this is the most positive way to resolve the situation.

(Continued)

Table 9.9 (Continued)

Conflict position	Description
Competing	High assertiveness and low cooperation: This position is relevant in situations where a decision is needed to avoid a disagreement derailing progress and there is a senior person who is prepared to make the decision. The project sponsor may be required to decide on a way forward where the stakeholders are unable to agree and escalation has resulted.
Compromising	Medium assertiveness and medium cooperation: This position is relevant in situations where it is not possible to identify an option that would satisfy all needs. It requires all stakeholders to accommodate other stakeholder's needs to a certain extent. Care needs to be taken with a compromise as there is a risk of all stakeholders feeling dissatisfied with the outcome.
Collaborating	High assertiveness and high cooperation: This position is relevant where all participants are able to collaborate to identify a way forward that would meet everyone's needs. This is the most positive conflict position although it is not always achievable and it may be necessary to adopt one of the other positions.

Principled negotiation (Fisher et al., 2011) is an approach to negotiation that focuses on understanding participants' perspectives, interests and concerns and considering different options to resolve the situation. When applied carefully, this approach can help achieve a collaborative outcome that ensures a positive outcome for all stakeholders.

Process

The stages within the principled negotiation process are shown in Figure 9.19.

Figure 9.19 Stages of principled negotiation

The steps in this process are defined in Table 9.10.

Table 9.10 Stages of principled negotiation

Principled negotiation step	Description
People	Fisher et al. (2011) recommend that the people should be considered separately from the disagreement. Each stakeholder should be considered individually. The following questions should be considered regarding the stakeholders: • What are the genuine concerns of this stakeholder? • Are their any fundamental beliefs that are causing the stakeholder to have a particular perspective? • Has the style or language used when communicating contributed to the situation? • How might stakeholders be encouraged to understand each other's concerns and feelings regarding the situation?
Interests	Fisher et al. (2011) recommend that the focus should be on interests rather than positions. The potential for a positive solution that addresses everyone's needs exists where the relevant interests of all stakeholders are considered. The following questions should be considered regarding the stakeholders: • What benefit does the stakeholder believe will be achieved by adopting this approach or position? • Why doesn't the stakeholder want the suggested approach or solution? • What priority does the stakeholder apply to a particular requirement? • Are there any interests that are common to several or all stakeholders?
Options	Fisher et al. (2011) recommend that a variety of options are identified and evaluated before a decision is made. Time should be allowed to apply divergent thinking and ideate potential solutions to resolve the situation. The following questions should be considered regarding the stakeholders: • What ideas have the stakeholders put forward? • Are there any creative solutions that could meet the stakeholders' needs? • Are there any creative problem solving techniques that could be used to identify innovative options?

(Continued)

Table 9.10 (Continued)

Principled negotiation step	Description
Criteria	Fisher et al. (2011) recommend that decisions are based on objective criteria. Each stakeholder is able to evaluate the options based on objective criteria. This approach can help avoid the escalation of a situation into a conflict and ensures that the focus is on addressing the problem while taking the interests into account. Evaluation based on objective criteria also prevents more senior or assertive stakeholders from insisting on a particular solution. The following questions should be analysed to identify the objective criteria: • What are the costs associated with this option? • What are the benefits that would accrue from adopting this option? • What are the risks to the service that could arise from adopting this option? • What are the impacts that the option might have on the service? • What environmental constraints (such as legal or regulatory) impose a compliance requirement on the selected option? • What timescale would result from this option and is this acceptable?

Principled negotiation helps to achieve a positive outcome from a service disagreement. However, there can be situations where one stakeholder has greater influence over the situation and where this is leveraged, additional discontent can occur.

Fisher et al. (2011) recommend that the parties to the negotiation consider the absolute minimum they will accept. This is called the **Best Alternative to a Negotiated Agreement** (BATNA) and encourages stakeholders to ask: 'What would we do if our needs aren't met?' Thinking about the BATNA helps to ensure that any unacceptable solutions are declined.

Benefits of principled negotiation

The benefits of principled negotiation are shown in Figure 9.20.

Figure 9.20 Benefits of principled negotiation

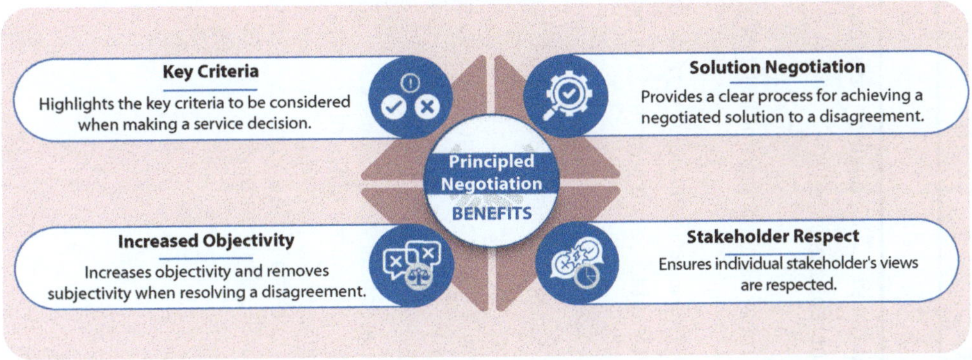

Example of principled negotiation

Table 9.11 shows an example of applying principled negotiation within the restaurant scenario. A disagreement has arisen between the restaurant owner and the restaurant manager.

The criteria provide a basis for evaluating each option and discussing with the stakeholders who are in disagreement.

CONCLUSION

Designing, developing and deploying a service requires engagement with stakeholders to ensure that a basis for value co-creation exists. Stakeholders tend to have different perspectives on a service, so engagement can be complex and require significant expertise if the stakeholder relationships are to work well. However, engaging with stakeholders can enable service design and service improvement.

The techniques described in this chapter help to engage effectively with stakeholders and should be used to conduct the range of stakeholder engagement activities. They offer insights that would not be found without applying them when analysing stakeholders and determining relevant engagement strategies.

Table 9.11 Example of principled negotiation for the restaurant scenario

Service	Processing diner payments	
Stakeholders and concerns	Restaurant owner	Wishes to introduce automated online payment system. Wants to cut costs and increase profits.
	Restaurant manager	Wants to ensure the payment service accommodates all diners. Wants to increase number of diners and volume of business. Has concerns that an automated online payment system will deter potential diners
	Waiting staff	Want to provide the best service to diners across all demographics. Have concerns that they will have to manage any unhappy diners.
	Diners	Different groups have different service expectations. Some want the payment service to be more efficient as there have been delays when waiting to make payment. Some diners want the current service to remain the same. Some diners are opposed to making online payments.

(Continued)

Table 9.11 (Continued)

Service	Processing diner payments	
Interests	Restaurant owner	Making a profit.
	Restaurant manager	Running a successful restaurant. Enhancing personal reputation.
	Waiting staff	Avoiding conflicts with diners.
	Diners	Receiving a great restaurant service. Avoiding problems while paying for a meal.
Options	(1) Retain existing payment service. (2) Implement smart phone payment system. (3) Provide each table with tablet where diners can access the bill and make payment. (4) Allow several payment methods. (5) Allow several payment methods and provide discount for online payment via new system.	
Criteria	Costs: cost of operation of each proposed payment service; disruptive effect of changing a service. Benefits: savings resulting from reduced staff costs; increase in customer satisfaction. Risks: reduction in customer satisfaction; negative feedback; use of social media to complain. Impacts: technological; processes; staff roles; culture. Compliance: information security requirements. Timescale: elapsed time to deploy revised service.	

10 GENERIC SERVICE DESIGN TECHNIQUES

Targeted demographic

INTRODUCTION

This chapter describes generic techniques that can be used to support the delivery of the services described within the Service Design Service Framework (introduced in Chapter 2). The techniques covered in this chapter are:

- interviews;
- storytelling;
- observation.

These techniques may be used to elicit information from a targeted stakeholder demographic. This contrasts with the techniques used to elicit information and insights from a distributed demographic of stakeholders (see Chapter 11).

Service designers should always select the technique most appropriate to the context in which they are working. If a technique is not helping to elicit the required information, it should be adapted to suit the context or replaced by another technique. Techniques should be used to further understanding and drive outcomes for the organisation and its stakeholders, particularly customers.

The techniques described in this chapter support the delivery of service design services and are also used in the delivery of services offered by other roles including user researchers, business analysts, business architects, change managers, project managers and product owners.

THE TECHNIQUES

Interviews

An interview is a one-to-one discussion between individuals. The technique involves the interviewer asking the interviewee questions to obtain insight. When applied in the context of service design the technique can provide an opportunity to build rapport with individual stakeholders. This often results in a depth of understanding that is unmatched by other investigation techniques.

The stages of an interview are shown in Figure 10.1 (adapted from Cadle et al., 2021) and described in Table 10.1.

Figure 10.1 Interview stages

Table 10.1 Interview stage descriptions

Stage	Description
Planning and preparation	The interview is planned, which requires consideration of the following: • **Why?** What is the purpose or goal of the interview? • **What?** Which topics will be discussed during the interview? • **Who?** Who will be interviewed? Will the interviewee agree to be interviewed? Who will be the interviewer? • **When?** What is the date and time of the interview? How long will the interview last for? • **Where?** Will the interview be face-to-face, virtual or via telephone call? Have all the arrangements been made to support this? • **How?** Will the interview be formal or informal in nature? Will questions be shared with the interviewee in advance? How will responses be recorded? An agenda is developed as a result of the planning activity. Typically, this is issued to the interviewee in advance of the interview to enable them to prepare. For external stakeholder interviews, permission may be required and could involve signing contracts or non-disclosure agreements.
Interview	The interview has three sections: • **Introduction:** The interviewer and interviewee introduce themselves, there may be some initial conversation to establish rapport, and the purpose and goal of the interview is confirmed. • **Questioning:** The question areas identified in the agenda are discussed. While the agenda defines an ordered list, the interviewer may decide to adapt the order and explore other relevant areas. • **Close:** The next steps or follow-up actions are identified, the interviewee is thanked for attending the interview and further means of communication (in case there are any additional queries) are agreed.

(*Continued*)

Table 10.1 (Continued)

Stage	Description
Follow-up	Post-interview actions are carried out, including: • sharing the interview transcript or recording; • carrying out any agreed actions; • reporting progress regarding the agreed actions.

There are various types of questions that can be used during an interview. The main types are described in Table 10.2.

Table 10.2 Question types

Question type	Description
Open	Open questions are used to elicit general thoughts about a situation, product or service, idea and opportunity. They encourage the interviewee to think broadly and lead to open information exchange. Examples include: • 'Tell me what you think about...' • 'What are your views on...' • 'What are the biggest frustrations that you encounter with...' • 'What do you feel about...' Interviewers often use open questions to begin interviews as these can aid with building rapport with the interviewee. If appropriately placed, this style of questioning can also help the interviewee to relax.
Closed	Closed questions result in short, specific answers, such as 'yes' or 'no'. This style of questioning tends to close down discussion and can be useful to: • **Frame a discussion:** For example, 'Are you happy with the product or service?' • **Obtain a definitive answer on a question or topic:** For example, 'Do you agree with the new policy on...' or 'Does the complaints department deal solely with customer complaints?' • **Gain control over an overly talkative interviewee:** This can be enabled by asking clear questions with limited alternative answers. For example, 'Is this a regulatory requirement?' Closed questions should be used with care as they can close down a discussion and risk breaking rapport.

(Continued)

Table 10.2 (Continued)

Question type	Description
Limited choice	Limited choice questions offer the interviewee a restricted set of options to choose from. For example: • Would you say that the product or service is better, worse or about the same as it was last year? • Which would you prefer, option A, B or C? Limited choice questions also need to be used with care.
Leading	Leading questions attempt to direct the interviewee towards a particular response. For example: • 'Do you agree that the latest product upgrade caused disruption to customers?' • 'It seems that option three is the best option – what do you think?' Leading questions can stimulate in-depth discussion if they cause the interviewee to reflect on their opinion. However, there is a risk that a nervous or inexperienced interviewee may agree with the question posed without really considering their answer.
Probing	Probing questions are used to follow up responses to other questions. They are used in order to find out additional detail on a particular subject. Examples include: • 'Can you tell me more about...?' • 'What did you mean when you said...?' • 'Does this mean that responsibility for resolving delivery issues will transfer to the new partner?'
Linking	Linking questions are used to make connections between different topics or parts of the conversation. Where used effectively, they help to build rapport as they demonstrate to the interviewee that the interviewer is listening and understands the information being provided. Examples include: • 'Is the delay in responses to queries linked to the change in processes earlier this year...?' • 'Would the hire of the new employee help with resolving the compliance issue that you mentioned?'

Applying interviews

Several example situations where interviews can be applied are explored within Table 10.3.

Table 10.3 Situations when interviews are relevant

Situation	Description
Internal stakeholder interview	Interviews can be used to obtain insight from a range of internal stakeholders such as: • **Senior stakeholders:** The sponsor of the change initiative and other senior or influential leaders and managers. • **Subject Matter Experts (SMEs):** Individuals who can offer detailed knowledge and expert guidance about a specific domain or process. SMEs may be employed by the organisation or may be external consultants with significant domain expertise (see below – external stakeholder interview). • **End users:** The users or prospective users of the existing (or proposed) product or service may be interviewed where an in-depth discussion with an individual is required. However, information from these stakeholders is usually obtained via group discussions or surveys (see Glossary of Terms and Techniques).
Customer interview	Interviews can be used to elicit information and obtain insights from those who can offer a customer perspective, including: • **Current customers:** current users or customers of the organisation's products or services. • **Former customers:** previous users or customers of the organisation's products or services. • **Customers of competitors:** customers of competitor products or services. • **Customer proxies:** people associated with the customer but who are not the customer themselves. For example, a parent or guardian could be interviewed, instead of, or in addition to, the interview of a child.
External stakeholder interview	Interviews can be used to obtain insight from a range of external stakeholders such as: • **Partners and suppliers:** representatives from other organisations that are partners or suppliers within the organisation's external ecosystem. • **SMEs:** external consultants who can offer detailed, expert guidance or information regarding a specific domain. • **Regulators and industry bodies:** representatives able to share the views of regulatory or other relevant industry organisations. Occasionally, it may be appropriate to interview a representative from a competitor. For example, where it would be helpful to collaborate regarding an industry initiative or proposed regulatory change.

Practical considerations

Table 10.4 describes practical questions and considerations related to the use of interviews.

Table 10.4 Practical considerations for the design and completion of interviews

Situation	Description
How much research is needed prior to an interview?	As part of interview preparation, the interviewer should conduct background research into the business situation. This aids with the preparation of interview questions and helps to ensure that the interviewer and interviewee have some shared understanding at the outset. For example, if interviewing a stakeholder about a particular product or service it helps if the interviewer has some understanding of the history of the product or service, its value proposition, the delivery approach and similar competitor products or services. Gaining an understanding of terminology and acronyms used in the business situation can also enable the interviewer to establish credibility. In situations where the interviewee has significant seniority or influence, it may be vital to conduct pre-interview research regarding the interviewee. This can influence the approach taken to arranging and executing the interview.
How significant is organisational culture to the interview approach?	It can be useful to reflect on the organisational culture when preparing for an interview. For example, where an organisation has a hierarchical, formal and risk averse culture, stakeholder interviews may require prior permission to avoid stakeholder engagement issues. Where internal interviews are taking place, it may also be problematic if the interviewer is deemed to be less or more senior than the interviewee. In contrast, an organisation where the culture encourages open and transparent dialogue between customers and employees may enable less formal preparation and interview conduct.
How should interviewee expectations be managed?	When conducting interviews the expectations of the stakeholder concerning future change need to be managed carefully and pro-actively. It should be made clear to any interviewees where the interview is part of a broader research activity. Interviewers should take care not to promise, or give the impression, that any changes suggested by the interviewee will be actioned.

(Continued)

Table 10.4 (Continued)

Situation	Description
Should interviews be combined with other techniques?	Interviews may be conducted with senior stakeholders before a focus group or a workshop is arranged. This helps the facilitator to clarify the objectives of the service design assignment and build rapport with the senior stakeholders. It also provides a means of identifying who should attend further research forums or be contacted for information. A range of other techniques can be used during an interview. Examples are storytelling (described below), prototyping and scenario analysis (see Glossary of Terms and Techniques).

Storytelling

Storytelling is a technique used to elicit information about unique human experiences and insights by encouraging a stakeholder (or group of stakeholders) to share 'stories'. These stories relate previous experiences and help identify where there were issues to be addressed or where exceptional service might be replicated. The technique may be used during interviews, meetings, workshops and focus group sessions.

Humans have for several thousands of years exchanged knowledge through stories. Storytelling provides insight into the perspectives, beliefs and expectations of either internal or external stakeholders. Stories often include aspects such as:

- ambiguity, inaccuracies and distortions;
- attached meanings, emotions experienced and interpretations of events;
- explanation of an end-to-end journey;
- knowledge of the situation or context;
- links to other subjects (for example, other events, situations or stories);
- personal anecdotes;
- warnings, lessons learned and guidance.

The storytelling technique can be applied during an interview (see previous technique) or within a workshop or focus group (see Glossary of Terms and Techniques).

For storytelling to be effective, the interviewer or facilitator needs to create an environment where the stakeholder (or group of stakeholders) feels comfortable sharing stories. This should be achieved as part of setting expectations for the interview, workshop or focus group.

One approach for the application of the storytelling technique is for the interviewer or facilitator to share a personal story (for example, about a personal experience with a particular organisation, team, product or service). Through this approach the researcher demonstrates storytelling behaviour – permission is subconsciously granted to others to share stories. As a result of an initial story being shared, some stakeholders will automatically start to share their own personal stories without being prompted.

A second approach (that can be combined with or used independently from the researcher sharing a personal story) is for the stakeholder(s) to be encouraged to share stories. Prompts for this could include the researcher asking questions such as:

- Can you tell me about a previous negative (or positive) customer or user experience?
- Can you tell me about a personal experience of this product or service?
- Could you share an example of working with this team or organisation?
- Could you share your journey as a customer or user of the organisation's products or services?
- Can you tell me about a time when you felt frustrated/delighted with a product or service?

The storytelling technique is often focused on stories related to positive or negative experiences with an organisation, a team or particular products or services. For stakeholders that are comfortable with sharing stories, the technique can feel less intrusive than in comparison to an interviewer or workshop/focus group facilitator asking questions. Where applied in these circumstances it is possible for the technique to aid in the development of rapport and shared understanding. To apply the technique effectively, the researcher needs to actively listen and reflect on the meaning of the stories shared.

Applying storytelling

Table 10.5 describes situations where storytelling may be used to elicit information.

Table 10.5 Situations when storytelling is relevant

Situation	Description
Formal and planned approach to storytelling	Storytelling can take place within the context of an interview, focus group or workshop on a formal and planned basis. This approach includes managing proactively any stakeholder expectations about the technique and can include: • providing an explanation of the purpose of the technique and its benefits; • adding storytelling to the agenda. Where the interview, workshop or focus group is part of a series, this approach provides each interviewee or participant with the opportunity to share their stories. The stories can then be analysed and compared across the various interviews, workshops or focus groups.
Informal or unplanned approach to storytelling	Storytelling can take place within the context of an interview, focus group or workshop on an informal and unplanned basis. This approach involves the technique being applied without the researcher providing an explanation of its purpose or benefits. This can include: • The interviewer or facilitator sharing a personal story or insight prior to or during the course of the interview, focus group or workshop. • The interviewee or participant naturally sharing stories as part of the discussion. Where the interview, focus group or workshop is part of a series, this approach could appear unbalanced if only certain stakeholders have shared stories. The significance of this will need to be assessed depending on the context. If necessary, follow up interviews, focus groups or workshops (to include the opportunity for others to share stories) may need to be considered.
Other storytelling instances	Storytelling can also take place outside of the context of an interview, workshop or focus group. For example, a stakeholder may share a story with the researcher during a different meeting or during a break. The story could provide insight into the stakeholders' perspectives, beliefs and expectations. Listening to and remembering the story could support wider stakeholder engagement activities (see Glossary of Terms and Techniques).

An alternative use of storytelling involves sharing stories when communicating, rather than eliciting, information. Where communication is the focus, storytelling may be used to clarify, reassure or persuade. Example situations are:

- when explaining possible business scenarios to stakeholders;
- when presenting to stakeholders who are apprehensive about the impact of a proposed change;
- when reporting information to senior stakeholders who need to be convinced about a proposed change.

In each situation, a relevant narrative, or 'story', can help stakeholders to visualise and recognise the real-world outcomes that may result from introducing a new product or service.

Practical considerations

There are a variety of practical questions and considerations related to the use of the storytelling technique. Several of these are described in Table 10.6.

Table 10.6 Practical considerations for the use of storytelling

How to select a story to share?	The researcher selecting a story to share, to help encourage stakeholders to share stories, requires consideration. Aspects to consider include: • **Authenticity:** The story should ideally be personal and authentic. Where the researcher shares a story that is not their own (for example, a story from a friend or colleague about a recent customer experience) this should be disclosed in advance. If appropriate, the rationale for sharing this particular story should be explained. • **Length:** The time taken to share the story should not be excessive. The emphasis should be on helping the stakeholders feel comfortable in sharing their stories – this can be achieved through the researcher sharing a succinct story. • **Impact:** Ideally the story shared will have a positive and thought-provoking impact. It should in some way aid the individual or group to think or reflect. • **Optics:** The story shared should be considered in advance from the perspective of the potential positive or negative influence that it may have on stakeholders. The impact on rapport between the researcher and the interviewee or workshop/focus group participants should also be considered. For example, if the story selected involves aspects such as breaching rules, violence or celebration of mistreatment of customers this could result in a negative perception of the interviewer or facilitator. This type of story could also influence expectations negatively in terms of outcomes of the broader service design initiative.

(Continued)

Table 10.6 (Continued)

Situation	Description
How to overcome scepticism about the use of storytelling?	Some stakeholders are sceptical about the benefits of the storytelling technique. This is often due to it providing an indirect (as opposed to direct) means of obtaining information. Where scepticism exists, it can be helpful for the service designer to highlight that the technique helps to build empathy and understanding of users and customers. In addition, it can be helpful to share that the technique is recognised and used by academic researchers. In addition, some individuals are not comfortable with sharing personal stories. This could be due to: • **Privacy concerns:** Helping to establish a safe and secure environment for sharing stories can assist here. Applying the technique on a one-to-one basis or discussing any privacy concerns in advance can also be beneficial. • **Relevance concerns:** Explaining the relevance of the technique can assist here. Highlighting the importance of both divergent and convergent thinking may also be beneficial (see Glossary of Terms and Techniques). • **Broader organisational culture:** Setting expectations for behaviour within the context of the interview/workshop or focus group can help here. In addition, researchers may benefit from discussing impediments and risks of the application of the storytelling technique – if these are managed and controlled it may be possible to alleviate these. Finding a sponsor that is willing and able to support the use of a range of research methods (including storytelling) is critical to the success of a service design initiative. The sponsor visibly supporting the technique can be beneficial. The creation of a successful history of effective design and execution of storytelling can aid in overcoming scepticism regarding the technique. Finally, the service designer should always adapt their approach to the context in which they are working. If scepticism surrounding storytelling cannot be overcome, alternative techniques should be considered.
How to build confidence and competence in using the storytelling technique?	Colleagues, friends and family all share stories at different times – both within and outside the work context. For example, a friend may have returned from a holiday and shared insights into aspects that have delighted or frustrated them. This is an instance where the service designer can practice applying the storytelling technique. Through asking questions about the story and reflecting on its meaning – the service designer can build both confidence and competence in using the technique. If this practice is repeated, over time confidence can be built in the application of the technique within the work context.

Observation

Observation is a primary research technique that involves watching and listening while work is conducted. This may be a real or simulated work situation. The technique allows the researcher to obtain in-person insight into the environmental context.

The technique can be applied to a variety of situations, including the researcher observing:

- employees completing activities;
- customers or users engaging with products or services;
- behaviours within environments such as physical locations or online platforms.

Observation provides the researcher with access to tacit knowledge. This is knowledge that individuals find difficult to explain or share with others. Service safari, ethnographic study and contextual enquiry are techniques that can help to elicit more detailed information.

The stages of applying the observation technique are shown in Figure 10.2 (adapted from Cadle et al., 2021) and descriptions are provided in Table 10.7.

Figure 10.2 Observation stages

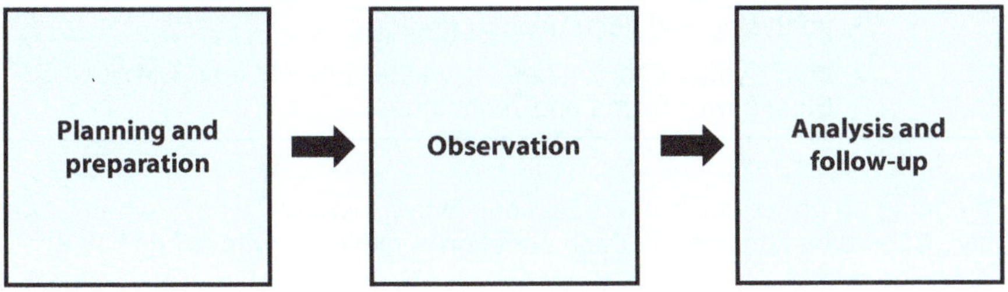

Table 10.7 Observation stage descriptions

Stage	Description
Planning and preparation	This involves considering the questions 'why?', 'what?', 'who?', 'when?', 'where?' and 'how?' in relation to the observation. These considerations are explored in further detail within Table 10.8.
Observation	This involves conducting the observation. There are three stages, as follows: • **Introductions:** The observer introduces themselves and builds rapport with the individuals being observed, confirming the rationale for conducting the observation, any expectations and the duration of the observation. • **Observation:** The main aspect of the observation. It is focused on the observer watching and listening to the activity or work, and documenting their observations. • **Close:** Agreeing next steps or follow up actions and thanking the participants for their time.
Analysis and follow-up	This involves analysing and sharing the findings from the observation. Examples include: • using insights from an observation to plan additional observations and assist with planning interview questions, workshop or focus group activities; • analysing and documenting findings; • identifying opportunities for waste removal (see TIMWOODS, Glossary of Terms and Techniques).

When planning an observation, the questions 'why?', 'what?', 'who?', 'when?', 'where?' and 'how?' should be considered. Each question is explored within Table 10.8.

Table 10.8 Observation planning and preparation questions

Planning consideration	Description
Why?	This consideration is focused on the goal or purpose of the observation. With a clear rationale, the likelihood of obtaining stakeholder support for the use of observation increases. The chances of successful design and execution of the technique are also enhanced.
What?	This consideration is focused on the specific activity, work or environment that will be observed. Before undertaking observation activity, the researcher should consider any legal, political, ethical or privacy concerns surrounding this. For example, it may not be appropriate to observe an individual discussing sensitive information with a manager, healthcare or legal professional.
Who?	This consideration is focused on three aspects. First who will be accountable for the organisation and completion of the observation? Will a single observer be used or is a team needed to complete this activity? Second, prior to the completion of observation it may be necessary to obtain permission from the individuals responsible for the environment in which the observation is planned. Examples include obtaining permission from: • the manager responsible for the activity within a department; • the owner or manager of a retail outlet (for example a retail outlet or coffee shop); • the individual responsible for an environment (for example the individual responsible for a park, shopping centre or online platform). Third, the individuals being observed. Aspects to be considered include: • **Breadth and range of individuals:** Do planned observations align with the purpose of the observation? Is the breadth and range of individuals balanced? • **Sourcing of individuals:** Who will engage and invite individuals to be observed? • **Management of individual expectations:** Who will be accountable for communication? How will individual expectations be managed? How will any questions from individuals about the observation activity be answered?

(Continued)

Table 10.8 (Continued)

Planning consideration	Description
When?	This consideration is focused on the specific timings of the observation. Aspects to be considered include: • **Date and time:** Is it appropriate to conduct the observation at the planned date and time? Are participants available? Does the date and time selected provide the observer with insight into both quiet and busy periods of activity? • **Duration:** How long will the observation last? Is the duration sufficient?
Where?	This consideration is focused on the location of the observation. There are two primary location options, virtual or in-person observation. Each has specific advantages and disadvantages. Virtual observation is conducted through use of video conferencing software. The observer uses functionality such as the sharing of cameras, microphones and if appropriate screens. This approach can lead to: • Reduced travel time and associated costs for the completion of observation activities (for example, a variety of remote individuals could be observed in different locations across the globe in a single day). • Reduced risk of injury or infection (particularly if the activity being observed is conducted within a hazardous or clinical environment). Virtual observation offers several disadvantages including: • Reduced insight for the observer into the environment. This is due to the observer being reliant on visual and auditory senses only. Significant reliance is also placed on the performance of supporting technologies.

Where? (Continued).

	The observer obtains no direct insight into aspects such as the: • smells present within the environment; • temperature of the environment; • texture of objects within the environment. • Reduced opportunity for the observer to build rapport with individuals being observed. For example, when an individual being observed goes for coffee break – the observer cannot easily join them for this. The second location option is for observation to be conducted in person. This approach can also lead to: • increased travel time and associated costs; • increased risk of injury or infection; • increased insight through the full range of the observers senses.
How?	This consideration is focused on the specifics of the observation itself. Aspects to be considered include: • **Standalone or series of observations:** Will the observation be a 'one off' or part of a broader series of observations? • **Recording:** How will insights from the observation be recorded? Will audio or visual recordings be used? Will the use of recordings influence behaviours? Has permission to record been obtained? • **Behaviours:** How will the presence of a researcher impact the behaviour of individuals being observed? How can expectations for behaviours be managed?

Applying observation

Several example situations where observation can be applied are explored within Table 10.9.

Table 10.9 Situations when observation is relevant

Situation	Description
Observing employee activity	When observation is applied to the context of an employee completing work, it enables the researcher to observe the environment in which this takes place. This includes challenges and opportunities faced by individuals that may not be mentioned during discussion in an interview, workshop or focus group. For example, an employee might need to spend time manually checking or transferring data between separate IT solutions. If this has a material impact on the delivery of the service, customer or employee experience this insight could be invaluable.
Observing customer activity	When observation is applied to the context of observing customers, the technique allows the researcher to observe both expected and planned uses of the product or service and also those that were not planned. For example, the customer could copy the terms and conditions for a product or service into an AI tool and request a summary. This insight could prove valuable for the design and testing of product terms and conditions.
Observing an environment	When observation is applied to the context of observing behaviours within an environment (such as a physical location or online platform) it allows the researcher to gain insight into the broader environment and the behaviours of actors within this. This can include actors such as employees and customers but will also include other actors (for example, relatives of customers/employees, third party providers and other nonstandard actors). For example, the observer could focus on a specific location such as a departure hall within an airport. The observer could as a result obtain insight into the range of actors and their interactions (for example, passengers, relatives, taxi drivers, thieves, cleaning and security staff). Due to observing the environment as a whole, insight into the broader problems and opportunities within this can be obtained.

Practical considerations

There are a variety of practical questions and considerations related to the use of the observation technique. Several of these are described in Table 10.10.

Table 10.10 Practical considerations for the design and completion of observation

Situation	Description
How to overcome legal, political, ethical or privacy concerns surrounding the use of the technique?	Where genuine legal, political, ethical or privacy concerns are raised in relation to the use of observation, the use of other investigation techniques should be considered.
How to reduce the anxiety level of individuals being observed?	If the 'why?' for observation is not clear or is not communicated – individuals being observed may feel anxious regarding its purpose. Employees being observed may be concerned about their employment. For example, they could imagine that the observation will lead to redundancy, a change in processes, line management or individual responsibilities. Likewise, customers being observed may be concerned about changes to the product or service. To reduce the risk of anxiety the reasons for conducting observation should be explained. Individuals being observed should also be able to ask questions surrounding this.
How to reduce the risk of changes in behaviour due to the presence of the observer?	The presence of an observer can impact the behaviours of individuals being observed. This is known as the 'Heisenberg principle'. The observer explaining the purpose of the observation to the individuals being observed and attempting to build some level of rapport with them can help. In addition, the observer should be mindful to attempt to blend in to the environment as much as possible. As a result, after some time has passed, those being observed are likely to revert to their natural behaviours. For example, an observer wearing a formal suit, holding a clipboard or pointing a camera at uninformed colleagues preparing a meal in a kitchen is highly likely to both get in the way and be noticed. In contrast, if the observer wears clothes similar to those in the environment and observes behaviour in an unobtrusive way, the risk of change in behaviour can reduce.

CONCLUSION

This chapter has focused on generic techniques that can be used to elicit information from a targeted demographic of stakeholders. These techniques are used to describe a situation or to observe how a situation develops. They may be augmented by a service safari to enable service designers to 'live' the service experience.

Service designers should consider the context in which the technique is being applied and, where necessary, adapt the use of the technique accordingly.

The development of a shared understanding of the techniques used in support of the delivery of service design services provides a foundation for collaboration and knowledge sharing between service design practitioners and their stakeholders. Over time, it is hoped that a shared toolkit of techniques can help develop continuous improvement for the service design profession.

11 GENERIC SERVICE DESIGN TECHNIQUES

Distributed demographic

INTRODUCTION

This chapter focuses on generic techniques that can be used to support the work conducted for any of the services described within the Service Design Service Framework (introduced in Chapter 2). The techniques covered in this chapter include:

- focus groups;
- workshops;
- surveys.

These techniques are used to elicit information from a distributed or broad demographic of stakeholders. This contrasts with the techniques focused on a targeted demographic of stakeholders, covered within Chapter 10.

While the techniques described here are used in support of the delivery of service design services, they are also used to deliver services performed by other roles. In particular, professional change roles such as user researcher, business analyst, business architect, change manager, project manager and product owner. When applying these techniques, the context and scope need careful consideration. While the application may focus on the features required of a product, it can also extend to cover the delivered service or even the entire customer journey.

THE TECHNIQUES

Focus groups

Description

A focus group is a means of uncovering perceptions about a specific product, service or business situation in an interactive group environment.

The technique enables the sharing of perspectives, ideas, beliefs and feedback from a range of participants and can be focused on the exploration of problems or opportunities. In contrast, workshops are often aimed at achieving consensus or achieving a specific objective (Cadle et al., 2021).

The stages of a focus group are shown in Figure 11.1 (adapted from Cadle et al., 2021).

Figure 11.1 Focus group stages

Each of the stages of the focus group is explored in Table 11.1.

Table 11.1 Focus group stage descriptions

Stage	Description
Planning and preparation	This involves considering the questions 'why?', 'what?', 'who?', 'how?', 'when?' and 'where?' in relation to the focus group. These considerations are explored in further detail within Table 11.2.
Focus group	This involves conducting the focus group itself. It involves three components: • **Introductions:** Includes aspects such as introducing the individuals, outlining the agenda, establishing rapport, confirming the purpose and goal of the focus group. • **Focus group content:** This is the main aspect of the focus group. It is focused on sharing of perspectives, ideas, beliefs and feedback from a range of participants. • **Close:** Includes agreement of any next steps or follow-up actions and thanking the participants for their time.
Analysis and follow-up	This involves analysing the findings from the focus group and completing any agreed actions. Examples include: • sharing insights, transcripts or focus group recordings; • thanking participants and providing any agreed participant rewards.

When planning a focus group, the questions 'why?', 'what?', 'who?', 'how?', 'when?' and 'where?' should be considered. Each question is explored within Table 11.2.

Table 11.2 Focus group planning and preparation questions

Planning consideration	Description
Why?	This consideration concerns the purpose of the focus group. With a clear rationale, the likelihood of obtaining stakeholder support for the use of the focus group technique increases. The chances of successful design and execution of the technique are also enhanced.
What?	This consideration concerns the specific topic of the focus group. For example, will the focus group be focused on a: • new or existing product or service; • problem or opportunity; • brand or organisation; • business situation (for example a proposal for change, innovation, department or team, policy, customer journey, scenario or persona).
Who?	This consideration concerns two aspects: Who will be accountable and who will attend? The first consideration identifies who will be accountable for the organisation and facilitation of the focus group. In some contexts, it may be appropriate for the organisation to facilitate the focus group using internal employees. Alternatively, an external third-party that specialises in the design and execution of focus groups can be utilised. The second consideration identifies the attendees of the focus group. Aspects to be considered include the: • **Breadth and range of participants:** Do planned attendees align with the purpose of the focus group? Is the range and breadth of participants balanced? • **Sourcing of participants:** Who will engage and invite focus group participants? • **Participant rewards:** Will attendees receive rewards for attending? Will rewards impact the breadth and range of participants? Will rewards impact participant behaviours? • **Management of participant expectations:** Who will be accountable for communication to participants? How will attendee expectations be managed? • **Permissions:** Has permission to capture and share data been obtained? Are participants expected to sign a contract with the organisers of the focus group?

(Continued)

Table 11.2 (Continued)

Planning consideration	Description
When?	This consideration concerns the specific timings of the focus group. Aspects to be considered include: • **Date and time:** Are participants available at the required date and time? Are participants in different time zones? • **Duration:** How much time will be allocated to the focus group? Is the duration sufficient given the planned agenda? Does the duration of the focus group align with participant expectations and rewards?
Where?	This consideration concerns the location of the focus group. For example, the focus group could be conducted using video conferencing software, on-site within the organisation or at a neutral off-site location. Aspects to be considered include: • **Availability:** Is the location available on the dates/times? • **Cost:** Are location costs within or outside of the available budget? • **Capacity:** Does the location have sufficient capacity? • **Accessibility:** Is the location accessible for attendees? Does the location have adequate transport links? Are technology platforms accessible and usable? • **Security:** Is the location secure? Are technology platforms secure? • **Optics:** Does the location of the focus group align with the wider environmental context and purpose of the organisation? For example, a charity hosting a focus group at an expensive location could be deemed to have misused charity resources.
How?	This consideration concerns the following aspects regarding the focus group: (1) **Standalone or focus group series:** Will the focus group be a 'one off' or part of a broader series of focus groups? (2) **Recording:** How will insights from the focus group be recorded? Will an individual be responsible? Will AI be used to complete recordings? Will audio or visual recordings be used? Will the use of recordings influence behaviours? Has permission to record the focus group been obtained? (3) **Agenda:** What is the agenda for the focus group?

(Continued)

Table 11.2 (Continued)

Planning consideration	Description
	Does the agenda align with the: • purpose of the focus group? • participant availability and expectations? • proposed focus group duration? A typical focus group agenda will include: • background to the focus group; • objectives of the focus group; • list of attendees; • timing, duration and location; • topics to explore; • confirmation of decisions made and next steps; • summary and close. (4) **Techniques:** Which techniques will be utilised during the focus group? For example: • personas; • lotus blossom; • customer journey maps, empathy maps; • prototyping, scenario analysis, storyboarding; • storytelling. (5) **Behaviours:** What behaviours are expected of focus attendees? How will behaviours be managed?

Applying focus groups

Example situations where focus groups can be applied are described in Table 11.3.

Table 11.3 Situations when focus groups are relevant

Situation	Description
Prototype demonstration and exploration	Focus groups can be used to demonstrate and obtain feedback on a prototype (see Glossary of Terms and Techniques). Where a prototype is used in conjunction with the focus group this can lead to: • obtaining insights into customer behaviours, needs, likes and dislikes; • validating assumptions; • uncovering problems or opportunities; • generating ideas for enhancement.
Problem or opportunity exploration	Focus groups can be used to explore a specific problem or opportunity. The intent here is to engage stakeholders to explore the nature of the problem or opportunity, uncover assumptions, identify where further research is needed and generate ideas for resolving the problem or grasping the opportunity.
Existing product or service exploration	Focus groups can be used to obtain insight into existing products or services. This can lead to: • obtaining insights into customer behaviours, likes and dislikes; • validating assumptions; • uncovering problems and opportunities; • generating ideas for product or service enhancement.
Brand or organisation	Focus groups can be used to explore a specific brand or organisation. The objective is to obtain feedback and insights about the brand and the organisation's reputation.
Business situation	Focus groups can be used to discuss a business situation where improvement is needed. Examples include a: • proposal for a change; • new (or existing) policy; • customer journey, scenario or persona.

The approach used to design and execute a focus group needs to be decided before organising the session. Alternative approaches used to design a focus group are described in Table 11.4.

Table 11.4 Focus group design options

Design option	Considerations
Engagement of a third-party specialist provider	The engagement of a third-party specialist provider to organise and facilitate a focus group can offers several advantages including providing access to: • **Specialist skills and knowledge:** Access to skilled and knowledgeable professionals that are able to design, organise and execute focus groups effectively. • **Focus group participants:** Access to a broad range of participants willing to attend focus groups. • **Purpose built locations and technologies:** Access to specialist locations and/or technologies that aid with focus group facilitation and analysis. This can include audio and video capture equipment and specialist AI tools. • **Independent facilitators:** Access to facilitators that are neutral and objective – they are unencumbered by the bias that would otherwise influence internal employed facilitators. • **Risk mitigation:** Research conducted is not visibly connected to the organisation. For example, a soft drinks manufacturer could use a focus group, organised via a third-party provider, to obtain insight into perceptions regarding the relationship between soft drinks and dental hygiene. The manufacturer can decide if it wants to acknowledge funding this research publicly. When engaging a third-party specialist to support the delivery of a focus group there are also several potential disadvantages: • **Increased costs:** The costs associated with sourcing and using third party focus group specialists. • **Impediments to information exchange:** The third-party specialist may limit access to primary focus group events or recordings. • **Misinterpretation of focus group insights:** The third-party specialist may have limited knowledge of the context, domain or industry for the focus group. • **Intellectual property risk:** The third-party specialist may share insights with others inadvertently. A robust contract that provides a foundation for the relationship with the third-party specialist is a prerequisite. When conducting focus groups, many organisations seek to augment external third-party specialist resources with internal employees. This helps to establish credibility and confidence in the completion of focus groups and, over time, can also help to build employee confidence and competence in the completion of focus groups.

(Continued)

Table 11.4 (Continued)

Design option	Considerations
Direct employee engagement with external customers	The direct engagement of external customers by internal employees within focus groups offers several advantages including: • **Increased direct customer engagement:** Employees within the organisation engage with customers, users and other external stakeholders during focus groups. This helps employees to gain insights and awareness regarding the voice of the customer. If used regularly, this approach can help to create a wider culture where it is routine to interact with and listen to customers. • **Reduced reliance on third-party specialists:** Employees build knowledge and skill in the design, organisation and execution of focus groups. Accordingly, the costs associated with engaging third-party specialists and any impediments to information exchange are avoided. The direct engagement of external customers within focus groups, by employees, has several potential disadvantages including: • **Risk of reputational damage:** Employees that do not have the knowledge and skills associated with the design and execution of focus groups may inadvertently damage customer relationships. This could result in reputational damage for the organisation. • **Risk of facilitator bias:** Employees facilitating focus groups are at risk of being influenced by their own bias. This bias stems from them being employed by the organisation organising the focus group.
Employees acting as proxies for customers	The use of employees as proxies for customers is relevant for organisations that have a direct relationship with their customers. For example, a customer (or user) facing retailer, financial services provider or government department could opt to arrange the focus group using internal employees as proxies. This can include the employees organising, facilitating and participating in the focus group. Advantages of this approach include: • **Reduced short-term costs:** The cost of external third-party specialists, external participant rewards and venue hire can be avoided. • **Reduced risks:** The risk of the focus group inadvertently sharing information or raising external customer expectations of change are avoided.

(Continued)

Table 11.4 (Continued)

Design option	Considerations
	Disadvantages of this approach include: • **Risk of participant bias:** Due to being employed by the organisation the views of the employees are inherently biased. This may limit the value of focus group findings. • **Limited breadth of demographic represented:** The organisation's employees may not represent some of the demographic categories targeted by the research. For example, they may not be able to offer insights from those below working age, in full time education, not employed or are retired. In addition, the views of individuals that have no prior knowledge or experience of the organisation, its products or services are also excluded. In addition, there is also a risk of broader cultural impact of using employees as representatives of the customer. Repeatedly using this approach could be interpreted as suggesting that the organisation's culture does not support value co-creation with customers.

Practical considerations

There are a variety of practical questions and considerations related to the use of the focus group technique. Several of these are described in Table 11.5.

Table 11.5 Practical considerations when designing and running focus groups

Consideration	Hints and tips
How to gain senior leader support for use of the focus group technique?	Finding a sponsor that is willing and able to support the use of a range of research methods (including focus groups) is critical to the success of a service design initiative. If senior leaders do not support the use of a focus group, the reasons should be investigated and, if possible, any impediments and risks managed. A track record of effective design and execution of focus groups within the organisation can help to build confidence in using the technique.
How to encourage participant engagement?	Finding a broad range of participants who are prepared to engage in focus group activities can be challenging. To combat this issue the organisation may need to engage specialist third parties. An alternative approach would involve building confidence and competence in using focus groups through using employees as proxies for external customers. This approach could be extended to include the friends and families of employees. Over time, through continual review of lessons learned and enhancement of the approach, confidence and competence in the engagement of participants can be increased.
Is the focus group a one off or part of a series?	If the focus group is likely to be repeated in the future (for example, on a quarterly, biannual or annual basis) the approach used in the design and execution of the focus group could differ. If the design and execution of the focus group is subject to change, the likelihood of accurate trend analysis diminishes.

Workshops

Workshops aim to achieve consensus, uncover insights and achieve predefined objective(s) in an interactive group environment. While workshops can on occasion include external stakeholders, they are predominantly facilitated and attended by internal employees.

The stages of a workshop are shown in Figure 11.2 (adapted from Cadle et al., 2021) and are described in Table 11.6.

Figure 11.2 Workshop stages

Table 11.6 Workshop stage descriptions

Stage	Description
Planning and preparation	This involves considering the questions 'why?', 'what?', 'who?', 'when?' 'where?' and 'how?' in relation to the workshop. These considerations are explored in further detail within Table 11.7.
Workshop	This involves conducting the workshop itself. A typical workshop agenda includes the following: (1) background to the workshop; (2) objectives of the workshop; (3) list of attendees; (4) timing, duration and location; (5) topics for discussion/ techniques to be used; (6) confirmation of decisions made and next steps; (7) summary and close.
Analysis and follow-up	This involves: • analysing the information gleaned during the workshop and any decisions made; • sharing insights, transcripts or workshop recordings; • thanking attendees for their participation; • conducting any agreed follow-up actions.

Table 11.7 Workshop planning and preparation questions

Planning consideration	Description
Why?	This consideration concerns the overall aim to be addressed by the workshop. This can include a mix of: **Achieving consensus:** For example, building stakeholder awareness and engagement for a new or existing: • product or service; • project; • strategy; • approach or policy. **Uncovering insights:** For example, exploring a: • persona or user role; • problem or opportunity; • scenario; • product or service – including associated definitions. A clear rationale increases the likelihood that the workshop planning, design and execution will be effective.
What?	In addition to achieving consensus and uncovering insights, workshops can also aim to achieve specific objectives such as: • to identify specific problems with a business process; • to generate ideas about a proposed new service. Situations where a workshop may be relevant are described within Table 11.8.
Who?	This consideration concerns three aspects. First, who will be accountable for the organisation and facilitation of the workshop? Aspects to be considered include: • **Facilitator relationship with workshop participants:** Does the facilitator have an existing relationship with workshop participants? Will any existing relationships influence (either positively or negatively) the achievement of workshop objectives?

<table>
<tr>
<td>Who? (Continued)</td>
<td>

- **Facilitator competence and experience:** Does the facilitator have the necessary level of competence and experience to organise and facilitate the workshop? Will any support be required?
- **Facilitator bias:** Will the facilitator remain objective? Will the selected facilitator undermine or enhance the credibility of workshop outputs or decisions?
- **Co-facilitators:** Will additional facilitators be required to support the facilitation of the workshop?

Second, who will attend the workshop? Aspects to be considered include:

- **Expertise of participants:** Do the attendees have the required knowledge and expertise to effectively engage in the content of the workshop? Are those with the required expertise available to attend the workshop?
- **Seniority of participants:** Is the seniority of participants balanced? Do participants have sufficient authority for any required validation?
- **Breadth and range of participants:** Do the planned attendees represent a sufficient breadth of expertise, and viewpoints?
- **Relationships between participants:** What is the nature of the relationships between planned attendees? Could pre-existing relationships between participants influence (either positively or negatively) the workshop?
- **Application of other techniques:** Have attendees provided insight via other techniques (such as a survey or an interview)? What insights were obtained from these techniques? Do the insights provide help with planning and executing the workshop?

Third, who will scribe the results from the workshop. Aspects to be considered include:

- **Scribe relationship with the facilitator(s):** Will the facilitator and scribe work well together?
- **Scribe relationship with workshop participants:** Will any existing relationships influence (either positively or negatively) the achievement of workshop objectives?
- **Scribe competence and experience:** Does the proposed scribe have the necessary level of competence and experience? Will any support be required?
- **Scribe bias:** Will the scribe remain objective in the documentation of outputs? Will the selected scribe undermine or enhance the credibility of workshop outputs?
- **Use of AI:** Will AI be used to support or replace the scribe? Does the intended use of AI align with organisational policy?

</td>
</tr>
</table>

(Continued)

Table 11.7 (Continued)

Planning consideration	Description
When?	This consideration concerns the specific timings of the workshop. Aspects to be considered include: • **Date and time:** Are participants available at the required date and time to attend the workshop? Are participants in different time zones? • **Duration:** How long will the workshop last? Is the duration sufficient given the planned agenda?
Where?	This consideration is focused on the location of the workshop. Aspects to consider align with those discussed for focus groups (see Table 11.2).

How?	This consideration concerns the structure and organisation for the workshop. Aspects to be considered include:
	• **Standalone:** Will the workshop be a 'one off' or part of a broader series of workshops? Should the objectives be decomposed into sub-objectives and a duration applied to each?
	• **Recording:** What technologies will be used in support of the workshop? Will an online or physical whiteboard be used? Will AI be used to record? Will audio or visual recordings be used? Has permission to record the workshop been obtained?
	• **Techniques:** What techniques will be utilised during the workshop? This could include techniques covered elsewhere within this book. For example:
	  • personas;
	  • lotus blossom, brainwriting/brainstorming and affinity analysis;
	  • customer journey maps, empathy maps;
	  • service blueprints, value stream analysis, value proposition and service definition canvas;
	  • prototyping, scenario analysis, storyboarding;
	  • business readiness assessment;
	  • storytelling.
	• **Behaviours:** See Table 11.9: How should participant behaviours be managed?

Applying the workshop technique

Several example situations where workshops can be applied are explored within Table 11.8.

Table 11.8 Situations when a workshop is relevant

Situation	Description

Project initiation	Workshops can be used to engage stakeholders in the launch of a new project or initiative and to explore aspects such as:
	• terms of reference/project initiation document including:
	  • objectives;
	  • scope;
	  • constraints;
	  • authority;
	  • risks and impacts;
	• stakeholders and associated communication plans;
	• resources, timescales and plans.
	Stakeholders are provided with an opportunity to share their views on the project and to shape its future progression. When applied effectively, this can provide the project team with a means of identifying the level of stakeholder resistance or support.

Problem or opportunity exploration	As with focus groups, workshops can be used to explore a specific problem or opportunity and to engage with relevant stakeholders. A workshop can help to elicit information about the nature of the problem or opportunity, understand different views and perspectives and uncover assumptions
Divergent thinking/idea generation	Workshops can be used as a mechanism to generate ideas about a particular problem/opportunity or solution (see design thinking, Glossary of Terms and Techniques).
Output exploration and validation	Workshops can be used as a mechanism to create and validate deliverables and other outputs. For example, a workshop could be used to create and validate an empathy map or a storyboard (see Glossary of Terms and Techniques).
Other business situations	Workshops can be used to explore almost any business situation. Example topics include: • strategy; • organisational structure; • policy; • customer or user preferences; • competitor behaviour; • key supplier or partner; • regulatory or compliance rules or guidelines.

Practical considerations

Practical considerations related to the use of workshops are described in Table 11.9.

Table 11.9 Practical considerations for the design and completion of workshops

Consideration	Hints and tips
Can 'workshop fatigue' be avoided?	Some organisations view workshops as a default means to address business situations. Where this approach persists, there is a risk that stakeholders become tired of attending workshops and become disillusioned or disengaged with the workshop technique. This can lead to stakeholders failing to attend or participate fully in workshop activities. Service designers should be careful to avoid the trap of 'using workshops by default'. When a workshop is suggested, they should be comfortable asking 'why?' and, if appropriate, suggesting an alternative technique or range of techniques. When applying the workshop technique service designers should be mindful of the concept of co-creation. This should help ensure that workshop agendas, activities and outputs are co-created with stakeholders.
What is the ideal ratio between workshop facilitators and attendees?	In general, an experienced facilitator should feel comfortable facilitating a group of between 10–12 attendees. Where a larger workshop is necessary (above 12 attendees) the facilitator may need the support of co-facilitators. The ratio between co-facilitators and attendees should stay roughly the same. For example, if there is a need to facilitate a workshop with 20–24 attendees, the main facilitator would need the support of one other facilitator.
How should participant behaviours be managed?	Facilitators need to consider the workshop attendees and consider how they may prefer to engage in the discussion and how to manage unhelpful participant behaviours. It is helpful to set out expectations regarding engagement and behaviour at the outset of the workshop. This also provides a basis for reminding participants should they fail to adhere to the expectations during the workshop. Where a participant continually demonstrates behaviour that does not align with the agreed behaviours, the facilitator may need to conduct a one-to-one discussion with the participant. This can help to determine if there are other factors affecting the participant's behaviour and whether an alternative means of participating is needed.

(Continued)

Table 11.9 (Continued)

Consideration	Hints and tips
How can a facilitator manage conflict?	Some level of disagreement is to be expected within a workshop. The facilitator should explain at the outset of the workshop the behaviour expected from participants should conflict situations arise. Where a conflict situation arises, the facilitator should remain calm and recognise and acknowledge the conflict. The facilitator may consider pausing the workshop and conducting separate discussions with those in conflict and possibly allow individuals time to reflect. A recognised approach such as the Fisher, Ury and Patton principled negotiation process can be helpful (Fisher et al., 2011). This approach comprises four steps: (1) Separate the people from the problem. (2) Focus on the interests rather than the positions adopted. (3) Identify different options available to resolve the situation. (4) Define criteria to help evaluate the options objectively.

Surveys

Surveys are often referred to as 'questionnaires' and are used by organisations for many reasons. For example, customers may be asked to provide an 'evaluation' stating how satisfied they are with a product or service, or they may be asked for information about their requirements regarding a particular service or product.

A survey uses questions to obtain information from a group of stakeholders. The stakeholders may be distributed geographically, or there may be a large volume of stakeholders. Surveys can be used to collate both quantitative and qualitative data.

A survey consists of three sections. These sections are explained in Table 11.10.

Table 11.10 The sections of a survey

Section	Description
Heading	This section sets out the purpose of the survey and any instructions or information about its completion and submission.
Classification	This section is used to capture data about the survey respondent such as: • Demographic: for example – age, gender, salary, address, nationality, qualification level; • Role: for example – job title, department, length of service, grade.
Data	This section contains the questions to be answered that are specific to the topic or situation under investigation. Questions may elicit quantitative or qualitative information.

Formal research surveys use all three sections described in Table 11.10. They provide a foundation for rigorous analysis of the data collected in combination with insights obtained about the respondent from the classification section. The design of this type of survey can take longer as the data section needs to be very precise.

Some surveys are less formal and focus solely on the 'data' collection section, possibly with an overview 'heading' section. For example, an airport asking customers to rate the 'check-in' experience might provide a device with three emojis representing 'happy, mediocre, unhappy'. The heading section for this type of survey may be a short instruction such as 'rate your check-in experience'. Similarly, some surveys can ask respondents to provide a 'thumbs up' or 'thumbs down' response to a question. Figure 11.3 provides an example of each of these types of survey.

Figure 11.3 Survey examples using emoji icons or thumbs (Image sourced from Microsoft 365 library of creative content)

Heading section

The heading section sets out the purpose of the survey and any instructions or information about its completion. The heading section is described in Table 11.11.

Table 11.11 The survey heading section elements

Element	Description
Survey title (or name)	The survey title (or name) identifies the survey to the potential respondent and enables it to be distinguished from other surveys. The title should capture the prospective survey respondents attention and encourage them to complete the survey. Example survey titles include: • customer satisfaction survey; • annual employee survey; • rate your baggage collection experience; • customer experience questionnaire.
Time to complete	The 'time to complete' element of the heading sets expectations for the respondent of the time needed to complete the survey. The information provided should be as accurate as possible. For example, if the time to complete is '10 minutes' and the respondent is only half way through the survey after 7–8 minutes, this indicates that the 'time to complete' is inaccurate. Consequently, there is an increased risk that the respondent will not complete the survey.
Submission deadline	The submission deadline is the latest date (and possibly time) by which the respondent should complete the survey.
Purpose	The purpose describes the rationale for the survey. The purpose should align with the survey title and encourage the respondent to participate in the survey.
Respondent reward	The respondent reward outlines any items that are available to survey respondents. For example, respondents may be entered into a prize draw or receive a gift following survey completion.
Return instructions	The return instructions provide the respondent with the information about returning the survey. Electronic surveys usually enable respondents to submit the survey with a click of a button. Paper-based surveys are rarely used as they require more effort to complete and return. Where a paper-based survey is used, clear guidance on returning the document is needed. This must include the return address and, possibly, a named person. The effort required to return a paper-based survey inevitably reduces the volume of survey responses.

(Continued)

Table 11.11 (Continued)

Element	Description
Legal notices	The legal notices element provides information on legal or compliance aspects that are relevant to the completion of the survey. For example, the legal notice may state how the data collected in the survey will be used, stored or shared (in line with data protection compliance requirements). This element may also include aspects such as how to consent to the data usage and storage, guarantees regarding anonymity and the way in which questions or concerns about the survey can be raised.

Classification section

The classification section is used to capture information about the survey respondent. The breadth, depth and range of questions asked in this section will vary depending on the context for the survey. For example, a survey of external customers would have a different classification section than a survey aimed at internal employees. Classification questions confirm the demographic of the respondent and may include questions that concern aspects such as age, gender, salary, address, nationality. If the survey is focused on internal employees, there are likely to be questions on aspects such as user role, department, length of service, grade.

The purpose of the classification section is to understand how the information (captured within the data section) relates to a particular demographic. For example, if an organisation wants to understand how a product or service would appeal to customers within the 18–25 years age demographic, the classification section provides a basis for identifying these respondents and analysing their responses.

The completion rate for a survey decreases when respondents are unable or unwilling to complete the classification section. Some respondents may refuse to complete the survey if they feel the questions asked are too intrusive or may even provide false information. This is a risk where the questions asked concern topics such as age or salary. A further risk of non-completion arises if the classification section contains too many questions and is very time-consuming to complete.

Survey designers sometimes omit the classification section where it is not felt relevant or helpful.

Data section

The data section contains the questions to be answered by survey respondents. The wording of individual questions requires careful consideration. Poorly worded questions can deter potential respondents from completing a survey and also impede the interpretation and analysis of survey results.

The volume and type of questions asked should be considered with regard to the context, the desired information outcomes and the likely motivation of potential respondents. An example of a limited survey is shown in Figure 11.4.

Figure 11.4 Example survey for a taxi service

Reply to this text to rate your driver using a number:

5 = Amazing
4 = Good
3 = Ok
2 = Poor
1 = Unacceptable

The example question shown in Figure 11.4 doesn't request classification information, but the software used for the survey is likely to be linked to a specific driver and provide the classification information. Taxi service software applications are typically linked to individual customers and record personal information. Therefore, the respondent information is known, as is the date and time of the journey and rating response. The heading section is not formally utilised in this example, but the question and the context when it is posed provide sufficient clarification.

When using short surveys such as that shown in Figure 11.4 survey designers should be aware of response fatigue. For example, if a taxi driver takes the same customer on the same journey on each working day of the year, it is unlikely that the customer would want to complete the survey on each and every occasion. If the organisation persists in sending the survey at the end of each journey, it could frustrate the customer and detract from the overall customer experience.

A variety of different approaches may be used to design survey questions and response scales. Example survey questions and response scales used to elicit quantitative data are shown in Figure 11.5.

An alternative approach to the style of survey questions shown in Figure 11.5 is to ask questions focused on eliciting qualitative data. This style of question can be used independently or in combination with questions aimed at eliciting quantitative data. Example questions aimed at eliciting qualitative data are shown in Figure 11.6.

Figure 11.5 Example question types and response scales aimed at eliciting quantitative data

Binary questions		
	Yes	No
Would you recommend the product to a friend?		
Did you find the product easy to use?		

Numerical questions					
How would you rate the following:					
	Very dissatisfied				Very satisfied
	1	2	3	4	5
Product quality					
Price					
Product packaging					
Staff responsiveness					

Likert scale questions					
How would you rate the following:					
	Strongly disagree	Disagree	Neutral	Agree	Strongly agree
I find the service easy to use					
I liked using the service					
I am likely to recommend the service to a friend					
I am likely to purchase the service again within the next 6 months					

Figure 11.6 Example question types and response scales aimed at eliciting qualitative data

Free format response area	
Which part(s) of the customer experience did you enjoy the most - and why?	
What else could we do to improve the customer experience?	
Do you have any further comments or suggestions?	

Using surveys

Several example situations where surveys can be applied are explored within Table 11.12.

Table 11.12 Situations when surveys are relevant

Situation	Description
Survey repeated at regular time intervals	Surveys can be sent out at regular time intervals such as on a monthly, quarterly, biannual or annual basis. For example, many organisations may use a survey on an annual or biannual basis to obtain feedback from employees or customers. The use of a survey in this situation can help obtain insights into trends – such as changes in likes, dislikes or behaviours – over a designated period of time.
Survey focused on individual transactions	Surveys can be sent out in connection with an individual transaction. For example, an organisation could request that a customer provides feedback following the completion of a specific activity such as responding to a customer service enquiry. The use of the survey in this situation can help obtain feedback and identify trends where immediate, rectifying action is needed.
Survey as a 'one off' activity	Surveys can be used to explore opinions as a 'one off' activity. For example, the survey could be initiated in order to explore a specific business situation such as: • proposal for a change; • new innovation; • department or team; • new (or existing) policy; • product or service; • specific brand or organisation; • specific event.

Practical considerations

Table 11.13 identifies practical questions and considerations that survey designers should be aware of when creating and distributing a survey.

Table 11.13 Practical considerations for the design and completion of surveys

Consideration	Hints and tips
When and how will the survey be distributed?	A variety of different technologies are available to assist in the distribution of surveys. Several technologies also enable immediate access to survey response data. When using technology, survey designers should ensure that it is sufficiently robust, usable, accessible and secure. If survey respondents are unable or unwilling to use technology to respond to survey questions, alternative methods (such as a paper-based survey) may need to be considered. The timing of survey distribution can impact response rates positively or negatively. For example, sending a question about a hotel 'check in' experience six months after the hotel stay is unlikely to yield high response rates. In comparison, asking hotel customers as they log in to the hotel Wi-Fi to rate the hotel 'check-in' experience is likely to yield a higher response rate.
Will the survey be repeated in the future?	If a survey is likely to be repeated in the future (for example, on a quarterly, biannual or annual basis) the approach used in the survey questions and response scales should allow for quick comparison between different survey instances. If questions between individual instances of the survey are subject to change, the likelihood of accurate trend analysis between the survey instances diminishes.
How will data be protected?	The data captured within a survey should be protected by design. An assessment of the type of data captured, the applicable laws and compliance obligations and the commercial value of the data should all be considered. If necessary, specialist advice and guidance on these aspects should be sought.
Can the survey be combined with other investigation techniques?	If positioned in advance, it is possible to investigate survey responses in additional detail using techniques such as interviews, focus groups or workshops. Permission should be sought from respondents prior to contacting them to conduct additional investigation.

CONCLUSION

This chapter has focused on generic techniques that can be used to elicit information from a broad demographic of stakeholders. These techniques require thought and preparation in order to be applied effectively and obtain relevant information. These techniques have been applied for many years and are proven to be highly beneficial when researching views and eliciting information. The techniques are used by many change professionals, including business analysts, user researchers and business architects. They are also essential techniques within the service design toolkit. However, service designers should consider the context in which they intend to apply these techniques to ensure they use them flexibly and adapt them accordingly.

12 SERVICE DESIGN FRAMEWORKS

INTRODUCTION

Service design has emerged as a relatively recent discipline that has much to offer organisations. The toolkit of techniques available to service designers is extensive and many result from established disciplines, such as business analysis. However, there are also many established frameworks that, when applied, offer service designers the opportunities to review a situation or service from different perspectives and gain additional insights.

This chapter introduces the following methods and frameworks:

- Soft Systems Methodology (SSM);
- Service Design Gaps Model;
- Culture Pyramid;
- Capability Analysis and Leverage Model (CALM);
- Change Paradigm Model.

These approaches offer a wealth of views that may be used during the investigation, analysis, definition and deployment of services.

SOFT SYSTEMS METHODOLOGY

Chapter 1 introduced systems thinking and SSM, which was developed by Professor Peter Checkland (1981). SSM offers an approach to applying systems thinking to business situations, which are often complex and require effective investigation, analysis and option evaluation before determining which actions to take.

An adapted version of SSM is illustrated in Figure 12.1.

Figure 12.1 Application of SSM to the service context

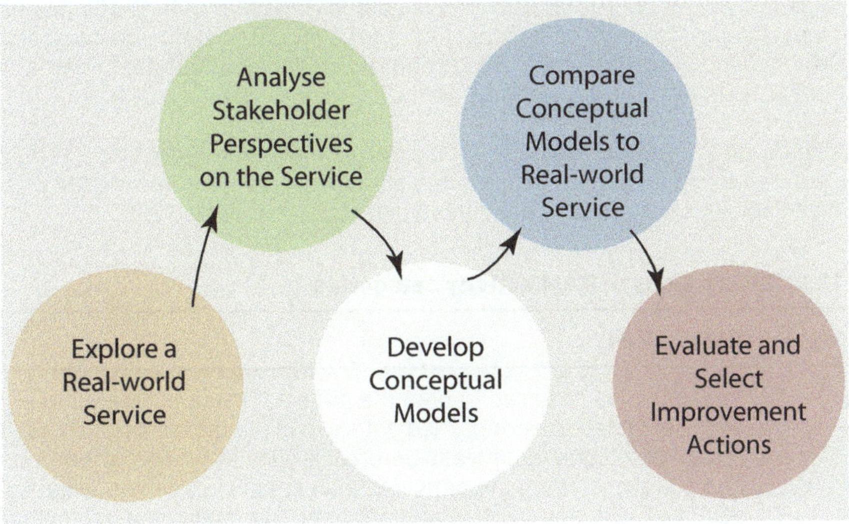

The stages of this model are defined in Table 12.1.

Table 12.1 SSM stages from Figure 12.1

Stage	Description
Explore a real-world service	Service designers apply a range of investigative techniques to explore the characteristics and concerns regarding a service. Visual representations are developed for the service using techniques such as rich pictures and fishbone diagrams (see Glossary of Terms and Techniques).
Analyse stakeholder perspectives on the service	Service designers apply relevant service design techniques to identify stakeholders and analyse their different viewpoints regarding the service. Perspective analysis using CATWOE (see Glossary of Terms and Techniques) is a key technique used in this stage.
Develop conceptual models	The defined stakeholder perspectives are modelled using conceptual activity modelling techniques. Value Stream or Business Activity Modelling are key techniques used in this stage. These models represent an ideal future service.
Compare conceptual models to real-world service	The conceptual models are compared with the representations of the current real-world service. Gaps and inconsistencies to be addressed are identified during this stage.
Evaluate and select improvement actions	Options to address the gaps and inconsistencies are identified using techniques such as ideation and divergent thinking. These options are evaluated to consider their viability, feasibility and desirability. This results in the identification of the improvement actions to be taken.

Modelling perspectives using business activity models

A Business Activity Model (BAM) provides conceptual models of the activities needed to fulfil a particular stakeholder perspective. These models help the service designer to obtain a holistic view of the activities required to develop and deploy an effective service that meets stakeholder requirements.

Value stream diagrams also provide a conceptual view of the activities required to deliver a service but focus on realising the customer's value item. A BAM offers an alternative view as it categorises activities as described in Table 12.2.

Table 12.2 Descriptions of BAM activity categories

Category	Description
Planning	The activities required to plan the different aspects related to a service. These are concerned with capability elements such as staff resources, technical infrastructure, Service Definition, promotion and suppliers. Planning activities also set performance targets, such as OKRs and KPIs, which are used to monitor the performance of different aspects regarding the service.
Enabling	The activities that acquire or replenish the resources needed to deliver the service. These activities are dependent upon the planning activities. For example, where the staffing requirements are determined during planning, the development of the staffing capability is enacted during enabling.
Doing	The activities concerned with the delivery of the service. These activities tend to be summarised so may be modelled as one or two activities.
Monitoring	The activities that are concerned with monitoring the performance of the different elements that are required to deliver the service. Monitoring activities apply the measure defined in the planning activities to determine if the anticipated performance has been achieved. It may be necessary to take action where there are discrepancies between the anticipated and actual performance.
Controlling	The actions taken to address issues identified during monitoring. This activity is typically drawn as one overarching activity because any of the other activities modelled may need to be revisited to determine the required actions.

An example BAM for the restaurant scenario is shown in Figure 12.2.

Figure 12.2 Example BAM for the restaurant scenario (note: P = planning, E = enabling, D = doing, M = monitoring C = controlling)

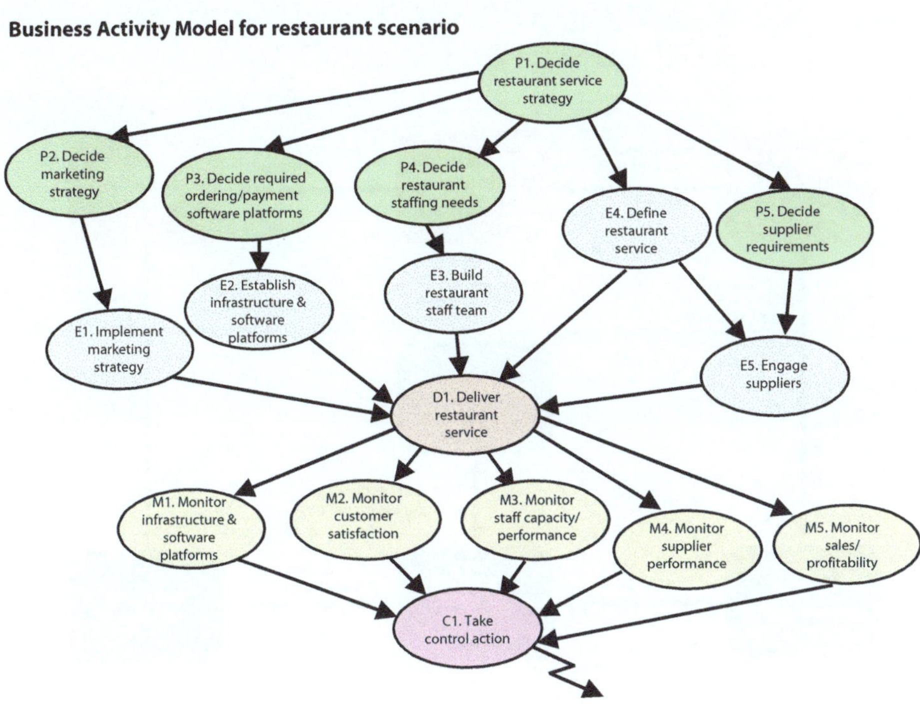

SERVICE DESIGN GAPS MODEL

The Gaps Model of Service Quality (Bitner et al., 2010; Parasuraman et al., 1985) identified key areas where there may be an inconsistency between different aspects of product delivery. For example, the 'customer gap' concerns the gap between the service expected by customers and the service they perceive to have been delivered.

The Service Design Gaps Model has been adapted from this model to align with service design work. This version of the model is shown in Figure 12.3.

Figure 12.3 The service design gaps model (Adapted from Bitner et al., 2010; Parasuraman et al., 1985; © Assist Knowledge Development)

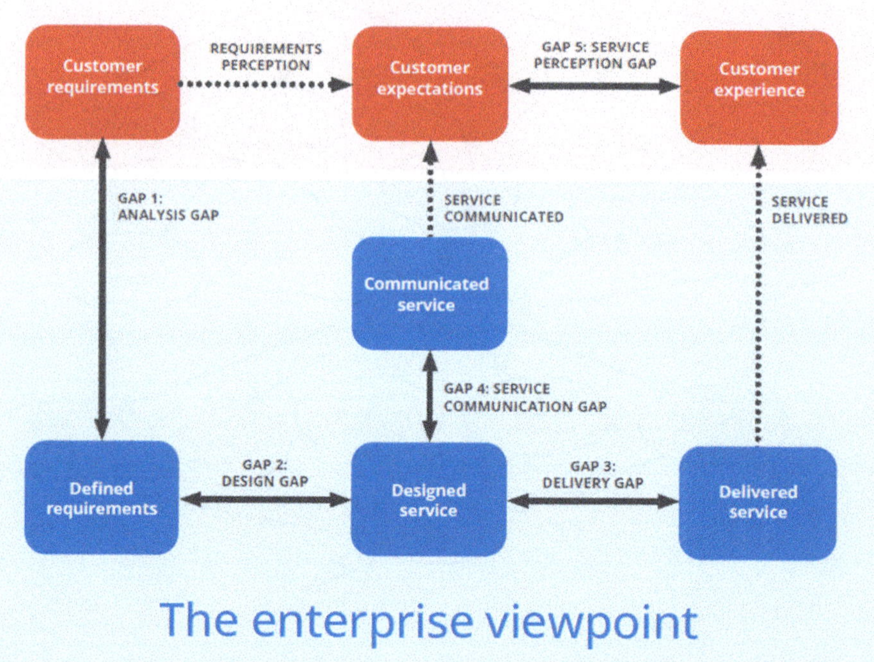

The five gaps identified in the service design gaps model are described in Table 12.3.

Table 12.3 The five service design gaps

The SD gap	Description
Gap 1: the analysis gap	The gap between the customers' requirements regarding the service and how the service requirements are defined by the organisation. This results from a failure to apply effective requirements engineering techniques.
Gap 2: the design gap	The gap between the defined service requirements and the designed service. This results from a failure to understand the service requirements and, accordingly, design the services that the customers want and expect.
Gap 3: the delivery gap	The gap between the designed service and the service delivered to customers. This results from a failure that occurs during service delivery, despite the service design meeting the customer needs.
Gap 4: the service communication gap	The gap between the designed service and the service promises made to customers. This results from a failure to communicate accurately the characteristics of the service offered by the organisation.
Gap 5: the service perception gap	The gap between the service expected by the customer and the service experienced by the customer. This may result from any of the other gaps.

The adapted model highlights two viewpoints involved in service delivery: the customer and the enterprise.

- The customer viewpoint concerns gaps resulting from a comparison of the following:
  - The original requirements that the customer has regarding the service. These determine why a customer engages with an organisation to purchase a service.
  - The expectations held by the customer regarding the service. These determine how well the customer expects to feel regarding a delivered service.
  - The actual experience encountered by the customer.

  Comparing the requirements to be fulfilled, the actual service provided and the perception of the experience causes customers to hold a view regarding the organisation and the standard of service offered. This view may be positive where all requirements are met and the service provided left a good impression. Alternatively, there may be situations where the requirements are not fulfilled or, even where they are met but the experience wasn't positive; in these situations, customers tend to be unhappy and may complain. Even worse, they may decide not to engage with the organisation but switch to a different service provider. Receiving complaints about a service helps organisations to understand where improvement is needed. Where customers fail to engage, the organisation may not realise that the service did not meet the customer needs.

- The enterprise viewpoint is concerned with the activities required to develop and deploy a service. Where these activities are not carried out consistently and with the required level of expertise, the gaps described in Table 12.3 can result and, accordingly, diminish the service provided.

Where service designers apply the gaps model, they are able to analyse issues raised regarding the customer perception of the service. This analysis should identify the root causes of problems by asking the following questions:

- Were the different types of customer requirements analysed and defined? Did this include non-functional and customer experience requirements in addition to defining the service features to be delivered?
- Was the service designed to fulfil the defined requirements?
- Did the delivered service align with the service design and fulfil the required value proposition?
- Did the service communications raise customer expectations or make promises that have not been fulfilled by the delivered service?

Customers may raise issues about a delivered service at any point in their customer journeys. The Service Design Gaps Model offers a framework for analysing where a service failed to meet customer needs and uncovering the root cause of these issues.

CULTURE PYRAMID

Organisational culture has the potential to support the quality of Service Deployment. Within organisations, there may be defined values that influence the culture but, equally, there may be unacknowledged shared values or beliefs that also have an impact. Service designers need to consider the culture of the organisation and ensure that they understand the implications this culture might have regarding a service.

Some organisations wish to develop a service culture where the staff are focused on delivering service excellence. Inevitably, this requires clear values that are communicated by the leadership. Without this, the staff involved in delivering the service may have different views on the service standards to achieve. An effective service culture can only develop where the customer expectations and requirements are known.

Organisational culture is defined as follows:

> The shared values and beliefs that are taken for granted by members of an organisation yet drive strategy, tactics and behaviours.
>
> Paul and Lovelock (2019)

The nature of organisational culture has been extensively researched. Schein's view of culture is represented in Figure 12.4.

Figure 12.4 Levels of organisational culture (Schein, 2016)

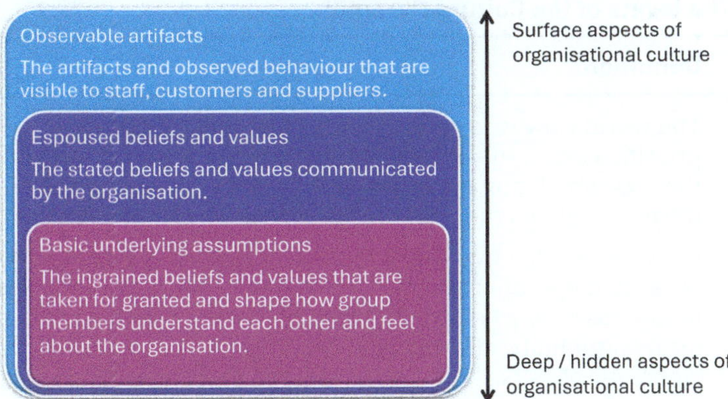

These three levels reflect how individuals hold underlying assumptions about their colleagues and the organisation. These assumptions underpin and provide a rationale for the set of shared values held by those working within the organisation. These values are then demonstrated by the behaviours of those working in the organisation. The underlying assumptions and shared values levels are rarely expressed or observable. However, they underpin the behaviours workers demonstrate that are evident to those engaging with the organisation, such as customers.

The Culture Pyramid defines how the leaders' world view directs the formal and informal elements that express the cultural aspects of an organisation. The Culture Pyramid model is shown in Figure 12.5.

Figure 12.5 The culture pyramid (© Assist Knowledge Development)

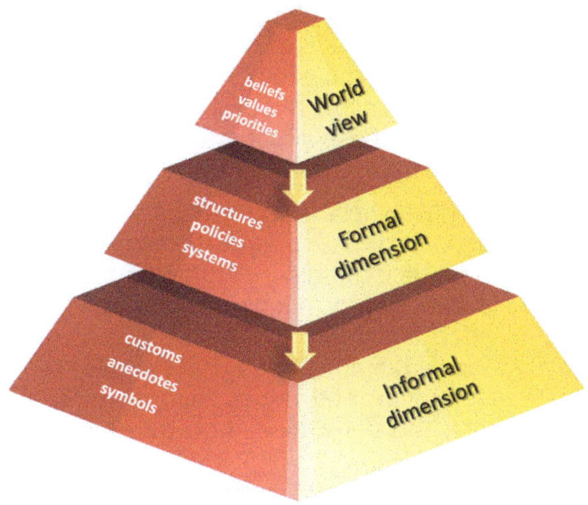

The three levels represented in the Culture Pyramid are defined in Table 12.4.

Table 12.4 The levels of the Culture Pyramid

Level	Definition
The world view	The world view is formed by the leaders' values, beliefs and priorities about the organisation. This determines how they perceive the 'system' that is the organisation, and informs their VMOST and the expectations they have for those working in the organisation. For example, the owners of the restaurant have a world view regarding the rationale that explains why the restaurant exists. In this case, they believe that the restaurant is embedded in the local community, offering high-quality meals using local produce wherever possible. They also want the employees to be from within the community and the restaurant to meet the needs of that community.
Formal dimension	The formal dimension comprises the structures, processes, policies and systems that determine how the organisation is governed and managed. These elements also determine the working practices that define how the organisation should operate, the rules and procedures to be applied and the measures used to assess performance. For example, the restaurant staff are organised into serving and cooking teams, both with a line manager. The teams apply several policies such as the restaurant's health and safety policy. The teams also use the meals ordering and delivery system.
Informal dimension	The informal dimension concerns the everyday behaviours that may be perceived within the organisation. The employees have assimilated and interpreted the world view and formal dimension and have a tacit understanding of the organisational culture and accepted ways of working. The cultural web (Whittington et al., 2019) identifies aspects such as stories, symbols, rituals and routine, and these are all areas where the informal dimension of the cultural pyramid may be perceived. Anecdotes told about previous incidents or experiences, and the reaction to those situations, often highlight cultural attitudes prevalent in an organisation. For example, the owners in the restaurant scenario believe in offering good service and have formalised this view in the restaurant's Service Definition. All the employees are made aware of the world view and formal definition when joining the team. This knowledge, coupled with their perception of the behaviours demonstrated by the other restaurant employees, provide a basis for their assumptions and values regarding the organisational culture. In turn, this determines how they behave when working at the restaurant.

The Culture Pyramid defines three levels that may be used to analyse an organisation's culture. This approach takes a 'top-down' view of culture, evaluating the beliefs and values of the senior leaders and considering how these are developed into formal definitions that are interpreted at the informal level.

CAPABILITY ANALYSIS AND LEVERAGE MODEL (CALM)

There are many aspects to consider when introducing a new service or enhancing an existing service. While the Gaps Model described earlier is concerned with the entire process from customer requirements to customer experience, CALM looks at the capability gaps between an organisation's current state and the target state to be achieved. The model is shown in Figure 12.6.

Figure 12.6 CALM approach (© Assist Knowledge Development)

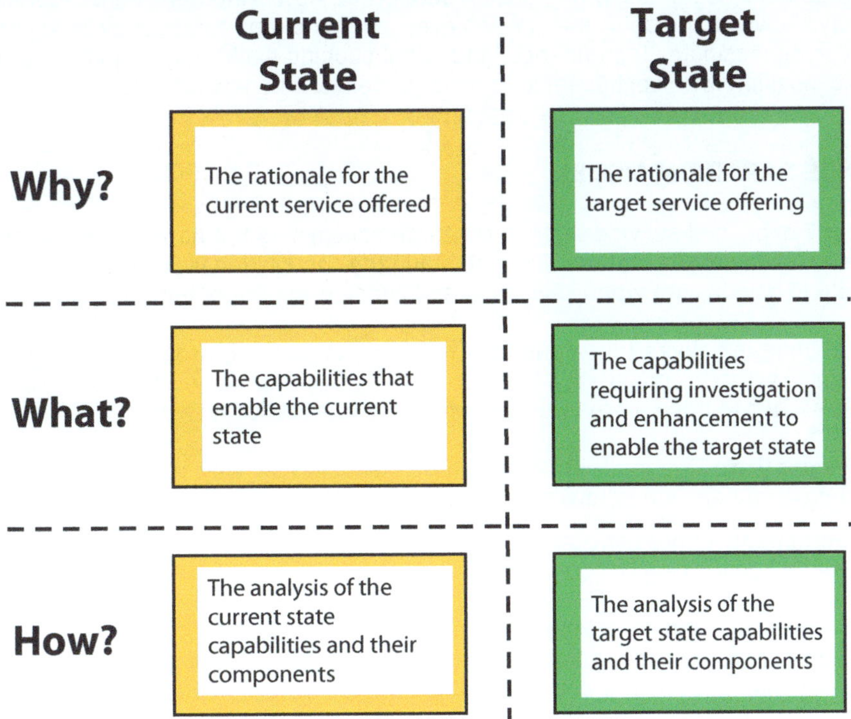

While the CALM approach typically focuses on building or enhancing an individual capability, it may be applied to an entire service by considering all the capabilities that service requires.

CALM identifies three aspects regarding service change:

(1) Why? What is the underlying rationale for the current and target service offerings? For example, within the restaurant scenario, there may be new food trends that the owners wish to embrace. This may be due to the development of new technology, increasing customer expectations or the receipt of negative comments regarding the limitations of the current service.

(2) What? Which current capabilities should be investigated and revised to meet the target state? For example, the current *Cook meals* capability may not support extending the restaurant service to encompass the new food trends.

(3) How? Which capability elements support the current state but may need enhancement or augmentation to support the target state? The POPIT™ model is helpful to identify the different elements that form a capability and clarify where change is needed to develop the target service capabilities. In the restaurant scenario, POPIT™ may identify that the extended service requires a capability uplift involving additional cooking skills (people), revised cooking tasks (processes) and new equipment (technology). In further detail, the 'how?' element helps identify the ways in which the uplift may be achieved: equipment purchase may be via options such as leasing or loan finance; additional cooking skills may require staff training, possibly with certification, in order to deliver the new food items.

CHANGE PARADIGM MODEL

Chapter 1 explained service science research concerning the nature of value and the relevance of value co-creation. Understanding the contrasting views of S-DL and G-DL can help to gain insight when reviewing and considering improvements to a service.

Many change initiatives falter due to a tendency to apply approaches, methods and techniques without considering the context and whether any adaptation would be beneficial. Two mindsets are often evident in these situations:

- **Pragmatism:** Dealing with a problem in a practical way to suit the particular context, rather than following fixed theories, ideas or rules.
- **Dogmatism:** Expressing an opinion or belief as if it were an undeniable fact, without considering the context or evidence.

The Change Paradigm Model represents the combinations of the two logic views and the pragmatic/dogmatic mindsets. The model clarifies the different results that may ensue depending upon the combination of views adopted. This model is shown in Figure 12.7.

Figure 12.7 The change paradigm model (© Assist Knowledge Development)

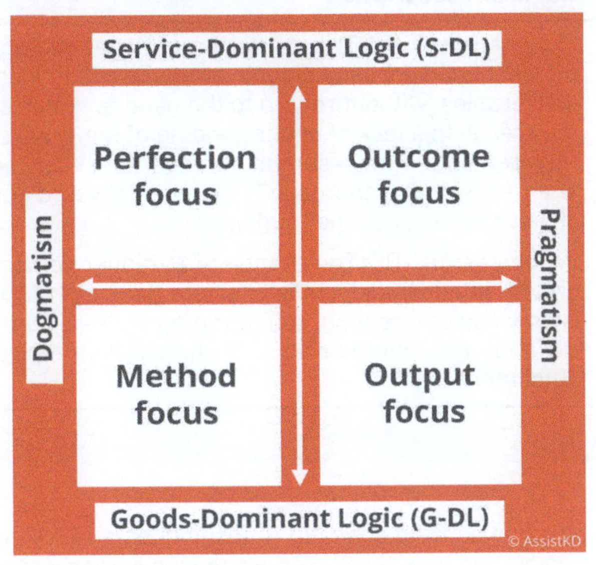

The four quadrants in the Change Paradigm Model are described in Table 12.5.

Table 12.5 Elements within the Change Paradigm model

Quadrant title	Quadrant description
Perfection focus	Dogmatism/S-DL: The change practitioner demonstrates a fixed mindset in applying service thinking principles. This may delay the service changes as the focus is on ensuring every aspect of the work is completed, irrespective of its relevance to the context.
Method focus	Dogmatism/G-DL: The change practitioner demonstrates a fixed mindset and is concerned to follow the designated method or approach without questioning its relevance. This can be highly risky as practitioners may undertake tasks in a systematic way without reviewing whether they enable progress for the organisation. While following predefined steps may offer a sense of security, without any contextual adaptation the result may not offer any benefit and could fail to achieve the requirements.

(Continued)

Table 12.5 (Continued)

Quadrant title	Quadrant description
Output focus	Pragmatism/G-DL: The change practitioner demonstrates a growth mindset but is focused on delivering the predefined product or deliverables, without regard to the need for value co-creation. This may result in a lack of understanding of the value expectations and requirements, with assumptions regarding value being relied upon. The risk with this approach is that the delivered output fails to be of value to the customer audience.
Outcome focus	Pragmatism/S-DL: The change practitioner demonstrates a growth mindset and applies service thinking principles. The focus is on value co-creation, collaborating with stakeholders to adapt the approach where necessary and always keeping the desired outcome in sight.

CONCLUSION

Service design professionals have a wealth of techniques and frameworks available to aid them when conducting their work. Service design is rarely prescriptive, requiring a creative, experimental mindset that encourages feedback. This chapter has explained additional frameworks that can support service designers with their work, offering ways of viewing situations that can supplement the more recognised design approaches. The aim is to augment the service designer toolkit and offer different ways to gain insight into service issues.

This book has described an extensive range of techniques and frameworks available to service designers. While not exhaustive, the value proposition offered by this book concerns the following aspects:

- Features/functionality: Techniques and frameworks for thinking, analysing and reframing.
- Quality: Clear descriptions with worked examples to support application and adaptation.
- Choice: A variety of approaches that enable the service designer to select and adapt depending upon the context.
- Price/availability: The approaches offered do not require investment in expensive products or delays in use; they are available to all service designers wishing to use them.
- Image/brand: The aim of this book is to enhance the role of the service designer and the reputation of the service design discipline.
- Relationships: The SDSF (Chapter 2) is intended to offer a basis for promotion and clarification of the service designer role, enabling improved working relationships with stakeholders.

The hope is that service designers will engage with the book contents and realise increased value from their work.

BIBLIOGRAPHY

Ackoff, R., 2016. Systems, messes and interactive planning. In *The social engagement of social science, a Tavistock Anthology, Volume 3: The socio-economic perspective*, 3, p. 417.

Alter, S., 2008. Service system fundamentals: Work system, value chain, and life cycle. *IBM Systems Journal*, *47*(1), pp. 71–85.

Bitner, M. J., Zeithaml, V. A. and Gremler, D. D., 2010. Technology's impact on the gaps model of service quality. In Maglio, P. P., Kieliszewski, C. A. and Spohrer, J. C. (eds.), *Handbook of service science* (pp. 197–218). Springer.

Brown, T., 2019. *Change by design*. Harper Business.

Cadle, J., Paul, D., Hunsley, J., Reed, A., Beckham, D. and Turner, P., 2021. *Business analysis techniques: 123 essential tools for success*. BCS Publishing.

Collins, J. C. and Porras, J. I., 2002. *Built to last: Successful habits of visionary companies*. Random House.

Checkland, P., 1981. *Systems thinking, systems practice*. John Wiley & Sons Ltd.

Dixon, M., Freeman, K. and Toman, N., 2010. Stop trying to delight your customers. *Harvard Business Review*, *88*(7/8), pp. 116–122.

Edvardsson, B., Gustafsson, A., Kristensson, P. and Witell, L., 2010. Service innovation and customer co-development. In Maglio, P. P., Kieliszewski, C. A. and Spohrer, J. C. (eds.), *Handbook of service science* (561–577). Springer.

Fisher, R., Ury, W. L. and Patton, B., 2011. *Getting to yes* (3rd ed.). Penguin Books.

Hall, E. T., 1976. *Beyond culture*. Anchor Books.

Hunsley, J., Paul, D., Banner, V., Greenhalgh, M. and Rothwell, V., 2025. *Business architecture: A comprehensive guide*. BCS Publishing.

Kano, N., Seraku, N., Takahashi, F. and Tsuji, S. A., 1984. Attractive quality and must-be quality. *Journal of the Japanese Society for Quality Control* (in Japanese), April 1984.

Kaplan, D. and Norton, R., 1996. *The balanced scorecard*. Harvard Business School Press.

Lemon, K. N. and Verhoef, P. C., 2016. Understanding customer experience throughout the customer journey. *Journal of Marketing*, *80*(6), pp. 69–96.

McCurdy, M., Connors, C., Pyrzak, G., Kanefsky, B. and Vera, A., 2006. Breaking the fidelity barrier: An examination of our current characterization of prototypes and an example of a mixed-fidelity success. In *Proceedings of the SIGCHI conference on human factors in computing systems* (pp. 1233–1242). Montréal, Québec, Canada.

Osterwalder, A. and Pigneur, Y., 2010. *Business model generation: A handbook for visionaries, game changers, and challengers*. John Wiley & Sons.

Osterwalder, A., Pigneur, Y., Bernarda, G. and Smith, A., 2014. *Value proposition design: How to create products and services customers want* (Vol. 2). John Wiley & Sons.

Parasuraman, A., Zeithaml, V. A. and Berry, L. L., 1985. A conceptual model of service quality and its implications for future research. *Journal of Marketing*, *49*(4), pp. 41–50.

Parasuraman, A., Zeithaml, V. A. and Berry, L. L., 1988. SERVQUAL: A multiple-item scale for measuring consumer perceptions of service quality. *1988*, *64*(1), pp. 12–40.

Paul, D. and Cadle, J., 2020. *Business analysis* (4th ed.). BCS Publishing.

Paul, D. and Lovelock, C., 2019. *Delivering business analysis: The BA service handbook*. BCS Publishing.

Paul, D. E., 2018. *Defining the role of the business analyst*, published doctoral thesis, Henley Business School.

Porter, M. E., 1985. *Competitive advantage: Creating and sustaining superior performance*. Simon and Schuster.

Reichheld, F. F., 2003. The one number you need to grow. *Harvard Business Review*, *81*(12), pp. 46–55.

Ross, J. W., Beath, C. M. and Mocker, M., 2019. *Designed for digital: How to architect your business for sustained success*. MIT Press.

Schein, Edgar H., 1988. *Organizational culture*, Sloan School of Management. MIT Press.

Schein, Edgar H., 2016. *Organization culture and leadership* (5th ed.). Wiley.

Scholes, K., Johnson, G. and Whittington, R., 2005. *Exploring corporate strategy* (7th ed.). Financial Times Prentice Hall.

Seddon, J., 2008. *Systems thinking in the public sector*. Triarchy Press.

Senge, P. M., 1990. *The art and practice of the learning organization*. Century Business.

Senge, P. M., 1997. The fifth discipline. *Measuring Business Excellence*, *1*(3), pp. 46–51.

Sinek, S., 2009. *Start with why*. Penguin Random House Group.

Taylor, F. W., 1911. *The principles of scientific management*. Harper & Brothers.

Thomas, K. W. and Kilmann, R. H., 2007. *Conflict mode instrument*. CPP, Incorporated.

Thompson, P., 2025. *Designing digital solutions.* BCS Publishing.

Vargo, S. L. and Lusch, R. F., 2008. From goods to service(s): Divergences and convergences of logics. *Industrial Marketing Management*, 37, pp. 254–259.

Vargo, S. L. and Akaka, M. A., 2009. Service-dominant logic as a foundation for service science: Clarifications. *Service Science, 1*, pp. 32–41.

Vargo, S. L. and Lusch, R. F., 2016. Institutions and axioms: An extension and update of service-dominant logic. *Journal of the Academy of Marketing Science*, *44*(1), pp. 5–23.

Ward, J. and Daniel, E., 2012. *Benefits management: How to increase the business value of your IT projects.* Wiley.

Whittington, R., Regnér, P., Johnson, G., Angwin, D. and Scholes, K., 2019. *Exploring strategy.* Pearson.

Wieland, H., Polese, F., Vargo, S. L. and Lusch, R. F., 2012. Toward a service (eco) systems perspective on value creation. *International Journal of Service Science, Management, Engineering, and Technology (IJSSMET)*, *3*(3), pp. 12–25.

Womack, J. P. and Jones, D. T., 2003. *Lean thinking*. Simon and Schuster/Free Press.

Online references

CMMI Institute: cmmiinstitute.com

Design Council: designcouncil.org.uk

Cambridge Dictionary: dictionary.cambridge.org

Standford d.school: dschool.stanford.edu

Merriam-Webster: Dictionary: www.merriam-webster.com/

Nielsen Norman Group: nngroup.com

PDSA Cycle – The W. Edwards Deming Institute: deming.org/explore/pdsa/

UKCSI – The state of customer satisfaction in the UK – January 2025 – Institute of Customer Service: www.instituteofcustomerservice.com/product/ukcsi-jan-25/

WCAG 2 Overview | Web Accessibility Initiative (WAI) | W3C: www.w3.org/WAI/standards-guidelines/wcag/

www.which.co.uk/policy-and-insight

GLOSSARY OF TERMS AND TECHNIQUES

A/B TESTING A technique used to test two or more variations of a product or service and then evaluate and compare the outcomes.

ACCESSIBILITY The degree to which all users, regardless of disabilities, are able to interact with services, processes and systems and achieve their goals. See *ACCESSIBILITY ANALYSIS*.

ACCESSIBILITY ANALYSIS The investigation and evaluation of the level of *ACCESSIBILITY* provided by an organisation's services, products, processes and systems.

ACTOR An individual, group of individuals or business system that carries out a business system's work activities.

ADAPTIVE SYSTEM A system that adapts to changes in its environment.

AFFINITY ANALYSIS A technique that seeks to identify and analyse connections and patterns between different items or activities.

AGILE An approach to software development based upon the Agile Manifesto that employs evolutionary development and incremental delivery.

ARTIFICIAL INTELLIGENCE A term used to define intelligence offered by automated machines and technology.

'AS IS' BUSINESS PROCESS MODEL A representation of a business process as it is performed currently.

BALANCED SCORECARD A strategic performance measurement template that encompasses both financial and non-financial measures of performance. There are usually four quadrants – financial, customer, process, learning and growth. The balanced scorecard was developed by R. S. Kaplan and D. P. Norton.

BAU See *BUSINESS-AS-USUAL*.

BENEFIT A positive gain to an organisation predicted to follow from carrying out a business change *PROGRAMME* or *PROJECT*.

BENEFITS DEPENDENCY NETWORK A visual representation of the investment objectives regarding a proposed change initiative, plus the benefits predicted to be realised from that initiative and the actions needed to secure the benefits.

BENEFITS MAP See *BENEFITS DEPENDENCY NETWORK.*

BENEFITS REALISATION A process that is concerned with the delivery of the predicted business benefits defined in a *BUSINESS CASE*. This process includes managing projects so that they are able to deliver the predicted benefits and, after the project has been implemented, checking progress on the achievement of these benefits and taking any actions required to enable their delivery.

BENEFITS REALISATION REPORT The deliverable produced from a *BENEFITS REVIEW.*

BENEFITS REVIEW A formal examination of the benefits expected from a business change initiative, the extent to which those benefits have been realised and the further actions needed to realise those benefits.

BLUEPRINT A diagram or model that represents a view of the organisation.

BRAINSTORMING A technique used during meetings and workshops whereby participants suggest ideas relating to a problem or issue. Brainstorming is based on the principles that an idea from one person will generate suggestions from others and that more suggestions will be generated if judgement is suspended until all participants have no further ideas to propose.

BRAINWRITING A technique used during meetings and workshops whereby participants are invited to write down ideas relating to a problem or issue. Brainwriting is based on the principles that an idea from one person will generate suggestions from others and that more suggestions will be generated if judgement is suspended until all participants have no further ideas to propose. This technique also encourages participation from those who are uncomfortable calling out ideas in an open forum.

BREAK-EVEN CALCULATION See *PAYBACK CALCULATION.*

BUSINESS ACCEPTANCE TESTING A service within the *BUSINESS ANALYSIS SERVICE FRAMEWORK* that is concerned with supporting business staff in testing new business and IT changes to ensure their acceptability.

BUSINESS ACTIVITY MODEL (BAM) A conceptual model that provides a holistic view of the activities needed to fulfil a particular stakeholder perspective. There are five types of activity included: planning, enabling, doing, monitoring and controlling.

BUSINESS ACTOR An individual or group with an active interest in a project. They may participate in the project because they have sponsorship or governance responsibility, or they conduct activities related to the business system. See *STAKEHOLDER*.

BUSINESS ACUMEN The ability to apply knowledge and understanding to enable an organisation to work effectively within the particular environmental context. The application of business acumen enables informed and positive business decision-making that aids the organisation in achieving strategic and tactical outcomes.

BUSINESS ANALYSIS A specialist discipline that co-creates value for organisations through delivering the services defined within the *BUSINESS ANALYSIS SERVICE FRAMEWORK*.

BUSINESS ANALYSIS SERVICE A business function that delivers *BUSINESS ANALYSIS* services and provides associated capabilities.

BUSINESS ANALYSIS SERVICE FRAMEWORK A framework that identifies a standard portfolio of services that may be offered by a *BUSINESS ANALYSIS SERVICE*. The standard services are: SITUATION INVESTIGATION AND PROBLEM ANALYSIS; FEASIBILITY ASSESSMENT AND BUSINESS CASE DEVELOPMENT; BUSINESS PROCESS IMPROVEMENT; REQUIREMENTS DEFINITION; BUSINESS ACCEPTANCE TESTING; BUSINESS CHANGE DEPLOYMENT. These services are subject to adaptation and customisation in order to meet the needs of a particular organisation.

BUSINESS ANALYST A business change professional who delivers *BUSINESS ANALYSIS* services and possesses the skills and knowledge required to deliver these services.

BUSINESS ANALYST ROLE An advisory role that carries out some or all of the services within the *BUSINESS ANALYSIS SERVICE FRAMEWORK* in order to ensure the effective deployment of business changes and use of technology in line with the needs of an organisation.

BUSINESS ARCHITECTURE A discipline focused on building shared understanding of the organising logic for an organisation. The discipline encourages a holistic approach that enables informed and aligned strategic and tactical decision-making.

BUSINESS ARCHITECT A person who carries out *BUSINESS ARCHITECTURE* services and possesses the skills and knowledge required to deliver these services.

BUSINESS ARCHITECTURE SERVICE A business function that delivers *BUSINESS ARCHITECTURE* services and provides associated capabilities.

BUSINESS ARCHITECTURE SERVICE FRAMEWORK A framework that identifies a standard portfolio of services that may be offered by an internal *BUSINESS ARCHITECTURE SERVICE*. These services are subject to adaptation and customisation in order to meet the needs of a particular organisation. The standard services are: SITUATION INVESTIGATION AND PROBLEM ANALYSIS; FEASIBILITY ASSESSMENT AND BUSINESS CASE DEVELOPMENT; BUSINESS ARCHITECTURE GOVERNANCE, BLUEPRINT DEVELOPMENT AND MAINTENANCE; TARGET OPERATING MODEL (TOM) DESIGN; STRATEGIC ROADMAP DEVELOPMENT.

BUSINESS-AS-USUAL (BAU) The standard, ongoing, operational activities carried out by an organisation.

BUSINESS CAPABILITY MODEL A model that provides an abstract, conceptual representation of what an organisation has the ability or motivation to do.

BUSINESS CASE A document that describes the findings from an investigative study and presents a recommended course of action for consideration by senior management. A business case typically includes an introduction, management summary, description of the current situation, options considered, analysis of costs and benefits, impact assessment, risk assessment, recommendations, plus appendices that provide detailed supporting information.

BUSINESS CHANGE GOVERNANCE AND REPORTING A service within the *CHANGE MANAGEMENT SERVICE FRAMEWORK*. This service is concerned with defining, communicating and executing change governance standards and processes.

BUSINESS CHANGE LIFECYCLE A visual representation of the stages that an organisation carries out to identify, evaluate, specify and implement business change. The stages involved are alignment, definition, design, implementation and realisation. Each stage is governed by and contributes to the development of the *BUSINESS CASE* for change.

BUSINESS DESIRABILITY The extent to which a change proposal is aligned with an organisation's strategic objectives, culture, operating model and market position. See *BUSINESS FEASIBILITY* and *FINANCIAL VIABILITY*.

BUSINESS DOMAIN A sector of the economy or an industry.

BUSINESS ENVIRONMENT See *EXTERNAL BUSINESS ENVIRONMENT*; *INTERNAL BUSINESS ENVIRONMENT*.

BUSINESS EVENT A business event initiates a business process, which is an organisation's response to the occurrence of an event. There are three types of business event: external, internal and time-based.

BUSINESS FEASIBILITY The degree to which a proposed course of action is compatible with the strategy, structure and culture of an organisation and the business domain within which it operates. See *BUSINESS DESIRABILITY*; *FINANCIAL VIABILITY*.

BUSINESS INFORMATION MODEL A model that provides an overview of the sets of *INFORMATION* (or 'information concepts') used to conduct the work of an organisation. Also known as an 'information concepts model' or 'enterprise data model'.

BUSINESS MODEL ANALYSIS An analysis of the core logic that determines how an organisation is constructed to deliver products and/or services within the context of its *ECOSYSTEM*.

BUSINESS MODEL CANVAS A generic template used to describe the core elements of an organisation's business model, including the value proposition, key revenue streams, activities and customer segments. The business model canvas was developed by Osterwalder and Pigneur (2010).

BUSINESS MOTIVATION ANALYSIS The analysis of the rationale that underlies how an organisation acts or behaves.

BUSINESS PERSPECTIVE See *STAKEHOLDER PERSPECTIVE*.

BUSINESS PROCESS A linked set of tasks performed by an organisation in response to a business event. The business process receives, manipulates and transfers information or physical items, in order to produce an output that offers value to a customer. See *BUSINESS PROCESS MODEL*.

BUSINESS PROCESS IMPROVEMENT A service within the *BUSINESS ANALYSIS SERVICE FRAMEWORK* that is concerned with researching, analysing and defining current and proposed business processes, and applying gap analysis to identify actions required to implement the revised processes.

BUSINESS PROCESS HIERARCHY A structure used to decompose business processes into lower levels of detail. The levels of the hierarchy are enterprise, event–response (business process) and actor–task.

BUSINESS PROCESS MODEL A diagram showing the tasks that need to be carried out in response to a business event and in order to achieve a specific goal. See *SWIMLANE DIAGRAM*.

BUSINESS PROCESS REENGINEERING A holistic approach that is applied to redesign and optimise the efficiency of an organisation's processes.

BUSINESS READINESS ASSESSMENT A technique that is concerned with investigating and analysing business readiness for change.

BUSINESS RULE A structured, discreet and enforceable instruction or procedure that determines how an activity, process, task or step should be conducted. There are two main types of business rule: constraints that restrict how an activity may be performed; operational guidance that describes the procedures for performing activities.

BUSINESS STAFF The individuals or groups who carry out the work of an organisation and will deliver services to customers.

BUSINESS STRATEGY The long-term direction defined for an organisation in order to achieve the *VISION*, *MISSION* and *OBJECTIVES*.

BUSINESS SYSTEM A set of business components working together in order to achieve a defined purpose. These components are defined in the POPIT™ model. See *IT SYSTEM*.

BUSINESS USE CASE A function or feature that an *ACTOR* wants a *BUSINESS SYSTEM* to offer; it is a 'case of use' of the business system by a specific actor and defines the interaction between an actor and a business system.

BUSINESS USE CASE DESCRIPTION A description of the steps conducted within an individual *BUSINESS USE CASE*.

BUSINESS USE CASE DIAGRAM A holistic, conceptual representation of the features of a *BUSINESS SYSTEM*.

CALM Capability Analysis and Leverage Model. Provides a means of assessing an organisation's *CURRENT STATE* and *TARGET STATE* against the questions why, what and how.

CAPABILITY A task or action that an organisation has the ability or motivation to perform.

CAPABILITY MODEL See *BUSINESS CAPABILITY MODEL*.

CAPABILITY MATURITY MODEL INTEGRATION (CMMI) A model developed by the Software Engineering Institute of Carnegie Mellon University that consists of five stages, showing increasing maturity of operation. It provides guidance for improving the quality of processes.

CAPACITY The volume or quantity of items that may be delivered, data that may be stored or tasks that may be carried out.

CAPAGILITY The existence of motivation, leadership and capability that enables an organisation to respond quickly and effectively to business environment forces and take relevant action at pace. The term was first used by Chris Martin (Assist Knoweldege Development) at the IRM Business Analysis Conference Europe in 2019.

CATWOE A technique from the soft systems methodology that provides a framework for analysing and defining business perspectives. The acronym stands for: C – customer, A – actor, T – transformation, W – world view, O – owner, E – environment. See *STAKEHOLDER PERSPECTIVE*; *SOFT SYSTEMS METHODOLOGY*.

CHANGE PARADIGM MODEL A model used to assess the relationship between service-dominant logic and goods-dominant logic, and pragmatic and dogmatic approaches to change. The model clarifies the different results that may ensue depending on the combination of views adopted.

CHANGE MANAGEMENT A discipline focused on enabling organisations to move effectively and successfully from a current state to a desired target state, in alignment with strategic goals and priorities.

CHANGE MANAGEMENT SERVICE An internal service function that provides *CHANGE MANAGEMENT* services to its organisation.

CHANGE MANAGEMENT SERVICE FRAMEWORK A framework that identifies a standard portfolio of services that may be offered by an internal *CHANGE MANAGEMENT SERVICE*. These services may be subject to adaptation and customisation in order to meet the needs of a particular organisation. The standard services are: BUSINESS CHANGE DEMAND ANALYSIS; STRATEGIC ROADMAP DEVELOPMENT; BUSINESS CHANGE GOVERNANCE AND REPORTING; BUSINESS READINESS ASSESSMENT; BUSINESS CHANGE PLANNING; BUSINESS CHANGE DEPLOYMENT.

CHANGE MANAGER A person who performs *CHANGE MANAGEMENT* work.

CLASS A definition of the attributes and operations shared by a set of objects within a business system. Each object is an instance of a particular class. See *OBJECT.*

CLASS MODEL A technique from the unified modeling language (UML). A class model describes the classes in a system and the characteristics of their associations with each other.

CLOUD COMPUTING A general term for the delivery of hosted services over the internet.

COLLABORATION A means of working with colleagues and other stakeholders to achieve the desired outcomes in a culture that values trust, psychological safety, respect and information sharing.

COMPETENCE A general level of ability. Competence and competences are broad concepts that tend not to be focused on the achievement of a particular task.

COMPETENCY A specific skill at the level of ability needed to perform a particular task. Organisational competency is typically aggregated from competencies held by a group of individuals.

CONTEXT DIAGRAM An outline visual representation of a business or IT system, comprising a box or circle and the interactions the system has with external actors and systems.

CONVERGENT THINKING A thought process focused on evaluating ideas or options and deciding the most promising ways forward.

CORE PURPOSE An organisation's fundamental reason for being (Adapted from Collins and Porras, 2002).

CORE VALUES The defined set of principles that guide how a company acts and operates. Core values may or may not be written down (Adapted from Collins and Porras, 2002).

COST-BENEFIT ANALYSIS A technique that involves identifying the initial and ongoing costs and benefits associated with a business change initiative. Costs and benefits are categorised as tangible or intangible and a financial value calculated for those that are tangible. The financial values are analysed over a forward period in order to assess the potential financial return to the organisation. This analysis may be carried out using investment appraisal techniques. See *PAYBACK PERIOD* (or *BREAK-EVEN ANALYSIS)* and *DISCOUNTED CASH FLOW/NET PRESENT VALUE ANALYSIS.*

CREATIVITY The application of a range of techniques and skills to generate new ideas, options and solutions. See *DIVERGENT THINKING.*

CRITICAL SUCCESS FACTORS The areas in which an organisation must succeed in order to achieve positive organisational performance.

CULTURE The shared values and beliefs that influence how those working within an organisation behave, think and feel.

CULTURE PYRAMID A model that supports the analysis of an ORGANISATIONAL CULTURE. The model consists of three dimensions: the world view, formal dimension and informal dimension.

CURRENT STATE The current operating model in place within an organisation or business area.

CUSTOMER An individual or organisation that is the beneficiary of a product or service.

CUSTOMER CENTRICITY A viewpoint adopted by an organisation, business area or service where there is a focus on ensuring customer requirements and expectations are understood and met, and value co-creation enabled.

CUSTOMER EFFORT SCORE A means of measuring customer satisfaction that requires customers to rate how much effort they expended to resolve a problem with a product or service.

CUSTOMER EXPERIENCE A multidimensional construct focusing on a customer's cognitive, emotional, behavioural, sensorial and social responses to a firm's offerings during the entire customer journey (Adapted from: Katherine Lemon & Peter Verhoef, 'Understanding Customer Experience Throughout the Customer Journey').

CUSTOMER EXPERIENCE (CX) ANALYSIS A service within *the SERVICE DESIGN SERVICE FRAMEWORK* concerned with researching, analysing and defining the *VOICE OF THE CUSTOMER* and service value expectations.

CUSTOMER JOURNEY The activities, experiences and emotions encountered by a customer persona when accessing a service in pursuit of a particular goal or outcome. See *CUSTOMER JOURNEY MAP*.

CUSTOMER JOURNEY MAP A model of the activities, experiences and emotions encountered by a customer persona when accessing a service in pursuit of a particular goal or outcome.

DATA ITEM A specific item within a CLASS.

DATA ARCHITECTURE A discipline focused on building shared understanding of the organising logic of the data recorded and used across an enterprise.

DATA MODELLING An approach used to analyse, structure and represent data items.

DECISION TABLE A technique that is used to identify, model and analyse business rules using a table-based format.

DECISION TREE A technique that is used to identify, model and analyse business rules using questions and alternative pathways.

DESIGN BRIEF A document that outlines the business context, objectives, scope, deliverables, timescale, budget, authority and available resources for a design assignment.

DESIGN THINKING A human-centric approach focused on innovative problem solving and solution creation. It encompasses a process and set of techniques that encourage collaboration, ideation and experimentation (Tim Brown, IDEO).

DESIGNED ABSTRACT SYSTEMS Systems created by humans that are not physical artefacts and express ordered conscious thinking.

DESIGNED PHYSICAL SYSTEMS Systems that are physical artefacts created by humans as a result of conscious design.

DESIGN THINKING MINDSET A mindset based on the principles of *COLLABORATION, OUTCOME FOCUS, CREATIVITY, EXPERIMENTATION* and *CUSTOMER CENTRICITY.*

DIGITAL A generic term used to describe technologies that generate, store and process data in a consistent and interoperable format.

DISCOUNTED CASH FLOW (DCF) An investment appraisal technique that takes account of the time value of money. The annual net cash flow for each year following the implementation of the change is reduced (discounted) in line with the estimated reduction in the value of money. The discounted cash flows are then added to produce a net present value. See *NET PRESENT VALUE.*

DIVERGENT THINKING A thought process that encourages thinking broadly and expansively about potential problems and options. See *CREATIVITY; CONVERGENT THINKING.*

DOCUMENT ANALYSIS A requirements elicitation technique where samples of documents are examined in order to analyse the data recorded and the usage made of that data.

DOMAIN KNOWLEDGE A general understanding of the business drivers, issues, pressures, dynamics, finances and technologies of a business domain. See also *SUBJECT MATTER EXPERTISE.*

ECOSYSTEM See *INTERNAL SERVICE ECOSYSTEM* and *EXTERNAL SERVICE ECOSYSTEM.*

EMERGENT PROPERTIES The properties or outcomes that emerge when an entire system is in operation.

EMPATHY MAP A technique used to explore and document what a customer sees, hears, says and does regarding a received service. The technique can also be used to analyse and interpret what the customer thinks and feels.

ENTERPRISE ARCHITECTURE 'The fundamental concepts or properties of a system in its environment embodied in its elements, relationships, and in the principles of its design and evolution' (ISO/IEC/IEEE 42010:2011).

ETHNOGRAPHIC STUDY A form of *OBSERVATION* concerned with spending an extended period of time within an organisation, community or society in order to obtain a detailed understanding of its culture and behaviours.

EXPERIMENTATION An approach that involves testing ideas, options and proposed solutions to gain feedback and insights and increase understanding.

EXPLICIT KNOWLEDGE Knowledge that is foremost in an actor's mind and can be articulated with ease. See *TACIT KNOWLEDGE*.

EXTERNAL BUSINESS ENVIRONMENT The business environment that is external to an organisation and is the source of forces that have the potential to impact the organisation. Types of forces may include the introduction of new laws, social trends or competitor actions. See *PESTLE ANALYSIS*; *FIVE FORCES ANALYSIS*.

EXTERNAL SERVICE ECOSYSTEM The network of service systems that are separate legal entities from the organisation, and interact and engage with the organisation to deliver products and services. The relationship of each external service system with the organisation should be governed by a contractual arrangement.

FACILITATION An interpersonal *COMPETENCY* required of *SERVICE DESIGNERS* that allows them to prepare for and lead a meeting or workshop, and achieve the desired objectives or goals.

FEASIBILITY The degree to which a proposed course of action is viable given the business, technical and financial constraints imposed by the organisation and the environment in which it operates.

FEASIBILITY ASSESSMENT AND BUSINESS CASE DEVELOPMENT A service within the *BUSINESS ARCHITECTURE SERVICE FRAMEWORK*, the *BUSINESS ANALYSIS SERVICE FRAMEWORK*, the *SERVICE DESIGN SERVICE FRAMEWORK* and the *PROJECT MANAGEMENT SERVICE FRAMEWORK* that is concerned with evaluating the options to meet the business need and supporting the development of the business case for change.

FEEDBACK CAPTURE GRID A technique used to capture and organise insights from customers regarding a specific *PRODUCT* or *SERVICE*. The Grid is designed to capture positive feedback, constructive criticism, questions, and ideas.

FINANCIAL FEASIBILITY The degree to which a proposed course of action is compatible with the financial constraints and objectives of an organisation.

FINANCIAL VIABILITY See *FINANCIAL FEASIBILITY*.

FISHBONE DIAGRAM A visual technique developed by Dr Kaoru Ishikawa where a problem and its causes are represented as the skeleton of a fish. The head shows the problem and the spines radiating from the backbone represent the causes. The technique can also be used to analyse opportunities.

FIVE FORCES MODEL See *PORTER'S FIVE FORCES*.

FOCUS GROUP An interactive group meeting used to gather ideas and feedback about a specific product, service or issue.

FUNCTION A business area that is responsible for conducting a designated set of processes or activities and achieving specified operational business objectives.

GAP ANALYSIS The comparison of two views of a business system, the current situation and the desired future, is the aim of gap analysis, which is to determine where the current situation has problems or 'gaps' that need to be resolved. This leads to the identification of actions to improve the situation.

GOAL See *OBJECTIVE*.

HOLISTIC VIEW The representation and analysis of all elements within a business system, including the interactions between different elements. Models and frameworks such as *BUSINESS ACTIVITY MODELS*, *ECOSYSTEM DIAGRAMS* and *POPIT* may be used to take a holistic view of a situation.

HUMAN ACTIVITY SYSTEMS Systems that support a goal or purposeful human activity found in the real world. Human activity systems employ *NATURAL SYSTEMS*, *DESIGNED PHYSICAL SYSTEMS* and *DESIGNED ABSTRACT SYSTEMS*.

HYPOTHESIS An idea or explanation for something that is based on known facts but has not yet been proved.

HYPOTHESIS TREE A technique that provides a visualisation of a range of different hypotheses regarding how to solve a problem or opportunity.

IMPACT ANALYSIS The detailed, analytical consideration of the impact a proposed change is likely to have on a business system, including on those conducting the work.

INFORMATION A summarised view of both *DATA* and *METADATA* that typically presents data in a form that is relevant to an organisation and its operation.

INFRASTRUCTURE ARCHITECTURE A discipline focused on building shared understanding of the organising logic regarding the infrastructure applied across an enterprise. The infrastructure includes the hardware, cloud services, operating systems and communication networks.

INTANGIBLE BENEFIT A benefit to be realised by a business change project for which a credible value cannot be predicted in advance of the change deployment. See *TANGIBLE BENEFIT*.

INTANGIBLE COST A cost incurred by a business change project for which a credible value cannot be predicted in advance of the change deployment. See *TANGIBLE COST*.

INTERNAL BUSINESS ENVIRONMENT The internal characteristics of an organisation that affect its ability to respond to external environmental forces. Techniques such as *VMOST* analysis or *RESOURCE AUDIT* may be used to analyse the capability of the internal business environment.

INTERNAL SERVICE ECOSYSTEM The network of service systems that are internal to an organisation. Internal service systems interact with each other, and with the external service systems where relevant, to carry out the organisation's work.

INTERVIEW An investigation technique to elicit information from relevant actors. An interview agenda is prepared prior to the interview and distributed to participants. The interview is carried out in an organised manner, and a report of the interview is produced once the interview has been concluded.

INVESTMENT APPRAISAL A technique used to analyse the costs, benefits, risks and impacts of a proposed change solution. See *PAYBACK CALCULATION* (or BREAK-EVEN ANALYSIS) and *DISCOUNTED CASH FLOW/NET PRESENT VALUE ANALYSIS.*

ISHIKAWA DIAGRAM See *FISHBONE DIAGRAM.*

IT SYSTEM A set of automated components that work together to provide services to the system users. See *BUSINESS SYSTEM.*

IT SERVICE MANAGEMENT See *SERVICE MANAGEMENT.*

KAIZEN An approach that emphasises the need for continuous improvement, typically in incremental steps.

KANO ANALYSIS A technique developed by Noriaki Kano that provides a framework for prioritising customer needs.

KEY PERFORMANCE INDICATORS (KPIs) Specific areas of performance that are monitored to assess the performance of an organisation. Key performance indicators are often identified in order to monitor progress towards achieving defined critical success factors. Measurable targets are set for KPIs. See *CRITICAL SUCCESS FACTORS.*

KEY RESULTS Specific results that are monitored to assess performance.

LEAN/LEAN THINKING A philosophy focused on the systematic enhancement of the work conducted by an organisation. Lean makes extensive use of principles such as continuous improvement, waste reduction, enhancing value for customers, and enhancing flow and quality. Lean thinking advocates the following five principles:

(1) specify value;
(2) identify the value stream;
(3) flow;
(4) pull;
(5) perfection.

LOTUS BLOSSOM A technique used to structure a discussion about a business problem (or opportunity) and generate a range of ideas. The technique focuses on the expansion of an initial idea or problem placed at the centre of the lotus blossom diagram. The central concern is discussed, and ideas for themes associated with the concern and potential actions are identified.

MANAGEMENT SUMMARY A brief summary that provides an overview of the background, findings and recommendations within a document or report.

MIGRATION The process of moving an organisation from an existing business system to a new one.

MIND MAP A technique pioneered by Tony Buzan that represents an issue as a diagram with the name of the issue in the centre and the aspects associated with that issue shown as radiating branches.

MISSION The definition of what the organisation does or will do to achieve the organisation's VISION.

MoSCoW A prioritisation technique used to distinguish between four levels of priority: Must have, Should have, Could have, Want to have but won't have this time.

MOST Analysis An analysis of an organisation's mission, objectives, strategy and tactics to identify any inherent strengths or weaknesses. See *INTERNAL BUSINESS ENVIRONMENT*; *VMOST*.

MOTIVATION A reason or impetus for acting or behaving in a particular way. See *BUSINESS MOTIVATION ANALYSIS*.

NATURAL SYSTEMS Systems that are not designed or created by humans but originate from the natural world.

NAVIGATION PATH ANALYSIS A technique that provides detailed insights regarding how customer *PERSONAS* may access and navigate a *SERVICE* to achieve a predetermined goal.

NET PROMOTER SCORE (NPS) A means of measuring customer satisfaction that concerns how likely customers are to promote the organisation to others.

NET PRESENT VALUE (NPV) An amount calculated by totalling the present values for the cash flows predicted to result from an investment. The present value for each annual cash flow is calculated using the discounted cash flow approach. See *DISCOUNTED CASH FLOW*.

OBJECTIVE A defined, desired goal or outcome. An objective is used to guide and measure progress towards the completion of the *VISION* and *MISSION*.

OBJECTIVES AND KEY RESULTS (OKRs) A performance measurement technique that consists of a *GOAL* (*OBJECTIVE*) and from three to five measures (*KEY RESULTS*) that track progress towards the completion of the goal.

OBSERVATION A technique used to gain insights about a business situation by watching and monitoring work as it is performed.

OPTIONS The alternative courses of action analysed and described in a *BUSINESS CASE*.

ORGANISATIONAL MEMORY Information about an organisation's history that informs the current and future operation of the organisation.

ORGANISATION MODEL A model that represents an organisation and the external business environment within which it operates. The external environment encompasses the organisation's competitors, suppliers and customers.

OSCAR An acronym that helps to identify the areas to be addressed in a *PROJECT INITIATION DOCUMENT* or *TERMS OF REFERENCE*. The OSCAR elements are objectives, scope, constraints, authority and resources.

OUTCOME FOCUS A mindset that is concerned with maintaining a focus on achieving the desired business outcomes.

OUTSOURCING A process by which an organisation entrusts certain aspects of its operations to other organisations.

PAYBACK CALCULATION An investment appraisal technique where a cash-flow forecast for a project is produced using the current values of the incoming and outgoing cash flows; no attempt is made to adjust them for the declining value of money over time. See *DISCOUNTED CASH FLOW*.

PERSONA A concept associated with *USER ROLE ANALYSIS*. A persona is a representation of a *USER ROLE*, aggregating customers (or other stakeholders) who have common characteristics including behaviour, attitudes and needs. See *PROTO PERSONA* and *VALIDATED PERSONA*.

PESTLE A technique used to analyse the external business environment of an organisation. The technique involves the analysis of the Political, Economic, Socio-Cultural, Technological, Legal and Environmental forces that may impact upon an organisation. See *BUSINESS ENVIRONMENT*.

POPIT™ MODEL A model that was developed by Assist Knowledge Development and illustrates the elements that need to be considered by business analysts in order to provide a holistic view of a business situation. The POPIT™ elements are people, organisation, process information and technology. The POPIT™ model is also used to conduct gap analysis and business readiness assessment and provides a basis for a *TARGET OPERATING MODEL*.

PORTER'S FIVE FORCES A technique used to analyse the industry or business domain within which an organisation operates. The Five Forces Model was developed by Professor Michael Porter.

PORTFOLIO The suite of business change *PROJECTS* or *PROGRAMMES* for an organisation.

POWER/INTEREST GRID A visual representation of the relative importance of a project's stakeholders. A stakeholder's position on the grid represents the level of power or influence they may wield over the project and their level of interest in the project outcomes. Stakeholder management strategies are identified for each section of the grid.

PROBLEM ANALYSIS A systematic approach to uncovering the root causes of a business problem or issue and developing workable and acceptable solutions.

PROBLEM DEFINITION A technique to create a clear, succinct and documented definition of a problem.

PROBLEM STATEMENT See *PROBLEM DEFINITION.*

PROCESS See *BUSINESS PROCESS.*

PROCESS MODEL See *BUSINESS PROCESS MODEL.*

PRODUCT An item created by an organisation and delivered to customers.

PROGRAMME A group of *PROJECTS* that all contribute towards the achievement of a business objective and which, because of their interdependence, must be coordinated.

PROGRAMME MANAGER A role responsible for planning, directing and managing a *PROGRAMME.*

PROJECT A discrete piece of work that is required to achieve a defined objective and has a defined start and end date, an agreed budget and specified deliverables.

PROJECT CHARTER See *PROJECT INITIATION DOCUMENT.*

PROJECT ESTIMATION AND RESOURCE CO-ORDINATION A service within the *PROJECT MANAGEMENT SERVICE FRAMEWORK* that is concerned with identifying, estimating, resourcing and scheduling tasks required to deliver the project deliverables and achieve the project objectives.

PROJECT EXECUTION AND CLOSURE A service within the *PROJECT MANAGEMENT SERVICE FRAMEWORK* that is concerned with completing all the tasks required to achieve the project objectives.

PROJECT GOVERNANCE AND PROGRESS REPORTING A service within the *PROJECT MANAGEMENT SERVICE FRAMEWORK* that is concerned with defining, communicating and executing project governance standards and processes.

PROJECT IMPACT AND RISK ASSESSMENT A service within the *PROJECT MANAGEMENT SERVICE FRAMEWORK* that is concerned with identifying, analysing and managing project impacts, risks and dependencies.

PROJECT INITIATION DOCUMENT (PID) A document that defines the business context for a project or assignment. The PID defines the objectives, scope, deliverables, timescale, budget, authority and resources.

PROJECT MANAGEMENT A discipline focused on organising individuals and work activities to achieve project objectives within defined scope and constraints.

PROJECT MANAGEMENT SERVICE An internal service function that provides *PROJECT MANAGEMENT* capabilities to its organisation.

PROJECT MANAGEMENT SERVICE FRAMEWORK A framework that identifies a standard portfolio of services that may be offered by an internal *PROJECT MANAGEMENT SERVICE*. These services may be subject to adaptation and customisation in order to meet the needs of a particular organisation. The standard services are: SITUATION INVESTIGATION AND PROBLEM ANALYSIS; FEASIBILITY ASSESSMENT AND BUSINESS CASE DEVELOPMENT; PROJECT GOVERNANCE AND PROGRESS REPORTING; PROJECT ESTIMATION AND RESOURCE CO-ORDINATION; PROJECT IMPACT AND RISK ASSESSMENT; PROJECT EXECUTION AND CLOSURE.

PROJECT MANAGER A person who is responsible for delivering the objectives of a *PROJECT* and carries out *PROJECT MANAGEMENT*.

PROJECT SPONSOR A senior manager within an organisation who is accountable for the success of a project as a business undertaking, and who is responsible for making major decisions about its scope and direction and ensuring the required resources are available.

PROTO PERSONA A *PERSONA* derived from the observations and insights of the service designers or close colleagues.

PROTOTYPE A model, representation or simulation of a product or service. See *PROTOTYPING*.

PROTOTYPING A technique where a model, representation or simulation of a product or service is created and used to test assumptions, experiment, validate and obtain feedback.

QUALITATIVE DATA Data expressed in non-numerical values that describes experiences, opinions and observations.

QUANTITATIVE DATA Data expressed in numerical values that can be analysed to identify patterns and trends and to test hypotheses.

QUESTIONNAIRE See *SURVEY*.

RACI MATRIX A matrix that identifies the nature of stakeholder responsibilities regarding tasks or deliverables. The types of responsibility are: responsible; accountable; consulted; informed. A RACI Matrix (sometimes called a RACI chart) may be used to clarify service design projects or business as usual responsibilities.

RAG A means of classifying the state or progress of an individual task, output *SERVICE*, *PRODUCT* or *CAPABILITY* using the categories Red, Amber and Green.

REQUIREMENT A want or need requested by a stakeholder to be fulfilled by a service or product.

REQUIREMENTS DEFINITION A service within the *BUSINESS ANALYSIS SERVICE FRAMEWORK* concerned with the elicitation, analysis, and definition of requirements for business and IT system change initiatives.

REQUIREMENTS ENGINEERING A framework for the elicitation, analysis, validation, documentation and management of requirements.

REQUIREMENTS MANAGEMENT A stage of the *REQUIREMENTS ENGINEERING* framework and a governance approach that aims to ensure that each requirement is tracked from inception to implementation (or withdrawal) through all the changes that have been applied to it.

REQUIREMENTS VALIDATION A stage of the *REQUIREMENTS ENGINEERING* framework where the requirements are reviewed and approved by selected external stakeholders.

RESOURCE AUDIT A technique to analyse the assets held by an organisation. The resource audit considers five areas of organisational resource: tangible resources – physical, financial and human; intangible resources – know-how and reputation.

RESOURCE INTEGRATION The application and integration of capabilities and competencies to co-create value.

RICH PICTURE A free-format visualisation technique used to record information about a business situation.

RISK/RISK MANAGEMENT A problem situation that may arise with regard to a project or business situation. Potential risks are identified for each option in a business case, the probability of the risk occurring and the likely impact of the risk are assessed and suitable countermeasures are identified. See *BUSINESS CASE*.

ROOT CAUSE ANALYSIS The detailed examination of a perceived problem to identify the actual underlying causes.

ROUND ROBIN A technique used during meetings and workshops where each participant is asked in turn to provide input or suggest ideas regarding a problem, issue or opportunity.

SCAMPER A composite approach to problem-solving and idea generation that includes seven elements: Substitute, Combine, Adapt, Modify, Put to another use, Eliminate and Reverse.

SCENARIO A conceptual exploration of the ways in which business actors may interact with an organisation, business process, service or product. Each scenario is triggered by a business event that initiates a sequence of actions. A sequence of actions may lead to the desired outcome or to an alternative, sometimes less positive, outcome.

SCENARIO ANALYSIS A technique used to develop and examine future events and various possible sequences of actions that may occur.

SERVICE The application and integration of resources to realise beneficial outcomes for both service providers and their customers.

SERVICE BLUEPRINT A technique that provides a detailed visual representation of a *SERVICE*. A service blueprint represents an entire *CUSTOMER JOURNEY*, including the 'front stage' and 'back stage' elements. The customer-facing elements such as the activities, touchpoints and emotions are known as the 'front stage'. The 'back stage' elements support the customer-facing work and include the data, processes and applications. The service blueprint shows the interactions and connections between the front stage and back stage activities and resources.

SERVICE CAPABILITY ANALYSIS A technique that defines the capability requirements of a service. The areas to be considered are: the business outcome to be achieved; the business constraints imposed by the legal/regulatory requirements and organisational policies; the customer experience to be delivered; the technical constraints imposed by the organisation's technology policies and infrastructure; the utility to be provided to customers by the service and the *SERVICE QUALITY REQUIREMENTS*.

SERVICE DEFINITION A service within *the SERVICE DESIGN SERVICE FRAMEWORK* that is concerned with researching, analysing and defining current and proposed business services.

SERVICE DEFINITION CANVAS A template used to aid the discovery, analysis and communication of the elements that underpin a *SERVICE*.

SERVICE DEPLOYMENT A service within *the SERVICE DESIGN SERVICE FRAMEWORK* that is concerned with supporting the deployment of enhanced business services.

SERVICE DESIGNER A person who performs *SERVICE DESIGN*.

SERVICE DESIGN A professional discipline with responsibility for developing and enhancing an organisation's services in alignment with strategic priorities and customer expectations. The discipline encompasses four thinking approaches: *SERVICE THINKING, SYSTEMS THINKING, DESIGN THINKING* and *LEAN THINKING*.

SERVICE DESIGN SERVICE FRAMEWORK A framework that identifies a standard portfolio of services that may be offered by an internal service design service. These services may be subject to adaptation and customisation in order to meet the needs of a particular organisation. The standard services are *SITUATION INVESTIGATION AND PROBLEM ANALYSIS, FEASIBILITY ASSESSMENT AND BUSINESS CASE DEVELOPMENT, CUSTOMER EXPERIENCE ANALYSIS, SERVICE DEFINITION, SERVICE EXPERIMENTATION* and *SERVICE DEPLOYMENT*.

SERVICE DESIGN GAPS MODEL A model adapted from the gaps model of service quality (Bitner et al., 2010; Parasuraman et al., 1985). The service design gaps model identifies five areas where there is the potential for gaps between the service design activities, resulting in a less than optimal customer experience.

SERVICE ECOSYSTEM A network of interconnected service systems that support the delivery of an organisation's services and co-create value through service exchanges.

SERVICE EXPERIMENTATION A service within the *SERVICE DESIGN SERVICE FRAMEWORK* that is concerned with supporting the design and development of service prototypes.

SERVICE MANAGEMENT A discipline that is concerned with supporting an organisation in the design and delivery of services. IT service management involves the management of the IT service delivery to ensure business goals are met.

SERVICE OWNER The individual accountable for the design, development, deployment, and performance management of a service.

SERVICE QUALITY REQUIREMENTS Requirements that are concerned with service quality characteristics. For example, those identified within the *SERVQUAL* model.

SERVICE SAFARI A technique that involves a service designer gaining first-hand experience of a service. The technique is used to gain in-depth, personal understanding about a service.

SERVICE SCIENCE A research discipline that concerns the study and identification of the concepts, principles and activities related to service analysis and engineering. The term 'service science' is an abbreviation of 'service science, management, engineering and design', sometimes further abbreviated to SSMED.

SERVICE SYSTEM An *ACTOR* (or entity) engaged in the delivery of a product or service that supports or enables value co-creation with other actors.

SERVICE THINKING An interdisciplinary thinking approach focused on understanding the nature of value and the co-creation of value through the integration of actors' resources.

SERVICE USER ROLE A generic title for a role taken by an individual or group or actors who require access to a particular service.

SERVICE VALUE PROPOSITION See *VALUE PROPOSITION*.

SERVQUAL A model (Parasuraman et al., 1988) that comprises five dimensions: (1) tangibility: the physical facilities, equipment, and appearance of personnel; (2) reliability: the ability to perform the promised service dependably and accurately; (3) responsiveness: the willingness to help customers and provide prompt service; (4) assurance: the knowledge and courtesy of employees and their ability to inspire trust and confidence; (5) empathy: the caring individualised attention the firm provides to its customers.

SFIA and SFIAplus An extensive framework of skills and competency levels relevant to those working in the Information Systems industry. SFIAplus is the extended version provided by BCS, the Chartered Institute for IT.

SITUATION INVESTIGATION AND PROBLEM ANALYSIS A service within the *BUSINESS ARCHITECTURE SERVICE FRAMEWORK*, the *BUSINESS ANALYSIS SERVICE FRAMEWORK*, the *SERVICE DESIGN SERVICE FRAMEWORK* and the *PROJECT MANAGEMENT SERVICE FRAMEWORK* concerned with investigating the root causes of problems, identifying where a business need exists and shaping a project to address this need.

SIX SIGMA An approach to identifying process improvements with a view to decreasing the variability and improving the consistency of a process execution. The stages of a Six Sigma project are: define (the problem); measure (the data); analyse (the problem); improve (the process); control (the effectiveness of the solution).

SKILL An ability that is acquired by an individual, typically through a combination of learning and experience.

SMART An acronym used to ensure that objectives are clearly defined in that they are specific, measurable, attainable, relevant, time-bound.

SOFT SYSTEMS METHODOLOGY (SSM) A methodology that provides an approach to analysing business situations. SSM was devised by Professor Peter Checkland and his team at Lancaster University.

STAKEHOLDER An individual, group of individuals or organisation with an interest in a business change or a new or enhanced service or product. Categories of stakeholder include customers, employees, managers, partners, regulators, owners, suppliers and competitors.

STAKEHOLDER ANALYSIS The investigation and consideration of the stakeholders involved in a new initiative. Techniques such as the POWER/INTEREST GRID, CATWOE and RACI may be used to carry out stakeholder analysis.

STAKEHOLDER ENGAGEMENT An auxiliary service associated with the *BUSINESS ARCHITECTURE SERVICE FRAMEWORK*, the *BUSINESS ANALYSIS SERVICE FRAMEWORK*, the *SERVICE DESIGN SERVICE FRAMEWORK*, the *CHANGE MANAGEMENT SERVICE FRAMEWORK* and the *PROJECT MANAGEMENT SERVICE FRAMEWORK*. Stakeholder engagement is concerned with supporting project success through stakeholder collaboration, communication, and effective stakeholder relationship management.

STAKEHOLDER MANAGEMENT The definition of the most appropriate means of ensuring effective engagement with distinct categories of stakeholders.

STAKEHOLDER MANAGEMENT PLAN A formal document that defines the strategy to be adopted to engage with a specific project *STAKEHOLDER*.

STAKEHOLDER PERSPECTIVE A view of the business system held by a stakeholder. A business perspective is based upon the values, beliefs and priorities of the stakeholder, which are encapsulated in a defined world view. There may be several divergent business perspectives for any given business situation.

STAKEHOLDER PERSPECTIVE ANALYSIS An activity focused on understanding the view of the business system held by a stakeholder or set of stakeholders. See *CATWOE*.

STICKY NOTE SESSION A technique used during meetings and workshops whereby participants are asked to use individual sticky notes to record information or suggest ideas relating to a problem, issue or opportunity.

STORYBOARDING A technique that provides a graphical representation of the steps within a *CUSTOMER JOURNEY*.

STORYTELLING A technique used to elicit information and gain insight by enabling an interviewee to share 'stories' of experiences when engaging with an organisation, product or service. This technique may also be used when presenting information.

STRATEGIC ANALYSIS The application of formal techniques to analyse the pressures emerging from an organisation's external business environment and the level of internal organisational capability to respond to these pressures.

STRATEGIC ROADMAP DEVELOPMENT A service within the *BUSINESS ARCHITECTURE SERVICE FRAMEWORK* and *CHANGE MANAGEMENT SERVICE FRAMEWORK* that is concerned with the execution of strategic change.

STRATEGY The direction and scope of an organisation over the longer term. The strategy is defined in order to achieve the organisation's vision, mission and objectives.

STRESS TESTING A form of intense testing used to determine how an organisation will respond to potential adverse scenarios.

SUAVE A set of quality criteria used for defining business capabilities. The acronym stands for stable, unique, abstract, valuable, executive.

SUBJECT MATTER EXPERT A person within a project who offers *SUBJECT MATTER EXPERTISE*.

SUBJECT MATTER EXPERTISE A detailed understanding of the terminology, processes, constraints and technology of a specific business area, product line or service. See *DOMAIN/DOMAIN KNOWLEDGE*.

SUFFICIENCY The extent to which an organisation has *COMPETENCY* in a particular area, which is based in the main on the volume of employees who can provide the required level of *SKILL*.

SURVEY An approach used to obtain data during an investigation of a business situation. The data obtained is usually quantitative data, but it is also possible to obtain qualitative data using a survey. Surveys are useful to obtain information from a large or dispersed group of people.

SWIMLANE A row on a business process diagram/model that indicates the actor responsible for a particular task.

SWIMLANE DIAGRAM A technique used to model business processes. A swimlane diagram models the business system response to a business event. The model shows the triggering event, the business actors, the tasks they carry out, the flow between the tasks, the decisions and the business outcome. See *BUSINESS PROCESS MODEL*.

SWOT ANALYSIS A technique used to summarise the external pressures facing an organisation and the internal capability the organisation has available to respond to those pressures. The acronym stands for strengths, weaknesses, opportunities and threats.

SYSTEMS THINKING A thinking approach that takes a holistic, systemic view of situations, services or items, viewing each as a system with an underlying purpose and comprising a set of interacting elements that together result in the emergence of additional properties.

T-SHAPED PROFESSIONAL A concept that represents the need for individuals to have deep skills in their own professional discipline and broad, generic skills that span other disciplines and enable them to interact effectively with anyone working in those disciplines.

TACIT ASSUMPTION A belief on the part of an individual that information they hold is correct, without checking to ensure that this is the case. *EXPLICIT KNOWLEDGE/TACIT KNOWLEDGE*

TACIT KNOWLEDGE Information held about business procedures and operations that an individual does not articulate or explain. This may be due to a failure to recognise that the information is required or because there is an assumption that the information is already known. See *EXPLICIT KNOWLEDGE/TACIT ASSUMPTION*

TACTICS Information that describes the specific and detailed means by which a strategy is executed.

TANGIBLE BENEFIT A benefit to be realised by a business change project for which a credible, usually monetary, value can be predicted. See *INTANGIBLE BENEFIT.*

TANGIBLE COST A cost incurred by a business change project for which a credible, usually monetary, value can be predicted. See *INTANGIBLE COST.*

TARGET OPERATING MODEL (TOM) A model that illustrates how an organisation must be constituted in order to support the execution of its *STRATEGY* and the achievement of its objectives.

TARGET OPERATING MODEL DESIGN A service within the *BUSINESS ARCHITECTURE SERVICE FRAMEWORK* that is concerned with designing, defining, deploying and maintaining the *TARGET OPERATING MODEL (TOM)* for an organisation or business area.

TARGET STATE The desired target state for an organisation.

TASK A work activity carried out by a single actor in one place at a specific moment in time. The OPOPOT acronym is used to support task identification (one person, one place, one time). Tasks are represented within swimlanes on a *BUSINESS PROCESS MODEL* or *SWIMLANE DIAGRAM.*

TASK ANALYSIS A technique used to analyse the work conducted during a given task. Task analysis considers the event that triggers the task, the input information, the task outputs, the steps required to complete the tasks, the decisions relevant to the task, and the measures applied to the task.

TECHNICAL FEASIBILITY The degree to which a proposed course of action is compatible with the technical constraints and infrastructure available to an organisation.

TECHNICAL VIABILITY See *TECHNICAL FEASIBILITY.*

TERMS OF REFERENCE (TOR) An alternative name for a *PROJECT INITIATION DOCUMENT (PID)*, sometimes preferred for consultancy assignments such as a feasibility study. The *OSCAR* acronym may be used to develop a TOR.

TIMWOODS A tool for the analysis of *WASTE.* The TIMWOODS elements are: transport; inventory; motion; waiting; overproduction; overprocessing; defects; and skills underutilisation.

TOM See *TARGET OPERATING MODEL.*

UNDERLYING RATIONALE The fundamental set of values and beliefs that explain why a system exists, what it is designed to do and who the targeted audience is.

UNIFIED MODELING LANGUAGE (UML) A suite of diagrammatic techniques that are used to model business systems and software applications.

USABILITY The degree to which customers and other stakeholders are able to interact with services, processes and systems in order to achieve their goals. See *USABILITY ANALYSIS.*

USABILITY ANALYSIS The analysis of the degree of *USABILITY* regarding services, products, processes and systems.

USE CASE A feature that an actor wants a system to offer; it is a 'case of use' required by a particular actor.

USE CASE DESCRIPTION A definition of the interaction between an actor and a use case. A use case description may be formed using either text or a diagram, such as an *ACTIVITY DIAGRAM.*

USE CASE MODEL A technique from the unified modeling language (UML). A use case model is made up of a diagram showing the actors, the boundary of the business system or software application, the use cases and the associations between them. It may be supported by a set of use case descriptions.

USER EXPERIENCE A construct focusing on a user's cognitive, emotional, behavioural, sensorial and social responses to touchpoints underpinned by information technology.

USER ROLE A generic title for a role taken by an individual or group of actors who require access to a particular set of features offered by a business system or software application.

USER ROLE ANALYSIS A technique used to identify and understand the user roles that need to interact with a business system or software application.

VALIDATED PERSONA A *PERSONA* based on data, typically obtained from market or customer research.

VALUE The utility, experience and beneficial outcomes offered by a *PRODUCT* or *SERVICE* and determined by the *CUSTOMER*.

VALUE CHAIN A construct developed by Professor Michael Porter to identify the primary and support activities deployed within organisations to deliver a *value proposition* to their customers.

VALUE CO-CREATION The engagement and collaboration between *SERVICE SYSTEMS* to realise *VALUE* from delivered products and services.

VALUE PROPOSITION A clear statement of the value that an organisation offers customers through the delivery of a product or service.

VALUE STREAM A representation of the activities carried out by an organisation that collectively offers a product or service to internal or external stakeholders.

VISION The aspirational target state for an organisation is without regard to how this will be achieved. The state should be realised through the accomplishment of the 'mission'.

VISUALISATION An approach that uses pictures and diagrammatic illustrations to represent ideas, processes, data and options.

VMOST An extension of the *MOST* technique for an organisation where Vision is added to the Mission, Objectives, Strategy and Tactics.

VMOST ANALYSIS The investigation of an organisation's *VISION*, *MISSION*, *OBJECTIVES*, *STRATEGY* and *TACTICS* to determine how well it is defined, internally consistent, communicated within the organisation, and used to generate direction and commitment among staff. See *VMOST*.

VOICE OF THE CUSTOMER The view of a situation, system, service or product from the customer perspective.

WASTE Several areas, defined in *LEAN*, where possible process improvements may be identified. See *TIMWOODS*.

WORKSHOP A meeting run by a facilitator and attended by a range of selected business actors, for the purpose of eliciting, analysing or validating information. An agenda is prepared prior to the workshop and distributed to participants. The actions and decisions are recorded by a scribe.

WORK SYSTEM A work system is a system in which human participants or machines perform work using information, technology, and other resources to produce products and services for internal or external customers (Alter, 2008).

ZONE OF TOLERANCE A technique that defines the desired and adequate levels of customer service delivered by an organisation. The 'zone of tolerance' is the difference between the adequate and desired customer service levels.

INDEX

Note: *italic* page numbers indicate figures; **bold** page numbers indicate tables.